IN SEARCH OF THE TREASURE WITHIN: TOWARDS SCHOOLS AS LEARNING ORGANISATIONS

A European Educational Network

IN SEARCH OF THE
TREASURE WITHIN

TOWARDS SCHOOLS AS LEARNING ORGANISATIONS

This publication has been carried out with the support of the European Community in the framework of the Socrates programme. The content of this publication does not necessarily reflect the position of the European Community, nor does it involve any responsibility on the part of the European Community.

Rudi Schollaert (ed.)
In search of The Treasure Within:
Towards schools as learning organisations
Antwerpen/Apeldoorn
Garant, 2002
299 pp – 24 cm
D/2002/5779/87
ISBN 90-441-1306-2

Garant
Somersstraat 13-15, 2018 Antwerp (Belgium)
Koninginnelaan 96, 7315 EB Apeldoorn (The Netherlands)

CONTENTS

PREFACE

This publication is one of the outcomes of the first year of '*The Treasure Within*' Comenius Network on the evaluation of quality in education. It is the result of the joint efforts of some 24 educational institutions (schools and educational support organisations) from 10 European countries. The publication is basically a reflection of the issues raised during the first international conference organised by this network in Prague on April 26 and 27 2002. Organising a conference that attracts over 300 participants from 13 different countries and publishing a book containing state of the art contributions from 29 contributors, less than one year after the representatives of the partner institutions first set eyes on one another, is not a minor achievement. The dynamics and good-will that developed in such a short period is simply amazing. The more as most of the communication and the mutual tuning had to take place electronically.

As the co-ordinator of this network and the editor of this publication, I want to express my gratitude and admiration towards all those who so generously contributed, without weighing the efforts and time invested on pharmacist's scales.

Also a word of thanks to all those who worked behind the screens, particularly to Jane Jones for her proof-reading and to the people at VSKO. Without their persistent and selfless efforts that have gone virtually unnoticed by the outside world there would have been no publication, there would have been no web site. Our thanks also include our partners in Vienna and in Prague, who took upon them the burden to organise – to perfection – the meetings and the conference of year 1, and our partners in Ljubljana and Karlsad who committed themselves to taking upon them this heavy responsibility in year 2.

Finally, a word of thanks to the European Commission, without whose financial and moral support, *The Treasure Within* network would have remained a pipe-dream.

Practitioners, schools or other educational organisations interested in the activities of the network can find additional information on the website www. treasurewithin.com or contact the Network Co-ordinator rudi.schollaert@vsko.be

INTRODUCTION

This volume contains a first series of papers on a number of issues that were raised during the first international conference (Prague April 26-27 2002) of *The Treasure Within*, an educational network on quality in education. The contributions in this publication reflect to a large extent the content of workshop presentations or plenary lectures held at the Prague conference. Both presentations and papers draw upon work carried out by the network partners: experiences on the work floor, research findings or theoretical constructs. The reader will notice that some of the contributions still show unmistakeable traces of their origin as presentations. As a matter of fact, in some instances, an additional section, the epilogue, containing reflections made by conference participants, was added to the paper.

The overall aim of this network is - on a transnational European scale - to make a significant contribution to the empowerment and professional growth of the teaching profession and to the development of the internal expertise within schools. Indeed, as the learning of teachers is strongly affected by the institutional context in which they function, the network also aims to contribute to the deployment of schools as learning organisations par excellence, thus disclosing 'The Treasure Within'.

Apart from providing a communication platform for practitioners across Europe, the activities of the network include taking stock, making a comparative analysis and finding a common denominator for the areas of quality looked into. This publication is a first attempt at collecting the baseline information that will allow schools and educational organisations in Europe to identify common goals they want to go in search of. This process is to lead eventually to a common understanding of what constitutes quality on the one hand, but also to the transnational transfer and piloting of successful materials, models and approaches, taking into account national, local and institutional contexts.

The contributions in this volume, reflect the great variety and wealth of quality initiatives across Europe. In this respect, *The Treasure Within* is not simply a stack of gold bars, but a colourful variety of diamonds, emeralds, sapphires, and let's confess it, semiprecious stones. Indeed, the quest for the treasure is one of trial and error, and those who claim to have found the treasure chest might find themselves disappointed once they have opened the rusty lid.

A wealth of contributions indeed, although they differ in scope and range, rather than in their underlying philosophy. Accounts of down-to-earth experiences are juxtaposed with more theoretical papers and large scale case studies. However, it is striking to which extent the contributions show a concordance and agreement about what really matters. Therefore, rather than separating theoretical from practical contributions, the structure of this publication reveals the main areas in which quality in education is being pursued by *The Treasure Within* partners.

Part 1 contains two documents that aim to provide the onset for a framework. In chapter 1 Rudi Schollaert puts forward a few assumptions about what accounts for quality in schools. In chapter 2 Marc Van den Brande looks at quality from a wider perspective, suggesting a framework for looking at quality assurance systems from a national or even transnational point of view.

From this point onwards, the focus is completely on issues of internal quality care. In part 2 several contributors tackle the issue of reflection in action, one of the prerequisites for teams of practitioners to become the backbone of learning organisations. In chapter 3 Jane Jones suggests practitioner research as an opportunity to enhance quality in schooling, and in chapter 4 she presents a case study illustrating how practitioner research was successfully introduced in a primary school. In chapter 5 Sonja Sento□nik makes a link with the concept of agency, another major condition for quality in schools. In her article she claims that critical reflection contributes to teacher empowerment. In chapter 6 Thea Prinsen and Harry Verkoulen explore how teachers can be reflective practitioners.

In part 3 the attention shifts to another aspect of school quality: connectedness. Teachers can no longer afford to be Robinson Crusoe-like characters, doing their thing in the seclusion of their own private sanctuary, the classroom. In Chapter 7 Magnus Persson presents a case study on team building in a context of change, in the Karlstad area in Sweden. In Chapter 8 Stefan Petterson describes how this form of team building can provide an added value to the functioning of a specific primary school, whereas in chapter 9 Jezerka Beškovnik and Jelka Pe□ar bear witness of how a primary school can benefit from collaborative efforts among teachers.

Although change is omnipresent in this publication, part 4 deals specifically with change. In chapter 10 Danuta Elsner, Philip Whitehead and Felix Claus present the outcome of their joint, transnational effort: a checklist for change agents. In chapter 11 Karine Van Thienen asks and answers the question why teachers on the whole are so unwilling to change.

Part 5 takes the issues of teacher co-operation and joint reflection beyond the boundaries of the school walls. In chapter 12 Pieter Leenheer discusses how networks of schools in the Netherlands have been used as a lever for professional development. Chapter 13 offers an interesting comparison, as Daniela Bachi and Silvana Mosca describe an Italian concept of networking.

Although quality is the recurring theme in this volume, it is explored in a very specific way in part 6. In this part several authors look at projects, strategies and instruments that are specifically meant to promote the internal quality of schools. In chapter 14 Francesco Tadini describes how schools are supported in starting up a school-specific quality project. Chapter 15 takes this issue across national borders. In yet another joint transnational effort, André Elleboudt, Joaquim

Laplana and Alexandra Schrutz tell what they found out after having questioned 25 schools in 8 countries about the way they go about setting up internal quality projects. In chapter 16 Shân Mullett relates how the seeds of success are sowed in her school through departmental support. In chapter 17 Helmar Vyverman and Luk Van Canneyt present the DISO instrument, which allows schools to diagnose their strength and weaknesses, with the help of an external critical friend. In chapter 18 Karl Blüml provides a comprehensive instrument for the evaluation of quality in schools.

Part 7 refocuses the quality discussion on certain categories of stakeholders that were only marginally mentioned so far: parents and pupils. Taking into account the massive impact education has on children, involving parents and pupils is not an option, it is a must. In chapter 19 Jackie Denis gives an account of how the involvement of parents can improve dramatically if school management and teaching staff set up a structured dialogue with parents. In chapter 20 Peter Van de Moortel illustrates how feedback from parents can be a powerful self-evaluation tool for a school. In chapter 21 Eva Thomasson presents a powerful testimony of how the empowerment of pupils can contribute to the goals of education, and how it turns pupils into real change agents.

Part 8 again marks a another shift of focus. Its rationale being the fact that change has very little relevance as long as it does not have a beneficial effect on the primary process of teaching and learning. Several instances of quality at learner level are given in the final chapters of this publication. In chapter 22 Anna-Lena Groth gives useful suggestions as to how learning can be mapped. In chapter 23 Philip Whitehead presents a case for learner-centred writing classes. In chapter 24 Jezerka Beškovnik gives examples of team building for learners, respectively in the context of an international co-operation project, and in the context of foreign language learning.

Finally in the conclusion, Pieter Leenheer tries to distinguish a couple of consistent developments that obtain all across Europe in the present educational context. He also singles out a couple of common features within the great variety of issues dealt with in *The Treasure Within*.

PART 1
QUALITY IN EDUCATION

CHAPTER 1

SOME ASSUMPTIONS ABOUT QUALITY IN EDUCATION

Rudi Schollaert

Abstract

Quality in education cannot be adequately defined by simply transferring the principles that govern the market place to an educational context. Education has a moral purpose, as it has an overwhelming impact on the individuals in its care and on society in general. Quality in education is a shared responsibility of all the stakeholders involved: school management, teachers, authorities, but also learners and their parents.

Quality is a volatile concept. Not only does it depend on the values one holds, it is also subject to change. In a post-modern world, schools have a coherence building mission. Therefore they need to take a proactive stance and integrate change into their current practice and its underlying philosophy.

Top-down change has a very poor record of success. It often takes the attention away from what really matters: the primary process of learning. Change will only succeed if the key agents, teachers and school heads, have ownership of the innovation.

The Treasure Within is a Comenius Network on the Evaluation of Quality in Education. It is not about league tables nor about quality control, it is about the ongoing process of quality management. An essential feature of this is creating the internal conditions that will allow quality to emerge. These conditions include a focus on the primary process, the pursuit of agency and connectedness, and a reflective attitude.

What is quality in education?

Since time immemorial quality has been a controversial issue, not in the least quality in education. Everybody has – at some point in his lifetime and to some extent – been educated. That makes each single person an expert on what the school should do: your sister-in-law, your tennis partner, your greengrocer, and particularly your dentist, whose socio-political ideas you'd better not contradict, even if you were able to talk with your mouth open wide.

If people don't agree on what constitutes quality – and they don't – it is because they hold different values. In the post-modern world we inhabit, established certainties have all but vanished. In a society that has lost its coherence, people adhere to different, sometimes contradictory values, and therefore voice different, sometimes contradictory expectations towards education. Is this decline? Not necessarily so. A tolerant and democratic society that allows for diversity and difference of opinion seems to me by far preferable to a monolithic society that only allows one single truth to exist, even though this multi-faceted society has no absolute consensus on what constitutes valuable objectives for education. The tension between these diverse views results in a dynamic balance. This balance is laid down in what is called the curriculum (Standaert, 2001). Within this field of tension, schools have a coherence building mission: to offer their learners a consistent set of values that can be used as a key to dealing with the complexity of present-day society. For the sake of street credibility it does not suffice for schools just to offer these values, but, what is far more difficult, they are also expected to live up to them.

Quality and the market place

The concept of quality in education has been strongly influenced by corporate thinking about quality. In the early 90's companies such as IBM and Ford Motor Company voiced similar definitions of quality, which boiled down to the old adage of keeping the customer satisfied. This raises the question whether there actually is a customer in education, and if so, who that customer might be. To my mind there is an essential difference between the manufacturing of goods and the provision of education. Education is not a market commodity, it is a public good, just like health care. Rather than trying to define who the customers are (learners, parents, society), I would venture the term stakeholder. Stakeholders are all those who have their own specific responsibility towards the quality of learning. Besides the teachers, the school, the authorities, each individual has an overwhelming responsibility for his own learning. And in the case of children and adolescents, parents cannot simply delegate all responsibility for education to the school. Can you imagine a scene at a car-dealer's, in which a customer makes the following complaint: 'That's a really lousy car you sold me there. I have had it for a week, and it has already had two parking tickets and one speeding ticket, and to make things worse, yesterday it crashed into a tree.'

'Quality equals customer sat sfaction'

IBM

What this boils down to is that all stakeholders are responsible for the quality of education, and that schools and teachers are too often blamed for the problems of society. This awesome burden is too easily placed at the doorstep of the teaching profession. Paraphrasing Joyce, Calhoun and Hopkins (1999) it could be stated that teachers receive a relatively modest initial training and salary to go with it. Yet, they are asked to manage one of the most complex professional tasks in our society. They have little status, but awesome responsibility both for individual children and for the health of society as a whole.

If we want to apply the rhetoric of business to education, it seems only fair that schools should be expected to provide an added value and be made accountable for this, which raises the issue of quality control. The problem with quality control, particularly if based on output indicators is that it is post factum (Sallis, 1996). In other words, if this control shows that the quality is defective, it is too late for the actual learners involved. Did the great majority of the learners meet the attainment targets? What if they didn't? Better luck for them next time? You can repair a defective car, but you cannot make up for a faulty education. In terms of the market place, Sallis (ibid.) remarks that every learner should be entitled to a Rolls Royce. This, if at all, can only be achieved by ongoing quality care, call it quality management if you like.

The moral responsibility of education

However, stretching the metaphor of the market place would take me away from the point I would like to make: education as a public good. Or as Michael Fullan (1999) puts it: the moral purpose of education. Every school has a moral responsibility towards society as a whole as well as towards the learners in its care. Education is primarily a moral business because it makes all the difference in the lives of people – just think about your own childhood and adolescence - and hence it makes all the difference in the society these people inhabit. The belief that each child can learn, that each child holds a treasure within, and acting upon that belief will make a world of difference for the less able children, while at the same time moving marginalised groups into the mainstream of society. Inclusion does not only affect individual lives, it is a guarantee for an equitable, stable and therefore economically thriving society (Fullan, ibid).

Education in a changing world

Stability, however, is a relative concept. As I pointed out earlier on, education is keeping its finger on the pulse of society. A society that is in a permanent state of change, affected by scientific and technical breakthroughs, by economic or sociological shifts and by subsequent new ethical dilemmas. And that is the real change schools have to cope with. The change in curricula is only a surface feature of the actual changes taking place in society.

There are no certainties left nowadays. The only thing we can take for granted is that tomorrow will be different from today. In a society that is torn between the tensile forces of the old and the new, education is poised in a delicate balance. Rigidity looms at one end, chaos at the other (Stacey, 1996). As Michael Fullan (1999) eloquently sums it up: Learning takes place on the edge of chaos.

> 'Learning takes place on the edge of chaos'
>
> Michael Fullan

In post-modern society chaos theory has become a powerful and comforting sociological metaphor to illustrate how an individual can still have an impact on the world around him. And it is not only chaos theory that Fullan applies to education. He also has a fling at good old evolution theory. In evolutionary terms species have to adapt to a changing environment in order to survive. This is why giraffes have developed long necks. This is why chameleons have developed their camouflage. Fullan argues that there are two ways for people to survive in a changing environment: we wait for our bodies to change, or the more efficient solution: we change our minds. There is a synonym for changing one's mind. It is called learning.

> 'Learning is changing one's mnd'
>
> Michael Fullan

Consequently one of the major challenges for a school is how to deal with change by means of learning. There is no choice really. Change happens anyway, whether we like it or not. By taking a proactive stance we can prepare the ground and embed new developments in our existing practice. This approach allows us to stay on top of the events that are to come. It allows us to stay in charge, it gives us a sense of direction. If not we will be overtaken by the events and experience a sense of helplessness. People who can and will not see that they are preparing their learners for a society that ceased to exist 30 years ago, at the same time give up the opportunity to have an impact on society.

The figure below illustrates the dramatic inadequacy of fossilized teaching in a changing society.

One generation later

The problem with state-imposed innovations

The problems with inducing change are manifold. For one thing it is usually counter-productive to impose change in a top-down fashion. As Spanbauer (1992) would say: 'Change happens by degree, not by decree'. If we were to look back, each of us would be able to give any number of instances of major disasters in educational change. Particularly state-imposed initiatives are prone to disappear into the Bermuda triangle of educational innovation, and are never heard of again. Gone is the money, gone are the efforts. What remains is some driftwood: widespread cynicism on the shop floor and another boost to the self-fulfilling prophecy of failure.

> 'Change happens by degree, not by decree'
>
> Spanbauer

Quality is in the primary process

There are several reasons why top-down change and particularly state-imposed change has such a bad record of failure.

In the first place, they often focus on the wrong thing. They mainly focus on structural reform, thus creating a massive diversion of attention and energy away from what really matters in education, and that is learning. Research by Wang, Haertel and Walberg (1993) has shown that initiatives that focus on the primary process, i.e. the learning process and the facilitation of learning – teaching if you like – have a far greater impact than initiatives that are situated in what they call the periphery. In his inaugural address when taking up his professorship at the University of Sheffield, David Hopkins (1996) took this argument one step further. I quote "Unless school improvement strategies impact directly on learning and achievement, then we are surely wasting our time". Hopkins' definition of school improvement (ibid.) is that it 'is a strategy for educational change that focuses on student achievement by modifying classroom practice and adapting the management arrangements within the school to support teaching and learning'.

In order to realise this, we need to answer questions such as 'What kind of learning content or experiences do we want to expose learners to? How are we going to organise this exposure? How does this affect the teacher role? And even more important: how does this affect the learner role?'

The answer to these questions is provided by Joyce, Calhoun and Hopkins (1997). They claim that schools need to create powerful learning environments to enhance the quality of the primary process of learning and teaching. This quality depends on three variables: *content*, which is conceptual rather than particular, the *learning process*, which is constructive inquiry instead of passive reception, and the *social climate*, which is expansive instead of restrictive.

The belief that quality in education is reflected in the quality of the primary process is the first essential element in the rationale of *The Treasure Within*.

The internal conditions for improvement

The second reason why state imposed innovations tend to fail is the fact that they insufficiently take into account the complexity of the teaching profession (Sarason, 1990). A decision, however neat it may look in the file on the desk of the administrator, often fails to understand the range, the depth and the complexity of a teacher's job. Rationally constructed reform – making mission statements, setting goals and strategic plans – does not work, unless the internal conditions for change are met.

One of the characteristics of poorly managed innovations is bad timing. Effective change should allow for time for the innovation to be implemented. It is not unknown for politicians to think along the time lines of upcoming elections. These timelines usually do not run parallel with the time needed for implementation. The urge for politicians to score may even lead to a surfeit of innovations, which are often introduced on top of other changes that are yet to be implemented. A certain recipe to cause overload and fragmentation among the teaching profession and particularly among school heads. Teaching involves a high degree of emotional investment of the teacher. It requires great skill and competence from the teacher and in an unsupportive environment it may easily lead to burnout (Bascia and Hargreaves, 2000). Insult is added to injury by external innovations that make teachers powerless, innovations that do not provide resources to match the ambitious schemes, innovations that draw teachers' attention away from their students into administrative duties.

Agency

This takes us to the second essential feature of *The Treasure Within*: the concept of agency, which is the key to teacher morale. Agency is defined by Frost, Durrant et al.(2000) quoting Giddens (1984) as 'the human capacity to make a difference through the application of bottom-up power to change the structures which constrain and determine our actions'. If we expect teachers to take on responsibilities beyond what is going on in their classrooms, we have to give them power outside their classroom. This is what A. Hargreaves (1994) and D. Hargreaves and Hopkins (1991) call empowerment. If agency or empowerment is what makes teachers tick, the same must be the case for learners. Only if learners have some impact on what and how they are learning, will they accept, even claim ownership of their learning, hence will they be motivated to learn. Only if learners have some impact on their learning environment, i.e. the tear and wear of school life, only then will schools duly prepare them for active and constructive citizenship in their adult lives.

Connectedness

The third element of *The Treasure Within* philosophy takes us from the individual to the collective level. A school is a community, it is more than the sum of the individuals that are part of it. A positive interdependence, a feeling of connectedness is a major contribution to the conditions for school improvement. The concept of connectedness addresses issues such as mutual emotional support among school head, staff and students, taking a collaborative responsibility towards student learning and interests. In such a collaborative culture, diversity, conflict and resistance are essential ingredients. Your regular portion of friction is the price you pay for a true collaborative culture. Without it an organisation gets stuck in superficial agreement and consequently in immobility and make-believe.

People who are good at sciences will assure ordinary mortals that when the process of fusion occurs it produces five times the energy. Fusion is about joining, coming together, creating connection (Daft and Lengel 1998). Applied to social systems such as schools, this is a metaphor, but a powerful one. Five times the energy is the kind of energy needed to realise self-organising breakthroughs in complex systems such as schools. Connectedness, therefore, is a major way to achieve the moral purpose of education.

Reflection in action

The fourth element to find its place in *The Treasure Within* conceptual framework is the idea of the reflective practitioner. Individuals being able to make a difference and doing so in unison with peers or other stakeholders, is an essential feature of quality in a school. However, there is more. A systematic disposition towards reflection is an absolute must if one wants to achieve quality within a learning context. There is no way the teaching profession can escape its responsibility in this respect. If school heads, senior management and teaching staff do not want desk people 'who have not seen the inside of a classroom since they were children themselves' to make decisions above their heads, they cannot sit back and wait until somebody does their thinking for them, until somebody takes their decisions for them. Agency is not something that is granted to you, it is something that you claim, and that you work towards, given the support of a facilitating legislation in which local autonomy takes a central position. Given also an equitable share of material and human resources. This autonomy implies a reasonable degree of accountability towards society and towards the subsidising authority. It also requires a critical attitude towards the demands put on education. But also a critical attitude towards one's own performance, both as individuals and as an organisation. This reflective process is to result in an ongoing self-evaluation, in which the internal quality criteria are carefully weighed against the just requirements of society. This involves putting output indicators into the balance with those criteria that are not readily measurable, such as personal growth in the intellectual, emotional, ethical and spiritual domain.

Schools as learning organisations

In order to achieve this, school teams have to take charge of their own development, their own learning, individually and collectively. Schools are truly learning organisations, as learning is their core business. Learning organisations address present and future learning needs of their members through creating structured learning opportunities on the basis of day-to-day experiences. Hopkins (1996) offers a more comprehensive definition, stating that a school that rightfully carries the epithet of learning organisation is 'a professional learning community in which staff collaboratively set clear goals for student learning, provide a coherent programme, develop a consistent assessment policy and develop action plans to improve student learning, learning that integrates new knowledge into prior knowledge. This requires what is termed 'educational leadership', not only from school heads, but also from the whole teaching staff. Here we are back where we started: the ongoing process of quality management is a concern that is shared by the whole educational community within the school. In a changing world this implies that all practitioners should be change agents, experts who know how to use change forces for the benefit of their learners.

Conclusion

In summary, although it's still early days in the development of a conceptual framework for internal quality management in schools, I would like to put forward four distinguishing quality features as working hypotheses for *The Treasure Within*:

- Focus on the primary process of teaching and learning, thus creating a powerful learning environment.
- Agency: empowering people so that they can make a difference in things that really matter
- Connectedness: all stakeholders actively working together and supporting one another, as allies do, in achieving the moral purpose of education
- Reflection: developing one's school into a learning organisation, by critically examining current practice in the light of theory.

The implication of these features is that one cannot bring about quality simply by the application of instruments or even by means of well-conceived strategies, if at the same time, the four factors mentioned above are not being addressed. This supports the idea raised earlier in this paper that quality is all about the values one holds.

How does all this relate to *The Treasure Within* Network? The network is meant to be an international professional learning community, a European platform for partners and members to share experiences, and to reflect and act upon them. *The Treasure Within* network is about capacity building. Capacities for educational staff to develop leadership qualities, for engaging in strategic thinking, planning and action. Capacities for setting up structures that will help to implement, to anchor, to institutionalise good practice. Capacities for creating the conditions that will promote agency and connectedness: a collaborative and reflective school culture that is expansive, not restrictive, that has high expectations, but realistic ones.

The Treasure Within is about activating all the capacities that lie dormant in teachers and learners that are hidden inside, jewels waiting to be discovered and polished until they shine and their glare rubs off on others. *The Treasure Within* is about making tacit knowledge explicit, thus creating the conditions for good practice to be transferable to other schools, other contexts, other countries.

All those who are contributing to *The Treasure Within* Network are fellow travellers on a journey of discovery, they are pilgrims in quest of *The Treasure Within*. We are looking forward to regular accounts of their progress and their adventures.

For more information check out our web site www.treasurewithin.com or contact Treasurewithin@vsko.be

References

Bascia, N. & Hargreaves, A. (2000). *The Sharp Edge of Educational Change.* London: Routledge Falmer.
Daft, R. & Lengel, R. (1998). *Fusion Leadership.* San Francisco: Berrett-Koehler.
Frost, D., Durrant, J., Head M., & Holden G. (2000). *Teacher-led School Improvement.* London: Routledge Falmer.
Fullan, M. (1999). *Change Forces: The Sequel.* London: Palmer Press.
Giddens, A. (1984). *The Constitution of Society.* Cambridge: Polity Press.
Hargreaves, A. (1994). *Changing Teachers, Changing Times.* London: Cassell.
Hargreaves, D. & Hopkins, D. (1991). *The Empowered School.* London: Cassell.
Hopkins, D. (1996). *Powerful Teaching, Powerful Learning, Powerful Schools.* Inaugural Lecture at the University of Nottingham.
Joyce, B., Calhoun, E. & Hopkins, D. (1997). *Models of Learning – Tools for Teaching.* Philadelphia: O.U.P.
Joyce, B., Calhoun, E. & Hopkins, D. (1999). *The New Structure of School Improvement.* Philadelphia: O.U.P.

Sallis, E. (1996). *Total Quality Management in Education.* London: Kogan Page Ltd.

Stacey, R. (1996). *Strategic Management and Organizational Dynamics.* London: Pitman.

Standaert, R. (2001). *Inspectorates of Education in Europe.* Leuven: ACCO.

Wang, M., Haertel, G. & Walberg, H. (1993). *Toward a Knowledge Base for School Learning.* Review of Educational Research, 63(3).

Rudi Schollaert is director of the INSET and International Relations UNIT of VSKO, Belgium

CHAPTER 2

TRUST THE TREASURE

FROM CONTROLLING TO SUPPORTING QUALITY IN SCHOOLS

Marc Van den Brande

Defining quality

Imagine a school inspector counting the number of computers at school. Does it give an adequate view of the implementation of ICT in schools? And is this an indication of the quality of a school? Which criteria do you use to call a school 'good' or 'efficient'? What is quality?

A school effectiveness researcher called 'school quality' a subjective, evolving and manipulative concept.

Look at parents choosing the best school for their youngsters. Some parents are looking for a nice school culture or a hot meal every day whilst other parents do like the school to be at walking distance, or they like the school with the attractive playground, or the school that can boast large numbers of graduates from renowned universities. Or parents may have their own objectives for sending their children to a particular school. In this regard, school quality is an issue about which people can disagree. School quality can be interpreted by different people with different opinions. It is a highly subjective item.

The quality of schools is also an evolving concept. One can imagine that schools in the 1950's had other standards than those that they have now e.g. participation of pupils in schools was not an issue in 1950. Nowadays schools are assessed on their participative level!

And is quality not also a concept that is easy to manipulate? Look at school advertisements. By emphasising certain features schools show their best side. Every school considers that it is splendid, gives an outstanding education, employs the best teachers, …

A framework

In a recent report Andersen Consulting developed a framework for maintaining quality in schools. Although it seems to have been derived from an industrial setting it is easy to use in comparing quality assurance systems in different countries. Simply stated, schools have to realise goals, goals that are defined by society, the government, the ministry, the parliament. And the same society tries to control the output of schools by appointing a corps of inspectors. We can call this the external quality assurance system.

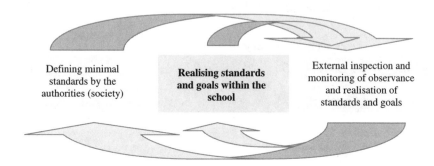

| Defining minimal standards by the authorities (society) | **Realising standards and goals within the school** | External inspection and monitoring of observance and realisation of standards and goals |

Fig. 1: Internal quality assurance system

But in an analogous way we can describe an internal quality assurance system. This is quite important as there is a shift in many countries from central steering to decentralisation. At least partial or functional decentralisation of educational governance is a major political issue. More quality and effectiveness of education is an essential motive for decentralisation policies but other arguments are also considered as a basis for legitimating this policy:
– Efficiency in the sense of budget control;
– Responsiveness to local communities;
– More democracy;
– More accountability;
– Creative human resources development.

The shift towards decentralisation empowers the stakeholders at lower levels and takes the debate on quality of schools to the micro level. Schools are increasingly asked to set their own goals, clarify their own procedures, develop their specific methods, evaluate their own organisation. Responding to this shift towards decentralisation, schools try to elaborate their own policy and establish their own quality assurance system.

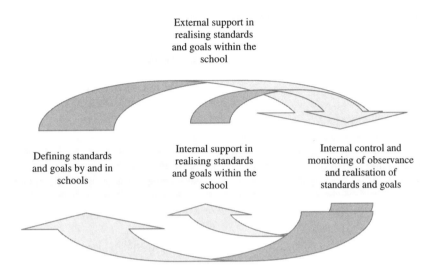

External support in
realising standards
and goals within the
school

Defining standards
and goals by and in
schools

Internal support in
realising standards
and goals within the
school

Internal control and
monitoring of observance
and realisation of
standards and goals

Fig. 2: External quality assurance system

Defining minimal standards as basis for quality assessment

The policy of decentralisation requires a guarantee that the system is fulfilling its objective, i.e. providing quality education for all. Therefore in different countries in Europe minimal standards were developed. We know this formulation of objectives as e.g. the National Curriculum (UK), 'Kerndoelen' or attainment targets (the Netherlands), Eindtermen (Flanders), Socles de compétence (French speaking part of Belgium). Moreover the ambition for norm and standard setting does not end at the borders of the nations. Supranational organisations try to establish a wide consensus concerning educational standards. We can refer to the indicators of the UNESCO, the OECD, the European Commission.

In May 2000 the European Commission published a European report on the quality of school education. The report was based on the work of the Working Committee on Quality Indicators. By describing these indicators the European Commission identified a number of quantifiable targets as a means of comparing best practice and as instruments for monitoring and reviewing the progress achieved. The 16 indicators fall into four areas: Attainment; Success and transition; Monitoring of school education; Resources and Structures.

AREA	INDICATOR
Attainment	1. Mathematics
	2. Reading
	3. Science
	4. Information and communication technologies (ICT)
	5. Foreign languages
	6. Learning to learn
	7. Civics
Success and transition	8. Drop out
	9. Completion of upper secondary education
	10. Participation in tertiary education
Monitoring of school education	11. Evaluation and steering of school education
	12. Parental participation
Resources and structures	13. Education and training of teachers
	14. Participation in pre-primary education
	15. Number of students per computer
	16. Educational expenditure per student

By defining these indicators the European Commission shows its ambition to provide a basis for school quality measurement and surveillance, especially at national level. It is an invitation to education ministers to engage in a global reflection on common goals for education systems in Europe. But the indicators will surely have an influence on the school quality assurance at a local level. Some researchers fear this technology of control which enables the monitoring and 'steering' of schools by applying such 'neutral' indicators (S. Ball, 1998). The search for 'Effectiveness' could in this way become a technology of normalisation. Predictability and efficiency are valued to the extent that schools would surely become dramatically more boring places than they are already (Angus, 1993). The European Commission is familiar with these critical opinions. In the European Report on the quality of school education it says that the search for effectiveness and comparability has to be approached with caution and open mind. Even the most robust of data conceal historical and cultural differences and values.

Controlling or supporting quality?

In most European countries we are familiar with the inspectorate of education. The major area of the inspectorate's responsibility is school quality control. In the most narrow formulation of their tasks the inspectorate has to consider whether schools are responding to legal regulations, i.e. whether the legal provisions are being adhered to by the schools. The inspectors control the degree of compliance with the legislation. In a broader interpretation of their responsibilities the inspectors face a range of different tasks: e.g. the assessment of the school development plan, the assessment of teachers, the advising of teachers and director, monitoring examinations, curriculum development, the development of evaluation instruments ...

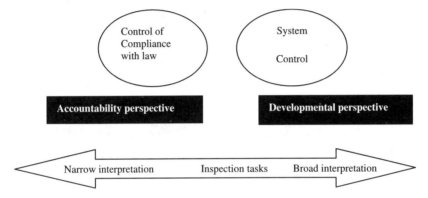

Fig. 3: Perspectives for inspection

The narrow interpretation of the inspectorate's tasks refers to the responsibility and the accountability of the school. Schools have to meet some well defined expectations of society. Inspectors must examine whether the school effectively fulfils this mandate. By means of instruments the inspector has to advise the authorities regarding accreditation and funding of the school. As long as norms and standards are clearly defined, there seems no problem. But who can ensure that all important features can be measured? That the instruments used are reliable and valid? That the instruments cover the range of tasks? One can imagine that schools and teachers may be captured in the interpretation of the standards by the inspector.

These difficulties can occur to the extreme if the inspectorate's tasks and responsibilities are broader than the control of compliance with legislation. Widening the role of the inspector to system control interferes with the responsibility of the schools in managing their own quality assurance system. The inspector's advice can even be in conflict with the agreements within the school.

Self evaluation as a basis for internal quality assurance

The increased school autonomy gives the different stakeholders in school the opportunity to develop their own quality assurance systems. Schools are responsible for monitoring and evaluating their organisation, the process and the output. In some countries schools have specific instruments for self evaluation at their disposal: checklists, questionnaires, observation sheets, function description and appraisal, pupil interview. Self evaluation becomes indeed a main topic in the process of the school development planning. The results of the self evaluation lead team members to formulate improvement objectives and to set common targets. It is a challenge for the stakeholders to find their own treasure within the school.

Has the inspectorate a role to play in this process? In my opinion this is not obvious. Interventions by a sanctioning body does not always fit in with the developmental perspective for the school. Empowering the stakeholders at school level means making them responsible for defining what they understand by quality in education and giving them 'ownership' of their part in the education system. If the leading people in this process really need some guidance or support, it would be desirable for them to be able to choose their advisers themselves.

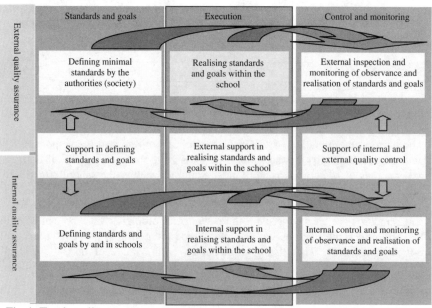

Fig 4: Total quality assurance system

Epilogue

During a workshop at the Prague 2002 Treasure Within conference, the presentation of this paper resulted in the following discussion taking place on the type of external controls that existed in the countries of the participants. The following points were made:

Italy:
There is no external inspection of any type. Some schools are in the process of establishing internal evaluation systems.

Sweden:
The Swedish system was for many years influenced by the English system but there has been a good level of debate in recent years and changes are taking place. National tests take place in the 5th and 9th years in school but there has been no external evaluation at Government level, the results were reported by the Swedish Authority on Statistics. Now there is an attempt to find a system to assess how pupils are performing and other factors are being taken into account in the interpretation of the statistics, for example a number of social deprivation factors. There is no evaluative interpretation of the final results which are averaged according to a weighted formula.

In the past an external inspection of schools only took place if a parent made a complaint. Previously when the National Agency visited a school they were looking to see whether the curriculum had been implemented, but recent changes mean that inspectors have a more specific role and they will have visited one third of all schools in Sweden in three years time. This new model includes a degree of support.

Slovenia:
The law is that schools will be inspected once every five years but this does not always happen. The report generated is short, three pages generally, and is not published. Inspectors only look at written materials and do not visit classrooms. If a parent makes a complaint then other inspectors who are specialists would come to observe the teacher.
A system of national examinations exists and the results of these examinations are important to the students because their future education choices are determined by the outcomes.

Belgium:
(French)
Schools are very autonomous and the role of state inspectors is to check if the curriculum is in place; they do not advise or comment upon its delivery. Headteachers are trained and some schools flourish and others are less successful. Teachers and parents are beginning to react and there are some initiatives underway.
There is no central examination system but there are national attainment targets which are decided by ministers.
(Flemish)
Inspection takes place once every six years and a team of five or six inspectors visits the school and register everything of importance. The indicators the inspectors use are context, input, process and output. Inspectors cannot advise but their reports influence the distribution of funding to schools.
There is no system of external examinations.

England:
There is a high degree of external control: regular inspection using a published framework which covers all aspects of the school's work. A poor report results in a high degree of support and intervention in the management of the school. Reports are published on the internet and a copy is sent to every parent and to local companies.

External examinations take place at ages 7,11,14,16,17, and 18. The results are published in the form of league tables showing schools in rank order.

Effects of external control:
The general feeling was that some form of external control was important to ensure standards in schools were sufficiently high. Advice and support were not always part of the system and therefore, where this was the case, there was no mechanism to help the schools improve their performance. If advice was given then this supported the school's internal quality management systems.

However too much control was likely to have a demoralising effect on teachers and pupils, particularly in circumstances where the reports were not favourable. Instead of helping a school to improve the control could have a negative impact for example reducing the number of good quality teachers that apply for posts with the school. In such a case it is possible that standards will decline even further.

References

Angus, L. (1993). The sociology of school effectiveness, *British Journal of Sociology of Education*, 14, 3, 333-345.

Andersen Consulting (2002). *Doelmatigheidsanalyse van de Inspectie van Onderwijs, de Pedagogische Begeleidingsdiensten en de Dienst voor Onderwijsontwikkeling*. Brussels, unpublished report.

Ball, S.J. (1998). Educational studies, policy entrepreneurship and social theory. In R. Slee & G. Weiner with S. Tomlinson (Eds), *School Effectiveness for Whom? Challenges to the school effectiveness and school improvement movements* (pp. 70-83). London: Routledge Falmer.

European Commision (2001). *European report on the quality of school education: Sixteen quality indicators*. Luxembourg: Office for official publications of the European Communities.

Maes, B., Vereecke, E. & Zaman M. (1999). *Inspectorates of Education in Europe, A Descriptive Study*. Brussels: Department of Educational Development.

Marc Van den Brande is co-ordinating director of the Pedagogic Department of VSKO, Belgium

PART 2

THE TEACHER AS REFLECTIVE PRACTITIONER

CHAPTER 3

PRACTITIONER RESEARCH: AN OPPORTUNITY TO ENHANCE QUALITY IN SCHOOLING

Jane Jones

Abstract

This paper promotes the construct of practitioner research principally as interactive and collaborative learning, and as a mechanism for effective professional development. I also suggest, and draw on a wide range of evidence in support, that practitioner research provides opportunities for an active exploration of teaching and learning at 'learner level'. Practitioner research which I define as systematic inquiry is hall-marked essentially by critical reflexivity and can be structured into the daily business of schools and become a driving force for school improvement, in various but modest ways.
It allows for creative inputs by all and respects a variety of adult learning styles. As with all things focused on educational change, it is not without its problems but I argue that these should not and need not be an overarching obstruction.

In sum, professional inquiry enables schools to provide meaningful and useful accounts of their work and performance to themselves, the local community and the research community at large. Joyce's interconnecting doors metaphor to describe the process of school improvement is used extensively and symbolically throughout.

Definitions and 'fuzzy' concepts

The rhetoric of school improvement and the rather fuzzy concept of school effectiveness have dominated current discourses of education for some time. The moral imperative of the need for schools to improve constantly and to consider and attempt to evaluate their effectiveness in terms of value for money and quality is undeniable. However the concepts of 'improvement', 'effectiveness' and 'quality' are very 'sticky' indeed and almost defy definition. Furthermore, assertions as to **how** to improve and **how** to become more effective are hugely contested. I would like to suggest that the processes involved do with certainty, have quite a lot to do with what goes on in the classroom and that no school improvement occurs unless it impacts on or derives from the core technologies of teaching and learning in the classroom. I would further suggest that what I term 'practitioner research' is a very sensible and fruitful way of engaging teachers (and other relevant and interested stakeholders as appropriate) in examining those core technologies and in thus providing opportunities to enhance quality in schooling. It would be useful to begin by considering what is meant by 'practitioner research' in this context.

Inside-out

The practitioners are, as above, those 'at the chalk face' or perhaps in our technological age, those 'at the interactive whiteboard'. Teachers themselves are predominant but the term practitioner is inclusive and extends to support staff of all kinds and at all levels, indeed all those involved in what Lave & Wenger call 'a community of practice', involving *"participation in an activity system about which participants share understandings concerning what they are doing and what that means in their lives and for their communities"*(1991, 95). Nonetheless, because there is a large measure of common ground, I use practitioner research and teacher research interchangeably in this paper. I have been greatly impressed by modest but important aspects of practitioner research taking place in 'Treasure' schools in Italy and Belgium, for example that includes parents, pupils, Inspectors and critical but professional friends in their undertakings. 'Research' for our purposes also needs defining before some practitioners/teachers take fright, frozen in a misconception that closes rather than opens doors to research possibilities for those 'at the interactive whiteboard' or, indeed, with the interactive whiteboard since I am currently working with a group of language teachers who are researching the possible impact of this tool on the quality of teaching and learning.

Some research is highly specialised and esoteric and it needs to be otherwise we could not make the necessary scientific advancements needed in our ultra-modern age. However, research is but a continuum of inquiry, the engaging or perhaps self-engagement of teachers in *"systematic, self-critical inquiry"* (Stenhouse, 1975) of the sort that thinking teachers naturally engage in, as shown in figure 1.

Investigation /inquiry   ⟶   specialised research

Figure 1: Continuum of research

Woolly staff room discussion it is not but the school staff room may, however, be a very fertile ground for launching such inquiry. Whatever it is that launches inquiry, it is important that it derives from a felt need to investigate, from a curiosity for and a desire to learn about the different realities of classrooms from **inside** the classroom, some of which are indisputably more effective than others. As Cochran-Smith & Lytle assert: *"Teachers' questions often emerge from discrepancies between what is intended and what occurs"* (1993, 14). We could put this very simply as 'something not working'! A very natural response is to seek to understand this phenomenon or, as Cochran-Smith & Lytle suggest: *"Teacher research stems from or generates questions and reflects teachers' desires to make sense of their experience – to adapt a learning stance or openness toward classroom life"* (ibid., 25). It is, as they conclude, an 'inside-out' not an 'outside-in' model of research and learning.

To summarise then so far, the construct of research I am using is underpinned by the following principles:
– A definition of research as 'systematic, self-critical inquiry'
– Such research is **by** or **with** and not **on** teachers
– An interest in making sense of classroom realities with a view to improving practice.

Learning communities

There is a common image of the 'researcher' engaged in lonely pursuit, a Sisyphian figure toiling up the mountainside, or, the oft-used image of the long distance runner. There is something to be said for private, individual reflection and the orientation of professionalism would indicate a need for self-improvement and for personally directed life-long learning. Each of us has special needs and interests and we should pursue them for the sake of self-learning and self-knowledge. As Senge writes:

"Personal mastery is the discipline of continually clarifying and deepening our personal vision, of focusing our energies, of developing patience, and of seeing reality objectively. As such, it is an essential cornerstone of the learning organisation-the learning organisation's spiritual foundation. An organisation's commitment to and capacity for learning can be no greater than that of its members" (1990, 7).

However, one's position as a member of a school community provides an opportunity to utilise one's skills, knowledge and sense of inquiry for the learning of the greater whole, for the school as a learning organisation or as a learning community, (the term I prefer on account of its inclusivity), which in turn contributes to the mosaic of learning invested in the bigger picture of the national, indeed cross-national European quest for greater school effectiveness and school improvement. It is this kind of analysis that highlights the role of the classroom teacher as a key agent of change in school improvement, modest though this contribution to the role may be. Too often, the role of teachers in change processes is marginalised instead of being yoked to a whole school approach to professional development and to school improvement within a realistic framework of what is possible, giving rise to my triangle of improvement opportunity thus:

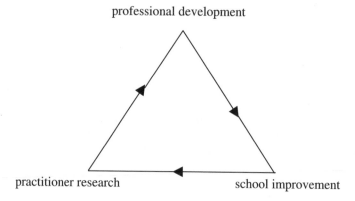

professional development

practitioner research   school improvement

Figure 2: Triangle of opportunities

Change processes

Paradoxically, enthusiasm for innovation and grandiose plans and probably unrealistic expectations can overwhelm colleagues on account of the perceived unbounded enormity of a project. The psychology of change processes is insufficiently considered in the framework of educational change. Alvin Toffler coined the phrase 'future shock' to describe: *"the shattering stress and disorientation that we induce in individuals by subjecting them to too much stress in too short a time"* (1990, 12).

Change involves, crucially, a reconciliation between what Fullan refers to as: *"the objective reality of change"* and *"the subjective realities embedded in people's individual and organisational contexts and their personal histories"* (1991, 43). Such personal histories cannot be ignored for, "if reforms are to be successful, individuals and groups must find meaning concerning **what** should change as well as **how** to go about it (ibid., 4). Change is not a passive process but an active engagement involving: *"new meanings, new behaviours, new skills and new beliefs"* (ibid, 77). This is a tall order for members of a traditionally conservative profession and the reason why change needs to be sensitively managed on a longitudinal basis. As Huberman & Miles wrote about their study of school improvement: *"Large scale, change-bearing innovations lived or died by the amount and quality of assistance that their users received once the change process was under way"* (1984, 273).

Where change, innovation and improvement are supported within a rich and coherent programme of staff development, then the combining of the two fields provides an outcome orientation with a process to achieve successful outcomes. The kind of staff development strategies central to the 'Treasure' philosophy, for example, skilled mentoring, peer coaching and action research have all been found to aid classroom and school improvement (Stoll & Fink, 1996). As a process orientation, it is most effectively underpinned by a collegial style of working, involving mutual sharing and assistance, of *"work related interdependence... concerned with personal availability, kindness and caring, where teachers and administrators make time for each other, even when very busy"* (ibid, 95).

Making time is very difficult for teachers. Interestingly, Huberman asserts that for most of the time, teachers learn alone. Indeed his study of 160 secondary school teachers indicated the most frequent scenario was that of 'the lone wolf' (2001, 145) with its solitary problem-solving, the pedagogical 'bricolage' of the individual artisan and its private, ruminatory 'tinkering'. In other words, he is suggesting that we do manage to find time for our own learning. However, adults clearly also learn powerfully in groups and since there is an especially strong 'discussion culture' among teachers it can, with a bit of 'pull and push', including an assault on the relative construct of time, encourage and sensitise teachers to the fact that their own personal theories are largely derived from their own practices and that there are several other possible and equally legitimate ways of constructing the same events and classroom realities. It is but a short step from experience sharing and what Schön calls *"reflections on action"* (1983) to collaborative experimentation and what Huberman calls *"exchanges in action"*, perhaps learning as 'packs' or 'networks of wolves'!

The gaze of the other

I have spent all of my professional life opening classroom doors, both literally and metaphorically speaking, as either a teacher or as a teacher educator. Classrooms are very special places and teaching a very special occupation. Teachers are, on the whole, quite special individuals with the necessary skills and the ability to touch young, developing minds. Much of this almost magical process takes place behind closed doors, insufficiently shared or observed by peers for example. Teachers, I would maintain, could also be touched by what they might see in the classrooms of their peers and improve or change their own professional skills by observing and incorporating new schemes into their mindsets for their own benefit and that of the whole learning community. Teachers have much to learn from each other and from their respective 'knowledge environments'; peer observation and peer coaching (and whatever else we might term 'peerwork') are at the heart of a culture of collaborative professional learning that encourages explicit counsel from peers who know how to respect the 'artisanship' of their fellow teacher'.

It is a role requiring skill and sensitivity. The skills are on the whole learnable although I would contend that these are not wholly in the grasp of everyone. 'Peerwork' can be very formalised as it is in one of our English project member schools in Essex, where all staff have 'buddied up' in pairs and have set about undertaking peer observation in a co-ordinated and systematic way. Everyone is involved as both observer and as the one observed at some point in time; all are exposed to 'the gaze of the other', *'le regard d'autrui'* as Sartre puts it, and actually a sort of self-controlling mechanism that persuades us to perform well when being observed. Critically, the unpredictable behaviour of the pupils and the very personal act of teaching serve as supreme levellers for all the teachers.

In other schools, 'peerwork' is more informal, more atomised within, for example, certain subject areas. In my last school for example, Maths and Modern Foreign Languages worked closely together both on a pedagogical basis (task - based learning more or less) and in terms of room proximity. Doors – yes, those doors again – were left open on the shared corridor and it was quite acceptable for colleagues to wander in and spend time in the classroom of a colleague, 'absorbing' if not exactly 'observing with a focus'. It led to the sensitisation to 'otherness' that is a key element in learning (Mason, 2002).

Learning from each other and theorising

Teachers, I am suggesting, have much to learn from each other and their 'knowledge environments' and it is this concept of two way learning that is at the heart of a culture of collaborative professional learning that includes peer observation as a matter of course. The axes of learning run in several directions, allowing, for example, new teachers to watch more experienced ones as well as the more experienced teachers to learn from the fresh ideas of the newly qualified teacher. The Humanities teacher can learn from the Scientist and from the Mathematician and vice versa, the less successful class manager from the more successful one and so on. The combinations are endless. Most teachers would agree that it is fascinating to see what goes on in a colleague's classroom; it appeals to one's professional curiosity. Indeed, as Brighouse and Woods comment, *'Teachers are natural researchers, in the sense that all teaching is based on inquiry and the response of the pupils provides ready evidence as to the effectiveness of various teaching and learning approaches'* (1999, 42). Peer observation moves teachers in the direction of working as co-researchers. Observation prompts reactions and questions and leads naturally to debate, challenge, problematisation, theory-making, suggestions and potential solutions to problems. The theorising, so often eschewed by classroom practitioners because of a misconception, *'is the bottom-up recognition of theory emanating from practice a means of forging personally meaningful links between theoretical knowledge about teaching and experience of the classroom'* (Wajnryb, 1992, 8-9). Theorising is thus: *"an important part of the teachers' learning experience and crucially, an opportunity to play a role in generating a knowledge base 'inside-out' emanating from neither theory nor practice alone but from critical reflection on the intersection of the two"* (Cochran-Smith and Lytle, op.cit., 15)

Labyrinths and gardens

Teachers can all benefit by adapting the effective practices of others, honing their own expertise further but, more importantly, providing as a team of teachers, a more coherent and more cohesive learning curriculum for the pupils, the ultimate beneficiaries. The curriculum can resemble a labyrinth for the pupils, *"a dark maze"* which offers *"bewilderment, frustration and confusion as each door [is] opened"* (Loughran, 1999, 86). Teachers must, in sum, learn to explore and examine the perplexities of their own maze through self-inquiry, embrace 'the open door classroom' and make peer observation a regular practice in their lives. It is known that we learn by keen 'noticing' and that during this process, we alter and enhance our personal constructs.

As Mason writes: *"Professional noticing is what we do when we see someone else acting professionally (teaching a lesson, leading a workshop, delivering a lecture…) and become aware of something they do (a task they set, a pattern of speech they employ, a question they ask…) which we think we could use ourselves"* (2002, 30).

Some schools are more receptive to this type of learning and have 'warmer' cultures than others do; indeed, this can be quite tangible. Cultures, however, are not static but are dynamic and are socially constructed by teachers, pupils, parents and other relevant stakeholders, shaped by their desires, needs, rituals, values and common interests (Nias, 1989). They are also buffeted by unpredictability, resistance and issues of contestation (Ball, 1987), a dimension of a school's subculture not to be underestimated. Given the evolving properties of schools, there is scope to develop in a school a culture of greater openness and receptivity. As far as peer observation is concerned, it is necessary to begin by declaring classrooms no longer as 'secret gardens', accessed, to continue the metaphor, only by the one lone gardener but rather as public gardens, with restricted visiting hours certainly to avoid unnecessary interruption but with beautiful blooms and horticultural skills to be appreciated by others who can then obtain ideas as to how to improve their own gardens.

In the reality of the school, colleagues can be timetabled to go into other colleagues' classrooms to do nothing other than to soak up the atmosphere in the first instance. Teachers can be paired up or can work in small groups and part of a school's designated professional development time earmarked for discussion of the observations and reactions. It is important that all comments, negative and positive are debated but a suitable challenge would be to consider how to transform the negative into positive, the not wholly successful to the more successful.

Such activities will invariably provide rich data for inquiry into the labyrinth of teaching and learning. Teachers are no strangers to data; in fact they are generators, collectors and receivers of substantial amounts of data. What teachers are not so good at is analysing the data; data often throw up discomforting features that we might prefer to keep under the carpet, for example. However the skills of objective interpretation are readily learnable, especially with an open mind that is ready to confront and to learn. The skills are underpinned by reflexivity, Schön's *'reflection in action'* and his concept of professionals as *'reflective practitioners'*, for as Bryant asserts:

"Research does not have to be something carried out by a special group of people called researchers but is in fact what any practitioner could do as part of everyday practice, given certain conditions. Reflective practitioners are ipso facto researchers into their own practice" (1996, 115).

Opening doors

One of the conditions might be a willingness to open doors. Of course, many 'doors', so to speak, are opened by those outside the school such as agencies involved in imposing national curricula, external inspection, publishable test and examination results, quality approaches such as Investors in People and, to some extent, the Governing Bodies of schools or School Councils. Stoll & Fink, also in 'doors discourse' mode, assert that: *"while opening mandated doors will certainly get people's attention, there is little evidence that they engender commitment on the part of people who have to implement the change. It is through opening as many internal doors as possible that authentic change occurs"* (1996, 48).

Through opening classroom doors, internally and on a mutually invitational basis, we can investigate teaching and learning (attempting to identify, describe and analyse teaching skills and other strategies, for example). We can also open many other conceptual doors, including that of self-evaluation and seek to make honest and constructive interpretations of, as David Silverman puts it so starkly, *'what is going on?'* in any particular scholastic arena in which we are interested (1985).

This door-opening metaphor has much to do with my construct of research. It resonates too with Loughran's construct as *"...seeking answers to questions...which are important in the teaching and learning environment"* (1999, 3). How we seek answers will thus depend on the questions and the type of evidence considered appropriate and useful. Quantitative and qualitative research methods both have particular uses and provide particular types of data; they can or should be complementary and not mutually exclusive; together they can help to construct a picture of 'what is going on' with the aid of quality indicators to reflect the qualitative nature of judgements to be made and of performance indicators to provide quantitative and statistical measures. One methodological approach shores up the weakness of the other. The data-rich picture obtained then can provide a basis for a conceptual shift from what Hopkins and Lagerweij refer to as the *"anecdotal evidence and perceptual data collected unsystematically"* (1996, 88) by teachers and to the posing of important questions that will seed an inquiry culture in preparation for more systematic research type investigations.

Such reflective processes engage us in utilising 'a vocabulary of practice' which facilitates thinking about our actions, evaluating responses and planning future courses of action. Where this is undertaken in a framework of shared reflection, Law & Glover suggest that: *"...it enables alternatives to be evaluated and future plans to be made through collaborative review and joint reflexive action"* (2001, 249).

Recent Italian research by Losito and colleagues (1998) on school-based and school improvement focused research, highlighted an interesting initiative of schools *'stopping to think'* for a whole day in allocated development time. Law & Glover also researched schools that offered the staff professional development time for *'structured reflection'* and for *'personal investigations'* linked to corporate expectations, of course – both examples of very creative use of time and certainly a luxury gift of quality reflection time for those involved.

Schools in their own cultural contexts and with their own needs will all have their own 'wish lists' of what needs improving or of what they would like to do differently and thus 'think about'; *autrement dit*, where doors need or might benefit from opening.

Two 'telling cases'

There are many examples of practitioner research that 'tell' of success, however modest. I will briefly tell about two cases, in which I have been involved, one from the 'inside', one from the 'outside'.

An 'insider' case

In my last school, we teachers became aware that although the school, as a true comprehensive, attracted a large number of able pupils (band 1 pupils according to performance data), someone somewhere suggested we were not making adequate provision for so-called able pupils. We became aware of this because:

- some parents complained about what they considered the inappropriate tasks being set for their children
- pupils deemed by consensus to be able were 'switching-off' or becoming disruptive in lessons
- exam results were adequate but did not excel where we had estimated they might.

I was one of the teachers in receipt of a letter from a disappointed parent who asked me whether I was an Art or a French teacher (I was a French teacher) on account of all the drawing homework I set (fairly common practice I am afraid to say in my subject area of MFL). Of course, I was piqued, angry and defensive as most teachers become when they are criticised, especially by a parent. I went, with great indignation, to see the head at some point who looked at me for a moment and then asked whether I would like to lead a task force to investigate the identification of and provision for able pupils and the creation of a whole-school policy for able pupils. This critical incident caused a seismic change in my professional stance. I wrote a gracious letter to the parent and became a researcher. I convened a cross-subject task force and my colleagues and I set to work. With support (some dedicated meeting time and very modest funding for the group from the head) and training (free from our partnership Higher Education Institute) we utilised questionnaires, we did interviews, we undertook observation and participant observation. We began with our own tacit knowledge to answer questions such as 'who do **we** think is able and what is our evidence?' before using our bit of funding to acquire some books and to visit other schools to help us articulate our definitions and policies. There was of course in built self and external evaluation, although in retrospect, this was probably insufficiently rigorous. This is just a brief insight into one modest piece of practitioner research. It was a motivating experience for a large number of teachers and associated colleagues and other stakeholders such as some parents. We had real ownership of our undertaking and came to realise we were involved in the shared construction of knowledge. Our views were respected, our suggestions enacted, practice embedded and sustained over time. We were made to feel valued and important. Thirteen years on, the policy still stands and has naturally, in an aware, improving school, evolved further. The main credit goes to the headteacher for her foresight and trust in our capabilities; she indeed was the lead learner. Whatever teacher empowerment means, I think this is it. The research process is represented in the open-ended flow-chart below:

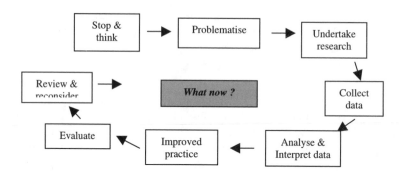

Figure 3: 'Insider' practitioner research open-ended flowchart.

An 'outsider' case

A very large primary school wanted to improve pupil behaviour. With clear policies for sanction and reward already in place, it wanted to 'investigate deeper'. The deputy head, very well read and an excellent example of a 'reflective practitioner', invited the entire staff to chose to work on one of four teams in a whole school research project. The four teams comprised the topics of multiple intelligences, EQ (emotional intelligence), language and learning across the curriculum and ICT across the curriculum, summarised in the diagram below:

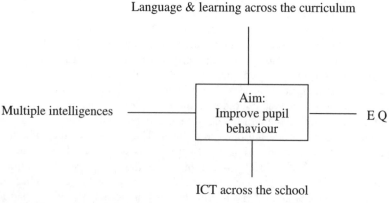

Figure 4: Axes of research

They have allocated meeting time and resourcing as appropriate. They have used a variety of research methods including literature review. As one of the outsider critical friends, with whom they engage, I have been afforded the occasional insight into this very creative research. If anything, it is superior to my first 'telling case' because every single teacher has been involved and because of its lateral thinking around the topic. EQ, for example, is relatively speaking, a fairly new input into the vast field on school management and leadership (although some would argue it is a new take on an old concept-interpersonal skills); in a pupil context it is incredibly innovative. The teams, as is always the case, work more or less effectively dependent to some extent on the quality of the team leadership but just as much on the quality and readiness of the team members. The most effective team has roles of responsibility for every single member.

I was, as an academic researcher, especially interested in the role of the team researcher. The one I interviewed searches the Internet and in libraries for associated literature and makes it available to colleagues, helpfully summarising it sometimes. She thus enables the group to articulate their <u>own</u> theories more effectively and to triangulate them with existing theories, a very good example of what Huberman calls: *"sustained interactivity between researchers and practitioners... that re-frames the goal of research from one of primarily informing the practitioner to one of jointly constructing knowledge through shared activity"* (1999, 291).

Knowledge boundaries are being extended by every single member of staff, including support staff; slowly but surely, practice is being transformed. The research project has included parents and pupils. The school has benefited from various spin-offs, for example, in the form of self-learning, the modifying of whole-school instructional practices and the interpersonal bonds which are significant. It is a fine example of an intelligent school utilising its own multiple intelligences.

So, what makes them work?

Some analysis of these two brief case slides will be useful if we are to be able to extrapolate potentially significant features that underpin their success (and I want to emphasise that success is always relative). In neither case did everything run smoothly, far from it. However, it seems to me that there are some overarching principles in operation, which include:

- In both cases, a research project was developed as a result of a real, felt need. It is well known that a felt need, on the part of practitioners to initiate change, to innovate, is a necessary precondition of teacher research (Stenhouse, 1975; Elliott, 1991).
- Processes and outcomes are both considered important. In both cases acceptable indeed stimulating ways of working have been found. However, a direct impact in the classroom has been clearly envisaged in terms of pupil achievement and behaviour and in terms of instructional practice.
- The quality of the research itself is a factor in terms of its structure, orientation, creativeness, evaluative mechanisms, rigour and leadership and whole-school support, for example. It is considered worthwhile.

– The enthusiasm factor of teachers is remarkable in both cases. This seems to me to have much to do with motivation. Williams & Burden separate the temporal dimension of motivation into three stages along a continuum:

> Reasons for doing something
> → Deciding to do something
> → Sustaining the effort, or persisting.

As they write: *"...motivation is more than simply arousing interest. It also involves sustaining interest and investing time and energy into putting the necessary effort to achieve certain goals"* (1997, 121)

– A door-opening culture and a willingness to learn. As Senge wrote: "The problem with talking about 'learning organisation' is that 'learning' has lost its central meaning in contemporary usage. Most people's eyes glaze over if you talk to them about 'learning organisations" (1990, 13). Nevertheless, if we use Handy's definition (1993) of a learning organisation as meaning:
  – an organisation which encourages learning in its people
  – an organisation which itself 'learns'
then the two 'telling cases' of practitioner action qualify their schools as learning organisations.

Problems arising

The above points are illustrative and not exhaustive. I suggest is it also useful to confront issues of concern and problem areas lest my own enthusiasm for practitioner research gives an overly rosy picture. There are in fact a great many problems or 'thorns'. To begin with, it seems to me that schools that have engaged in practitioner research are in the minority. Those irretractable problems of time, misconception and disinterest persist. Indeed, both 'telling cases' experienced these problems too but they were not defeated by them. It is highly likely that certain school cultures will be more supportive and enabling of practitioner research and other modes of community learning. Stoll & Fink have pulled together the cultural norms widely believed to underpin successful school improvement, a framework in which I am locating practitioner research:
– shared goals – 'we know where we are going'
– responsibility for success – 'we must succeed'
– collegiality – 'we're working on this together'
– continuous improvements – 'we can get better'
– lifelong learning – 'learning is for everyone'
– risk taking – 'we learn by trying something new'
– support – 'there's always someone there to help'
– mutual respect – 'everyone has something to offer'
– openness – 'we can discuss our differences'
– celebration and humour – 'we feel good about ourselves'
(op.cit., 92-8).

It is possible to map quite a few of these norms onto the 'telling case' schools and their practitioner research cultures. However, Stoll & Fink emphasise that: *"All schools are unique and may possess few, some or all of these norms"* (ibid, 1998). Furthermore each school has its own culture, its realities, its mindset of school life, its history, in sum its 'glue' that holds it together, more or less effectively, for better or for worse. It is certain (Prosser, 1999) that there are no quick recipes for reculturing.

I previously referred to the temporal nature of motivation. The initial flush of enthusiasm for a project in which we are interested will be a familiar sensation as will the almost inevitable plateau-ing out phase. As Cervantes declared, *'fore-warned, fore-armed!'* – and it can help to plan strategies to sustain interest with careful, creative action planning, injections of stimulus at well-judged junctures and a constant flow of feedback.

More of a problem perhaps is the emotional reaction to 'things going wrong', of uncomfortable data that may show practices, if not certain colleagues, in a bad light; of inter- if not intranecine relationships between and within teams, jealousies, fears and insecurities. Power relations shift in all directions and tension occur. There are always 'the resistors ' to contend with or what Brighouse and Woods call the 'energy consumers'; it is no easy task trying to turn the latter in to 'energy creators' or at best 'energy neutral'. It is a real problem considering how to find a way to 'energise' and to trigger motivation for all.

The emotional dimension ought not to be underestimated. Indeed, a teacher's emotional wellbeing, MacBeath & Mortimore (2001) claim, is an important influence on her/his capacity to engage in and sustain continuous learning. Solutions must lie in the domain of supportive interpersonal relationships and the aforementioned culture of openness. Teachers are especially vulnerable in another respect in so far as teaching is seen as a performance, in which case, audience response must be expected. As Gray & Freeman point out: *"Most teachers need the warm approval of their students to obtain the satisfaction they require from the job"* (1987, 47).

Such 'warm approval' is not always forthcoming from pupils and perhaps a greater fear is the 'audience response' of one's colleagues. My almost evangelical call to open doors will invariably involve critiquing of teachers' performance as well as pupil achievement. It is very hard to disentangle the personal and the professional in teaching when we teachers, in fact, invest so much of ourselves in our teaching personae. The art of constructive criticism is not in the gift of all colleagues.

One final point that I wish to raise in this paper in terms of problematics is what Andy Hargreaves calls *"contrived collegiality"* (1993) and Woods et al, rather more directly, *"collaborative overkill"* (1997). School management rhetoric is highly coloured by the notion of collaborative school planning, for example, and recent reform and innovation have most certainly increased the number of meetings teachers are required to attend, for one thing. However, as Woods et al comment: *"Debates and discussion are central to collaborative processes but if the only agenda is concerned with choices that are concerned with trivia... or there is no time to research fully the benefits and drawbacks of the new system, then teachers' commitment to collaboration becomes threatened"* (ibid., 31). It is, as they conclude on this point, *"the quality of the experience that matters"*, reflecting the heartfelt concern of Flemish headteacher Jackie Denis of the Treasure Project *"to improve the quality of debate with and amongst teachers"* (Oostende, January 2001).

And now what next?

There is , as the saying goes, much still to do, much to ponder, explore and to research. We know for sure that practitioner research can work in certain cultural contexts and we have a wide body of evidence indicative of cultures more favourable to such collaborative enterprises. What we really do not know for certain is what such a culture looks like or feels like to those inhabiting the particular context. Might it, for example, resemble what Smyth calls 'the dialogic school' in which teachers feel a need to: *"theorise and re-theorise what is going on, what works, how they know and how things might be done differently...and have feisty debates about alternatives"?* (1999, 73). And if so, where do they find the time and what do the teachers talk about?

As to the squeezing of teachers' time, Woods et al. refer to the recent 'intensification' of teachers' work and the rather unwelcome focus on their 'peformativity', especially in some cultures, but at the same time hint at the emergence of an 'extensification syndrome', *"a new empowerment of self"* (op.cit., 165) through a taking of control and a self-assertion. This would indicate powerful learning experiences taking place, in need of 'thick description' and microscopal investigation.

Ultimately, as teacher–researcher Ian Mitchell writes: *"It is teachers who determine what happens in classrooms... and one important advantage of teacher research is that it will generate the short-term contextual detail that teachers demand"* (1999, 63). This ties in nicely with Hopkins and Reynolds' predilection for 'short-term feedback loops', (loops being all the rage in current learning theory), on data obtained from school operational procedures in order *"to improve schools' level of intelligence concerning their operation"* (2001, 477). It is, I suggest, intelligence data we would wish to key into for research purposes and for the purposes of 'powerful learning' for ourselves.

They argue for more work on focusing school improvement on the 'learning level' because, and this is very relevant to the Treasure:

"Whilst not every school is an effective school, every school has within itself some classroom practice that is relatively more effective than other practice. Many schools will have within themselves classroom practice that is absolutely effective across all schools. With a within-school 'learning level' orientation, every school can benefit from its own internal conditions" (ibid., 467), and I would add , for we want doors opening outwards as well as inwards, from the

successful experiences and conditions of others. Credit and inspiration for the door metaphor is due to Joyce (1991) who first described the process of school improvement as a system of interconnected doors: practitioner research of whatever kind offers opportunities for those doors to be opened. We should not resist the opportunity to take a look both inside and outside.

References

Ball, S. (1987). *The Micropolitics of the School*. London: Methuen.

Brighouse, T. & Woods, P. (1999). *How to Improve your School*. London: Methuen.

Bryant, I. (1996). Action Research and reflective practice. In Scott, D. & Usher, R. (Eds.) *Understanding Educational Research*. London: Routledge.

Cochran-Smith, M. & Lytle, S. (1993*). Inside Outside. Teacher Research and Knowledge*. New York: Teachers College Press.

Elliott, J. (1991). *Action Research for Educational Change*. Buckingham: O.U.P.

Fullan, M. (1991). *The New Meaning of Educational Change*. New York: Teachers College Press.

Handy, C. (1993). *Understanding Organisations*. Harmondsworth: Penguin.

Gray, H. & Freeman, A. (1987). *Teaching without Stress*. London: Paul Chapman.

Hargreaves, A. (1993). Contrived Collegiality: the micropolitics of teacher collaboration. In Blasé, J. (Ed.) *The Politics of Life is School*. London: Sage.

Hopkins, D. & Lagerweij, N. (1996). The School Improvement Knowledge Base in Reynolds, D. et al. *Managing Good Schools*. London; Routledge.

Hopkins, D. & Reynolds, D. (2001). The Past, Present and future of School Improvement: towards the third age. *British Journal of Educational Research* 27(4), September 2001

Huberman, M. (1999). The Mind is its own Place: the Influence of sustained interactivity with Practitioners on Educational Researchers. *Harvard Educational Review*, 69(3) Fall 1999, 289-320.

Huberman, M. (2001). Networks that alter teaching. In Soler, J. et al. *Teacher Development. Exploring our own Practice*. London: Paul Chapman.

Huberman, M. & Miles, M. (1984) *Innovation Up Close*. New York: Plenum Press.

Joyce, B. R. (1991). The doors to school improvement. *Educational Leadership,* 48(8), 559-62.

Lave, J. & Wenger, E. (1991). *Situated Learning: Legitimate Peripheral Participation*. Cambridge: C.U.P.

Law, S. & Glover, D. (2000). *Educational Leadership and Learning. Practice, Policy and Research*. Buckingham: O.U.P.

Losito, B. et al. (1998). *Quality Evaluation in School Education*. ms.

Loughran, J. (1999). *Researching Teaching*. London: Falmer

MacBeath, J. & Mortimore, P. (2001). *Improving School Effectiveness*. Buckingham: O.U.P.

Mason, J. (2002*). The Art of Noticing. Researching your own Practice*. London: Routledge Falmer.

Mitchell, I. (1999). *Bridging the Gulf between Research and Practice*. In Loughran c.f. supra.

Nias, J. et al. (1989). *Staff Relations in the Primary School*. London: Cassell.

Prosser, J. (ed.) (1999). *School Culture*. London: Paul Chapman.

Schön, D. (1983). *The Reflective Practitioner*. London: Arena.

Senge, P. (1990). *The Fifth Discipline*. London: Doubleday.

Silverman, D. (1985). *Qualitative Methodology and Sociology. Describing the Social World*. Aldershot: Gower Publishing.

Smyth, J. (1999). *Researching the Cultural Politics of Teachers' learning* in Loughran c.f. supra.

Stenhouse, L. (1975*). An Introduction to Curriculum Research and Development*. London: Heinemann.

Stoll, L. & Fink, D. (1996). *Changing our Schools*. Buckingham: O.U.P.

Toffler, A. (1990). *Future Shock*. London: Pan Books

Wajnryb, R. (1992). *Classroom Observation Tasks*. Cambridge: CUP

Woods, P. et al. (1997). *Restructuring Schools, Reconstructing Teachers*. Buckingham: O.U.P.

Williams, M. & Burden, R. (1997). *Psychology for language teachers*. Cambridge: C.U.P.

Jane Jones is Head of Modern Foreign Language Teacher Education at the Department of Education Studies and Professional Studies, King's College, University of London, UK.

CHAPTER 4

PRACTITIONER RESEARCH IN THE PRIMARY SCHOOL: A CASE STUDY AND A 'JOLLY GOOD EFFORT'

Jane Jones

Abstract

I have elsewhere explained the rationale for practitioner research as professional development and as a concrete way for teachers to 'improve' their schools. I have also defined practitioner research as *'systematic self-critical inquiry'* (Stenhouse, op.cit.). The primary school provides a rich locale for research for many reasons that I will now expand upon.

From a methodological point of view, current, (as well as traditional) learning theories and the primary pedagogical community of practice tend towards investigation –focused learning, constructivism, both social and cognitive, research and inquiry driven modes of learning. This creates a warm and productive culture for practitioner research since it resonates with the core activities in the school.

Nias et al in their ethnographic study of primary schools were able to establish that: *'in general, there appears to be a broad consensus about what children should learn'* and where a culture of collaboration was strong, ' *a very broad consensus among the staff about teaching methods'* (1989, 48, op.cit.).

The primary school with its emphasis on the whole child and its cross-curricular map of learning provides conditions conducive to teacher collaborative learning since teachers are already engaged in much collaborative planning, possibly teaching, depending on the cultural context .It is but a few notches along the continuum of inquiry and research to begin researching together in the pursuit of organisational learning. Communication systems are often more successful and collegiality of the 'uncontrived ' variety in the primary school because of its lesser segmentation into subject pigeonholes. As Nias *et al* concluded: *'Two related features of the collaborative schools were that the staff spent a great deal of time talking to one another and that their conversations were usually a mixture of chat about themselves and discussion of their teaching'* (ibid., 79).

Teacher chat is a high level activity

I intend to describe and analyse one innovative, albeit small-scale piece of research that is taking place in a primary school where, to paraphrase Nias, the chat is a high-level activity. Their focus, a concern that many colleagues can doubtless identify with, is that of wishing to improve pupil behaviour. Instead of taking the usual route of evaluating and perhaps tweaking the system of sanction and reward, a very creative enterprise has been undertaken that has involved the whole school community in research activity and all of the teachers in one of four self-managing teams. Roles have been identified for all colleagues, thus respecting the varied learning styles and motivation of teachers themselves whose personal learning needs are often ill attended to. The project has framed the professional development of the school, giving it a sense of urgency and meaning in terms of relating to a felt need. The teams comprise: Multiple Intelligences, EQ (emotional intelligence), Language and Learning across the curriculum and ICT across the curriculum.

Multiple Intelligences (MI) theory derives from the work, of course, of Howard Gardner. He states, quite simply that all learners have the capacity to develop **at least** 7 types of intelligence, elaborated in the words below by MacGilchrist et al. (1997):
1   linguistic; the intelligence of words
2   logical-mathematical: the intelligence of numbers and reasoning
3   spatial: the intelligence of pictures and images
4   musical: the intelligence of tone, rhythm and timbre
5   bodily-kinaesthetic: the intelligence of the whole body and the hands
6   interpersonal: the intelligence of social understanding
7   intrapersonal: the intelligence of self-knowledge

Research activities have involved shared reading and discussion to provide a context. Many teachers have little time for reading but the provision of selected and focused reading has overcome that difficulty somewhat. They have then introduced the concept to the pupils and have asked them to reflect on the question: 'How am I smart?' and to research evidence for themselves to substantiate the claim. The assumption is that all children are smart in some way.

The evidence might include, for example, some justificatory writing, drawings, photos, testimonials from a friend or a family member or some sample of work. The evidence is mounted in a wall display for contemplation and sharing. The 'I can do' philosophy must give a potent message to the pupils about the capability of each one of them. Teachers have collected the data and analysed it. They have established for themselves that pupils have what Gardner calls *'individual profiles of intelligence'*, very useful information to share with colleagues who can then make fuller use, with the overt knowledge of the pupils and of their 'intelligence profiles'. As Gardner asserts: *'Assuming room for developing more than a single faculty along a single track, decisions of a far more focused sort must be made as well. In the case of each individual, those charged with educational planning must decide which means can best be mobilized to help that individual attain a desired competence'* (1983, 388).
Improving pupil behaviour is in evidence where pupils have developed self-esteem and reflexivity. MI across the school enables teachers to differentiate in a meaningful way.

EQ, otherwise known as emotional intelligence, is taken from the writing of Daniel Goleman. It is a theory that asserts that emotional literacy is as important as literacy in its traditional sense as well as academic and practical achievement. EQ involves personal growth and key skills that include: self-awareness, decision-making, the ability to manage feelings, handling stress, empathy, communication, insight, a sense of personal responsibility, assertiveness and the potential for conflict resolution. In England, this is the stuff of the so-called 'pastoral curriculum', often called personal, social and health education (PSHE), a compulsory element of the core curriculum that is timetabled usually once weekly. It doubtless exists in similar guises in other educational systems. The point it that it is misconceived to imagine that personal growth issues can be only relegated to a weekly slot; the subject of *'self-science'*, as Goleman calls it, needs interweaving across the whole of the schooling experience. Indeed, Goleman is right behind this case study primary school's attempt as he writes: *'Another way emotional lessons can be woven into the fabric of existing school life is through helping teachers rethink how to discipline students who misbehave'* (1996, 272).

Teachers have again explored the literature on the subject. When they felt comfortable with the concept themselves, they have introduced the idea to the pupils in a very specific way, in the activity now well known as 'circle time'. Bliss and Tetley describe it thus: *'When pupils meet together with their class teacher, sit in a circle in an enjoyable atmosphere of co-operation and take part in games and activities to increase self-awareness, awareness of others, self-esteem, co-operation, trust and listening skills'* (1997, 4). In research terms, the teacher in the group acts as participant-observer. All team members keep reflective diaries to record the events of each session and their personal reflections about them. In team meetings, these reflections are shared and discussed. Improved behaviour results because 'circle time' rules (e.g. the insistence on pupils listening to each other properly), having become phenomenally popular are adopted across the curriculum. Again a consistent message is given to all members of the community.

One member of the team mentioned that they had discussed EQ in terms of themselves and had established, for example, that EQ principles were just as important in staff relationships. As Loughran writes: *'In crowded and emotionally charged classrooms, peopled as they are at any given time with enthusiastic, disadvantaged and disenchanted students, teachers need to be able to draw upon self –awareness as a means of understanding their own behaviour and thus manage their feelings appropriately'* (1999, 220, op.cit.).

North American research on the interpersonal and emotional profiles of leaders indicated that some 80% of their success as leaders could be attributed to high EQ. It can be seen that there is a significant link with the MI team's point of focus, somewhat underplayed I found when I was 'critical-friending' but the staff were at least aware that they needed to develop coherent links across the teams.

The **Language and Learning across the curriculum** team was aware of its central role in terms of the present government's drive to raise the profile of literacy. This was not a problem. Indeed their work was deemed to be supportive to that drive but went beyond it in terms of its extended definition of literacy. Thus whilst basic reading and writing are considered important, this team was also stressing oral, aural and visual literacies, for example, as well as emphasising the need for children to develop critical language awareness. Ivanovic writes; *'the critical approach recognises that language can help to shape social practice'* (1990, 126). There was a strong attachment to the notion that language is power and that literacy as well as attending to spelling conventions, punctuation and sentence structure is about developing mechanisms for personal meaning-making. Research activities involved a considerable literature review undertaken by the self-styled team researcher. The team established a policy of coherent practice across the school and engaged, as peer experts, in peer coaching e.g. on correction techniques, handwriting scripts and literacy within subjects. They also undertook peer observation and focused observation of pupils.

In sum, here is one primary school in a very deprived area and of modest means that recognises the empowering nature of language as a tool for self-emancipation and of improvement.

The **ICT across the curriculum team** began by auditing the ICT capabilities of its own members. Whether by choice or by a little gentle persuasion, some members were in this team who were previously more or less at least computer-illiterate at the beginning. Somehow or other, the learning challenge had been confronted resulting in, as is often the case with ICT enthusiasts, an evangelical faith in the power and potential of ICT as a learning and teaching tool. The newly expert team then engaged in peer observation, peer coaching and very important for ICT instruction, continuing peer support. Most of their energies were directed at the staff, pupils having no fear of the array of technology *in situ*. Indeed when I was in the school, early morning watching the arrival of the pupils and the parents of many of them (a very rich observation period I have always found), many of the early arrivals went straight to a computer and started up some programme or other and got on quietly with whatever it was they were doing. It made for a peaceful and well-oriented start to the day.

The team was interested to consider how ICT can enhance teaching and learning and also to ease the burden of administrative load. This involved technical research on e.g. how to use the interactive whiteboard and its impact on learning, to investigate available resources for colleagues and to review them and to consider how to integrate all of these things into curriculum planning. Inroads had been made but, one team member lamented that there was the danger of the role quickly degenerating into one of technician hence the priority to capability – build in others. On a general level the team wished to emphasise that the benefits were essentially to do with sharing, e.g. the dissemination of lesson plans and ideas on the school intranet, and with the provision of opportunities for independent learning for the pupils, thus providing learning possibilities beyond the classroom, especially important for those in not especially supportive or literate households. The theme of pupil empowerment once again emerges strongly from this research perspective.

A success story: teachers reflecting on and in action

I have elaborated elsewhere on the conditions I consider necessary for successful practitioner research activities to develop. However, to sum up the key issues, I would suggest that the following are key factors:
- Activity focuses around a keenly felt need (such as unsatisfactory pupil behaviour)
- Engagement of the whole school community (that involved support staff, parental involvement, critical friends and pupil input and feedback) and thus effective community learning
- A lateral and imaginative approach to problem solving involving a wide range of investigation and research techniques
- Resources and time allocation
- Strong team leadership (better in some cases then in others but this is inevitable)
- Collaborative learning encompassing a wide range of teacher learning styles
- Supportive and imaginative leadership from the 'top'
- Observable impact and outcomes
- A desire to do better and a certainty amongst the staff that they could 'improve' their school.

The research project has not been without its problems but these are known about and have been confronted. It is even so, in my opinion, an unqualified success because real personal and organisational learning has taken place and individual teachers have engaged with educational change as active agents, making meaning of change for themselves to paraphrase Fullan (1991, op.cit.).

Webb comments that: '*the message to those engaged in practitioner research, which aims to initiate and sustain change going beyond the individual classroom, is that if it is to have maximum impact, an appropriate environment has to be created*' (1990, 252). We have, it seems to me, an example of such an environment in this school. I wrote in my introduction on the favourable conditions in primary schools for research activity again which are illuminated in this case study. Day *et al* also comment that: '*Primary schools have always taken the learning process seriously and much of what we do know about the ways to manage a learning in the classrooms have been developed by imaginative practitioners supported by insights and understandings from academic research*' (1998, 24). This school is a very good example of Huberman's construct of ' sustained interactivity' (written about elsewhere by me) between practice and theory, emerging as personalised theory for the school grounded in their own practice.

The school in fact has considered several management approaches to learning and has specifically opted for the Davies/Ellison model of 'self- managing teams'. It is a model designed to elicit high quality performance from the staff. The philosophy which needs no further comment is thus: '*The model suggests that, for high performance teamwork to occur, this alignment of power, information, resources and indeed rewards within the team structure is a fundamental prerequisite. This is in contrast with earlier approaches in which teams were used to deal with specific issues and/or solve particular problems without, necessarily, having large amounts of power and resources at their disposal. Under the new scenario, effective teamwork becomes far more than a nicety aimed at improving working conditions of staff, or even of achieving improved outcomes, and moves to the central pursuit of major driver in pursuit of high performance*' (1997, 150).

Epilogue

In a follow-up discussion to the presentation, colleagues present were asked to reflect upon their own multiple intelligences. They were asked to mind-map school research ideas. There follows two examples.

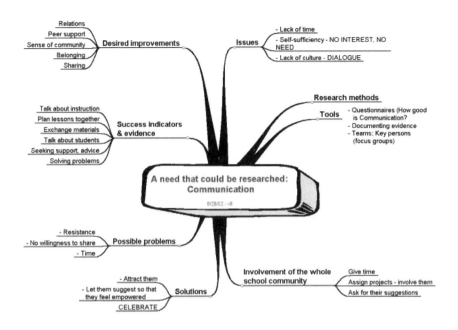

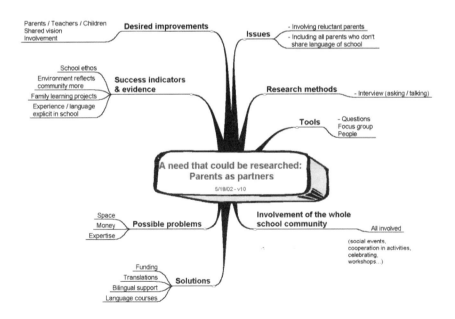

References

Bliss, T & Tetley, J (1997). *Circle Time*. Bristol: Lucky Duck Enterprises.

Davies, B & Ellison L. (1999). *School Leadership in the 21st Century*. London: Routledge.

Day, C. et al. (1998). *Developing Leadership in Primary Schools*. London: Paul Chapman.

Gardner, H. (1983). *Frames of Mind: The theory of Multiple Intelligences*. London: Fontana press.

Goleman, D. (1995). *Emotional Intelligence. Why it can matter more then IQ*. London: Bloomsbury.

Ivanovic, R. (1990). Critical Language Awareness in Action. In Carter, R. (ed.) *Knowledge about Language and the Curriculum*. London: Hodder & Stoughton.

MacGilchrist, B. et al. (1997). *The Intelligent School*. London: Paul Chapman.

Webb, R. (ed.) (1990). *Practitioner Research in the Primary school*. London: Falmer Press.

Jane Jones is Head of Modern Foreign Language Teacher Education at the Department of Education Studies and Professional Studies, King's College, University of London, UK.

CHAPTER 5

CRITICAL REFLECTION AS A MEANS OF TEACHER EMPOWERMENT

Sonja Sentočnik

Abstract

One of the essential goals of the curriculum reform in Slovenia which has been in progress since 1998 is to improve the quality of knowledge and to encourage life-long learning in students. In order to implement this goal, it is not enough that teachers have the knowledge of the subject matter and pedagogical skills; what they need in addition to the above is especially the ability to learn from day-by-day experience through systematic reflection. Why is this so important?

For some time now, we have been facing a far more rapid growth of information and technology than ever before, and this has important implications for education. With the changed conception of knowledge, learning has gained new meaning. Knowledge is not understood as a body of one-dimensional and unchanged truths any more, but as a dynamic, continuously changing structure. Therefore, it cannot be transmitted from the teacher to the students, but has to be constructed and re-constructed by the learner. Cognitive science, especially the constructivist branch, points out the importance of active knowledge construction, which requires a learning environment to support learning as an individualised construction of cognitive process. Teachers have found themselves in new, uncertain territories. Day by day they are facing the situations in which they are expected to perform the tasks they were not educated for. Also, they were educated in a completely different environment and were faced with different expectations. They have to give up the security of being in charge and knowing everything, and become facilitators instead, those who stimulate, animate and moderate the process of searching and discovering. In order to develop their students' abilities to become active learners and to seek understanding of complex problems, they need to know how to create situations for them from which they will acquire strategies for self-assessment and for monitoring their level of understanding, as well as to reflect on what works and what needs improving.

The meaning of reflection for quality teaching

The changes required by the curriculum reform implementation have put enormous pressure on teachers. In order to fulfil their new role, teachers have to take charge of implementing the reformed curriculum through an action research orientation. As Schon (1987) argues, it is not enough that teachers make informed choices and decisions based exclusively on the research findings of other people; instead, they have to rely also on their own "practitioner derived knowledge" (Smyth 1989) which is the most relevant for them and their situation. In other words, this means that teachers have to become autonomous professionals, who are able to make decisions in the light of their concrete pedagogic experience and good knowledge of their students' needs. It also means the ability to step back and reflect about the experiences of their teaching days, question decisions they have made, and learn from their reflections. Autonomy is essentially a capacity for detachment, critical reflection, decision making and independent action (Little 1991, in Kohonen 1999). Reflection is used to make teachers conscious of their beliefs and assumptions about teaching and learning by critically analysing their thoughts and actions. Through reflection, we can analyse our actions, decisions or products by focusing on our process of achieving them (Killion and Todnem 1991). But as Smyth (1989) points out, reflection itself is insufficient if it is not accompanied by action. Reflection is always the starting point of a dialogue between teachers and between teacher(s) and their headteacher, which should be challenging, raising doubts about assumptions and practices, especially those that have been taken for granted, reformulating them and testing how the changes work in the classroom situation, then reflect, discuss again, regulate them and try them out again.

Action research: promoting teacher reflection

In order to address the above issues,[1] we have developed guidelines for an instrument called portfolio, intended to document and evaluate individual teacher's progress and growth. We established a partnership with five schools, and within each school a group of 5-8 voluntary teachers was formed, led by a headteacher who had to guarantee his collaboration. We have also developed a model of supervisory collaboration with the project schools, and have tried to establish the network among the schools; pilot teachers and their headteachers have been offered ongoing support in the form of training and consultation, and we have organised regular meetings since the start of the project with all the participating members of pilot schools twice a year in order to create the need for the exchange of experience and ideas, beliefs and opinions, and thus develop the pilot team into the learning community. Pilot teachers were asked to give us feedback at regular intervals about the process of implementing the portfolio guidelines and how it affected their thinking, their work, and their relationship with their colleagues and headteacher. The headteachers were also required to report on the progress of the portfolio process and the changes it had caused. The goal of the project was to initially develop an inquisitive attitude in teachers towards their work which would gradually lead to critical reflection and the need for change, resulting in experimenting with new ideas, and ultimately, in improving the quality of teaching and learning. The partnership with schools was formed in order to ensure that the links between research and practice flow in both directions; the expectation that the insight of researchers would help shape the understanding of the practitioners, and the insight of practitioners would help shape the insight of the researchers has proved to be correct.

The portfolio process

The guidelines for the teacher portfolio initially lead teachers to the establishment of the *framework for their portfolio* which serves as a continuous reference within which they are going to collect and document their individual progress toward their personal/professional goals which are supposed to be aligned with their school's goals. First, the teachers write down their *school's vision statement*, and after that their *personal teaching philosophy*, their *mission* and their *vision statement* for the academic year ahead. It has to be pointed out, however, that the framework should not be viewed as fixed, but rather as subject to continuous revision and modification, which is in accordance with the expectation that the new attitude of enquiry and critical reflection will cause continuous growth and development of teachers and school community. The framework helps teachers select their priorities and define *the purpose of the portfolio use:* at the beginning of school year, they select two areas of their work that they would like to improve, and one area of their work that they think they are particularly good at.

Each teacher then meets with the headteacher to establish *clear, concrete goals* for the year, and to make *an action plan* for the implementation of the stated goals. The teacher is encouraged by the headteacher to think about the possible *strategies for implementing the goals* and the necessary changes in the instruction and her/his attitude toward students and colleagues to incorporate his goals. Teachers then pay attention *to date samples of their work*, and throughout the year *collect* the artifacts that document their growth within the selected areas. At least once a month they *select* the material which they believe documents best either their growth in their selected areas of growth, or their excellence in their strong area. They put the selected material in the portfolio and *write a reflection* about the reasons for selecting it and how it exhibits their growth/excellence. They can also express their concern raised by the selected material, difficulties they may have experienced in trying to reach their goals, and specific assistance they may need from their headteacher or supervisor.

Teachers are expected to meet at least three times a year with their headteacher for the so called *portfolio conference*: they are encouraged to present their portfolios, and after looking together through the portfolio discuss with the headteacher their development process and achievement of their goals. It is very important that the tone and the structure of these conferences is appropriate: the headteacher should not assume the role of a critic who would judge a teacher's performance and decide whether s/he deserves promotion or not. In such a case, the teacher would feel the need to defend her/himself and would hide the weak areas: the purpose of portfolio as a tool for development and growth would be lost forever. The appropriate role the headteacher should assume is the role of a critical friend and co-creator of knowledge about teaching and learning, which facilitates reflection about the meaning of the collected data in the portfolio, possible adaptation of the goals and re-definition of the necessary professional support.

At the end of the academic year, teachers are encouraged to write a reflection letter in which they look back and reflect about their strengths and the challenges, about the impact of the implemented changes on their students and on themselves, about their feelings and their plans for the future.

Findings

When we began the portfolio guidelines implementation, we realised that most of the schools did not have the vision statements written down; even when they claimed they had, it turned out to be a long description of the headteacher's wishes without a clear thread, and not based on the consensus of school communities. Unintentionally, the project started a process of vision building and engaged the school communities in discussions about their values and beliefs, which, though time-consuming, turned out to be an extremely efficient community building strategy. It has to be pointed out that the school community vision building process is essential for the portfolio (self)assessment implementation: it is a catalyst for clarifying ideas and reaching consensus about the quality teaching and learning, which determine the choice of entries for the portfolio.

Furthermore, we realised that teachers felt uneasy about self-assessment from the start, and were unwilling to engage in it. We decided to involve them in the process of defining clear criteria against which they would be able to measure their performance through self-evaluation instruments that would suit their teaching context. The application of the criteria has facilitated formative self-assessment, which in turn can support teachers in writing down their reflections. The latter has turned out to be the biggest problem, and the teachers are still mostly unwilling to provide them. When we talk to the teachers about their portfolios and the development they are supposed to have encouraged, they are willing to reflect back, but their reflections remain superficial: there is still a discrepancy between what teachers think they are doing in the classroom and what is actually happening. When we ask teachers why they do not write down their reflections, they admit that it is very difficult for them to write down what they think, and add that they never have enough time "to write down their thoughts nicely so that they would be good enough for the others to read them". These has led us to include the acquisition of reflecting skills into the project group training workshops: we have created the opportunities for the teachers to work collaboratively on case studies and reflect on them. Providing them with the structure and guiding them through a reflection protocol (for example as proposed by Hole and McEntee, 1999) has eased the tension and given them a degree of confidence, but we believe that a lot of practice and supervision are still necessary.

We have also noticed that the teachers often select artifacts for their portfolio that are not accurate representations of the development in the area of work they want to document with the portfolio. By means of supervision, we have been sensitising the teachers to the importance of their selectiveness, and also to the fact that portfolio cannot be used to document effective practice if the right evidence is not there. In order to prevent that portfolios become overwhelmingly large and time consuming, we have been working on reaching clear understanding about the types and amounts of material to be included as evidence in the portfolio.

Why we think portfolio assessment works

Since the start of the project, the number of voluntary participating practitioners has remained stable, and in one of the schools the number has doubled. We believe that this is a sign that teachers have found portfolios to be efficient tools for documenting and (self)evaluating their progress toward their personal and school goals. In another school, teachers have decided to find their critical friends in the neighbouring school, which has resulted in a voluntary inter-school collaboration and frequent classroom observations, as well as parallel experimenting with change and discussions after implementing it. Most teachers have written reflective letters and discussed in them the changes they have noticed about themselves, their weak areas and possible ways to improve them. From what teachers write down in their reflective letters, it has become clear that they have changed gradually from passive recipients to active designers of their own professional development and growth. Many of them write about the questionnaires they have prepared for their students in order to learn about their needs and verify whether the instruction had met those needs. This means that they have stopped being preoccupied with themselves and shifted their focus more on to the needs of their students. All the participating teachers have been actively involved in some sort of a presentation of portfolio process to their colleagues, which has improved their self-esteem immensly.

As Smyth (1989) points out, "reflection, critical awareness, or enlightenment on its own is insufficient – it must be accompanied by action..." Consequently, we can safely claim that the portfolio process has enabled the collaborating teachers to become more involved in making decisions concerning their school's vision and goals, which has empowered them and gave them a strong feeling of belonging. Reflection has helped them confront their problem and take responsibility for their actions and attitudes, as well as take control of their professional development.

Epilogue

Discussion with the participants after the presentation of this paper at a workshop during Prague conference was encouraged with the following questions:

1   If you used portfolio assessment as a teacher / with your teachers:
    –   What would be the most difficult part?
    –   What would be the easiest part?
2   Think of your particular situation:
    –   What would be the key for the success of the project?
    –   What would be the biggest threat to the success of the project?

The majority of the participants maintained that starting off the portfolio assessment would be the most difficult part. The reasons they enumerated were varied and in accordance with the specificity of their socio-cultural environment; some of them mentioned teachers' fears concerning their losing face if they admitted and revealed the areas of their professional work that still needed improvement. Some participants said that because of the lack of reflective culture in most of the countries they represented (Austria, Belgium, England, Holland, Ireland, Sweden) portfolio as an instrument of (self)assessment could become misused, and revealing areas of growth in the portfolio could mean that a young teacher would not get a tenure. This is especially the case in the countries (like Austria) where there are too many teachers and the selection criteria are not qualitative. Also, the role of the headteacher in all the countries present is mainly still perceived as the person in control who comes into the classroom to make judgements and not to support and coach. That is why they suggested that evaluation in a sense of making judgements about a teacher's work, and assessment should be separated, and they did not see the headteacher in the role of a critical friend. They could imagine that the teachers would reflect together with their peers, which is already successfully practised in some countries (e.g. Ireland). Some participants saw the difficulty in the teachers themselves: they could not imagine their teachers would want to invest additional time for assessing their own work, and saw the reason for that in the lack of awareness of the importance of reflection and self-assessment for professional growth. Some participants thought that choosing areas for improvement would be difficult, and they added that those areas should really be chosen because of a teacher's inner need for improvement, and not because of some outside pressure.

The participants maintained that the key to the success of the project would be creating a genuine need in teachers for continuous improvement and better quality of their work through portfolio assessment, as well as the climate of trust and non-threatening environment.

The dangers they saw for the success of the project was in the possible development of elitist groups in schools in the case that portfolio assessment was practised only by a limited number of teachers, and they suggested that portfolio assessment should be spread throughout the entire school as soon as possible.

References

Andrejko, L. (1999). The case for the teacher portfolio. *National Staff Development Council*, 19(4), 45-48.

Costa, A.L. & Kallick B. (1993). Through the lens of a critical friend. *Educational Leadership*, 51(2), 49-51.

Hole, S., & McEntee, G.H. (1999). Reflection is at the heart of practice. *Educational Leadership*, 56(8).

Killion, J.P. & Todnem, G.R. (1991). A process of personal theory building. *Educational Ledership*, 48(6).

Kohonen, V. & Kaikkonen, P. (1999). Exploring new ways of inservice teacher education: an action research project. *European Journal of Intercultural Studies*, 7(2), 42-59.

Sento☐nik, S. (1999). Portfolio, instrument za procesno vrednotenje u☐en☐evega in u☐iteljevega dela. *Vzgoja in izobraževanje*, XXX 3/1999, 15-22.

Sento☐nik, S. (1999). Pomen refleksije za kakovostno edukacijo. *Vzgoja in izobraževanje*, XXX, 5/1999, 40-43.

Shon, D. (1987). Educating the reflective practitioner. San Francisco: Jossey - Bass.

Smyth, J. (1989). Developing and sustaining critical reflection in teacher education. *Journal of Teacher Education*, 40(2), 2-9.

Wolf, K. (1996). Developing an effective teaching portfolio. *Educational Leadership*, 53(6), 34-37.

Sonja Sentočnik is an educational research specialist and teacher trainer at the National Education Institute, Slovenia.

---

[1] The author leads a research and development project called Reflective Education, which started in 1999 as part of the National Education Institute's annual plan with the aim of supporting the implementation of the national curriculum reform guidelines. The project team consists of 20 discipline-specific experts, two pedagogy researchers, 120 teachers and five headteachers.

CHAPTER 6

TEACHERS AS REFLECTIVE PRACTITIONERS

Thea Prinsen, Harry Verkoulen

Abstract

Schools in Europe are developing from institutes that 'deliver' existing knowledge to places where learners can 'construct' their own knowledge. (Schollaert, 2002). This leads to a shift in school organisation and teaching practice:
- places fit for the transfer of knowledge ('classrooms') are replaced by a variety of activity centres (workshops, information centres, discussion rooms, ICT supplies, etc);
- the focus is on the student ('the learner'), no longer on the teacher ('the supplier'). (Hopkins, 2001).

Therefore the relationships between pupils and teachers have to change dramatically. Pupils have to take more and more responsibility for their own learning processes and learning results. Teachers (as responsible adults) have to assist the pupils in doing so: they are coaching the youngsters in their development towards more competent (independent, responsible) learners. This certainly is a new role for the teachers, maybe even a new 'profession' for them. (Jones, 2002).

In the meantime there is another development among schools in Europe: more autonomy. Policies of decentralisation are being adopted in a great many countries, North and South. Despite a common language for describing these policies, however, these developments differ substantially. (Leenheer, 2002; Hopkins and Ainscow, 1994).

How does the 'new' idea on knowledge and the 'schools at the centre' phenomena effect learning and teaching? And how can we (headteachers, supporting organisations, politicians and others) be of help? Before entering this question, we will first analyze the necessity of change a little bit further.

Why this change?

Society changes towards a more complex and more demanding environment for citizens. Social structures are more and more based on responsibility for the individual (all individuals). New technical possibilities ask for a skilled and competent user. Human relationships function on another (bigger, different) scale (national, international, even global). And so on. Learning in the traditional sense gives insufficient tools and skills to people to deal with these demands. Schools (being the most powerful learning possibility that nations have) cannot step aside in this development. For the sake of the learner, schools have to change. New ways of learning are required. Inevitably. Teachers and learners are the key figures in making the school a place to learn. In search of these new ways of learning, teachers and students are our top track finders. They have to find the tracks and use them. Schools as support organisations have to change, according to the needs of pupils and teachers on their voyage of discovery. (Schollaert, 2002). Positive results are only possible when the school as a whole changes in the new, wanted, direction. (Hopkins and Ainscow, 1994).

Decentralisation is not an end in itself, but a means for achieving other ends or purposes. In some countries this is primarily motivated by the fact that it brings about a reduction of the budgetary burden of education on the public sector. Elsewhere there are educational ends: enhancing the quality of the curriculum by giving schools greater control over teaching programmes. Both options are rather different in their effect: cost reduction or democratisation of school governance. The nature and purpose of education is itself a matter of controversy. Is education an end in itself? Or has education to do with the nation's competitiveness and quality of life? Or is education a universal human right? Pieter Leenheer describes decentralisation and growing autonomy for schools as a trend: the situation can easily change with the change of political situations. Also the curriculum is an outcome of political controversy and therefore constantly changing. The role of management in schools (headteachers, teachers) is in this respect always uncertain; can they cope with this?

In this article we will focus on the position of teachers and students in the light of these developments. The common denominator for teachers and pupils is: learning. What's new on learning?

Learning in schools

The 'normal' situation in (secondary) education in Europe is transfer of existing knowledge (often referred to as: culture, heritage, science, content, curriculum, e.a.). The normal procedure in schools to do so is by telling (presenting, explaining): the teacher (on her own) active, the pupil (in a group: the class) passive. Education (in this sense) is about activity by the teacher, receptivity by the students (listening, repeating, taking notes, rote learning, reproducing).

Learning is mostly invisible. Popular opinion says that only in testing there can be some evidence of (the results from) learning. So the only way to prove whether or not learning has occurred, is by testing. Students, therefore have to prove their activity by the results of tests (and grades, derived from those tests).

Teaching often means delivering the words 'ex cathedra'. And pupils reproduce them. Repeating means: fulfil the requirements and getting full marks. But does the learner demonstrate knowledge? Has he learned something? Or is he just a parrot, repeating the words of the teacher? As Vigotsky (1962) said: they learn to 'cover up a conceptual vacuum'.

Learning shows itself as a result. The learner has gained new skills, new behaviour. Or he has other words in which he expresses his insight and understanding (not always new words, but always words with a new meaning, another significance or sense). This is not at all just like that: this newly gained behaviour comes forward in the tackling of problems, in the solving of problems and the performance on new tasks. These problem-solving abilities and new ways of coping with tasks did not use to be there before.

So it is new. Learning is gaining something new to the learner, or the group of learners (not only an individual can learn, also a team can learn to perform better than before). But does this 'gaining of new behaviour' require activity? Can't you just sit down, shut your eyes, and learn? Like a Buddha, or in a Yoga session?
Yes, it is possible. Because we can think. Our brain helps us in learning; we can re-think our deeds, our experiences and ask ourselves: are we satisfied with what happened? What went wrong and why do we think of it as 'wrong'? And not putting questions to ourselves still leads to activity of the brain: we start dreaming, or phantasizing. All kinds of associations do emerge. The human brain never sleeps.

A very powerful stimulus to the brain is our experience. What we have done, all that what happened with us or around us, goes through our mind (especially at quiet moments). But also when somebody asks us: did you do something, then? Were you there? What happened?
Expressing our thoughts in words gives us the need for words. Our own words, and in sharing them with others they can become meaningful for all the participants. Shared experience leads to shared language. Meaningful language. (Vigotsky, 1962).
Research on the use of language (pupils' language, teachers' language) can give us insight in what is meant by 'learning as developing language'. An example:[1]

Two of my students (Annemarie and Judith), both 16 years old, worked together on a task in physics. They were doing some experiments with lenses, bulbs, etc. All the questions I had written down in the instruction proceeded from the idea of light as is normal in physics: light is an entity on his own, darkness is no entity (it is just the absence of light).
For the girls there were *two* entities, necessarily linked together: light ánd darkness. To understand light, you need darkness, and vice versa. My text in the

instruction was incomprehensible to them. Learning through this chain of tasks was not possible, because of the block they felt in the use of teacher language that had no meaning for them.

So analysing the (teacher and learner) language is an important tool in practitioner research as proposed by Dr. Jane Jones (2002). Analysis of and reflection on the meaning of words, ideas, sentences (often even the whole *context* in which language is used) is necessary to understand each other in the classroom.

Teachers and change

Teachers are used to a relatively closed working environment: the classroom. Mostly they are alone with the class; preparing activities, as well as marking and grading afterwards, is also conducted by the teacher individually. Teachers are not familiar with working together with other teachers or supporting organisations. Most teachers do not regard pupils as co-workers, but as clients. They render an important service: they transfer knowledge.

The 'new learning' asks for a tremendous change in attitude of teachers. No longer it is 'transfer to the student', but now it is something like 'pupil, find out for yourself'. Until recently, teachers did the job for the learners. Now the (individual) student has to become active, has to discover new meaning, new insights (new knowledge) co-operating in the group or all by himself.

What is left for the teacher? The old speciality (telling, transferring, explaining) is no longer asked for. The new activity (something like guiding-from-a-distance, coaching from the side-line, analysing new knowledge represented by language-development) makes the teacher feel uneasy: it's like deserting, not taking the old job seriously. Certainly he is not prepared for any of these new duties. (Schon, 1987)

It is nearly impossible to develop this kind of new behaviour (the teacher's ánd the learner's) on your own. No wonder that a lot of teachers question the necessity of this change, even resist change. It puts everything you believe in, upside down. (Van Thienen, 2002)

On the other hand, most teachers are very much involved with their pupils, they care for them. A successful student (in gaining new insight, in completing a course, in passing an exam, in positive grading) means satisfaction for the teacher. So, pupils should benefit from change, otherwise this change has no real significance. And any proposed change has to benefit the teacher also, otherwise it's just another meaningless burden. (Van Thienen, 2002).

Improvement of learning in schools

The kind of activity, asked from pupils, mostly consists of listening. As I discussed earlier, for any type of learning to take place there must be a visible response from the learner. Students in a 'listening posture' may or may not be responding.

Experienced teachers could be able to detect from non-verbal cues whether or not any (inner) activity is taking place while they are addressing their pupils. Even then, it is uncertain whether or not this activity is related to the learning intended. It is always problematic, then.

Feedback is the process by which information about the results of activity is reflected back to the originator of the activity. Feedback is essential for effective learning. Unless one knows the effect of a given activity, one cannot adjust the activity to increase its effectiveness.

Thus it is quite crucial that teachers arrange suitable feedback for their pupils about the results of their activity. Improvement depends on feedback. All kinds of feedback, not only by teacher talk. Consequently, self-checking devices for learners are asked for. Or peer consultation. The key point is that pupils should be provided with precise information about the results of their actions. (Vigotsky, 1962)

The main task is to escape from the conventional 'delivery' mode described above. 'Delivering the curriculum' is often used as a synonym for 'teaching'. The use of such expressions betrays a trivial view of teaching and is a great obstacle to the development of the quality of learning in schools. (Hopkins, 2001)

Presenting stimuli for learning is just one element in the very complex operation aimed at structuring the learner's environment so as to lead to meaningful and transferable learning. A challenge for teachers! They have to provide imaginative and effective ways of structuring the learner's experiences by introducing interesting and relevant material and situations into the learning environment. Truly a 'rich', or, as David Hopkins (2001) put it, a 'strong' environment. Reflection is part of this necessary environment.

Professional development: reflection

Although there certainly is some resistance to change among teachers, there are also starting-points for growth and professional development in the current situation (Morse and Mazor, 1999). Every teacher has at some moment in his/her career made the choice of being a teacher: what is left from the ideals and hopes at the start? What moments of satisfaction can we recall? What kind of ambition is still there? Nearly all teachers care for their students: but do they reach the goals set? Is there something that can help to improve teaching and learning?

Discussing these questions with teachers gives moments of insight and can help change teaching practice. But it has to be done with scrutiny: careful planned, based on questions or subjects relevant to the teacher. (Sentocnik, 2002). There are procedures (reflective practices) that meet the needs of teachers. In our school (2College, Tilburg, The Netherlands) we developed several activities of the kind. A few examples:

Collegial consultation

A group of 6 teachers, accompanied by a professional coach, meets every week in a 90 minutes' session (six times in a row).

- Each session starts with a retrospective view on the earlier session and a 'warming up'.
- Then comes the written input of a real and recent problem ('case') by one of them.
- Several rounds of discussion: first putting questions to clarify; then asking questions to analyse and deepen the understanding of the case; making suggestions and propose actions. Each time a reaction is given only after each participant has written down for himself which question he/she would like to ask.
- The depositor reacts to these suggestions.
- At last a round of evaluation of the session.

The coach keeps strictly to the agreed order of events. Questions and reactions ought to be non-judgemental and supporting. In the last (seventh) session there is a round-up: What did we learn? What kind of follow-up is possible? What recommendations can we give to the headteacher?

Retreat

About 15 teachers and two coaches meet in a retreat-house for 3 days (2 nights) and engage in a series of activities (group sessions, individual writing, presentations, working in subgroups, e.a.). The participants can be colleagues from one institute, or they come from different schools.

The main goal is: going back to the origins of being a teacher. Why did you choose this profession? What did you learn from mistakes, problems? What are you proud of? What does it mean for future activities?

Important is the creation of a good atmosphere: relaxed, warm, open, safe. Each participant keeps records during the 3 days in a kind of log-book. In a series of activities (writing your biography, describing important moments in your career, interviewing some of the colleagues, making a drawing –a metaphor of what's teaching like?-, making a personal action plan, and so on) there grows more self esteem and a readiness to engage in new plans.

Working with pupils

Working with learners as partners in a common enterprise is very interesting and rewarding for teacher and student. Different ways of co-operation are possible; a few of these:

- Pupils Evaluate Teachers (PET). Each year a few classes fill in a questionnaire about the teacher's functioning as a teacher (questions like: Is he/she clear in asking questions? Do you understand the explanations? Is the homework relevant? Do you like working in groups?). The pupils answer these questions on a pre-set five-point scale. Afterwards a summary is made (mostly by a member of the management team, sometimes by the teacher himself) and this document is discussed in the class. Also this summary is the basis for an interview (teacher with the headteacher). A very powerful and rewarding instrument, especially while pupils are very serious and moderate in their evaluations ('they bring in the nuance', a teacher said to me).

- Resonance groups. Each activity in school where a working group (committee, project group, implementation group, etc) has the initiative, a group of pupils (about 6 to 10, invited by the working group) does take part in the discussions. Once or twice a month they join the meetings and comment on what has been done so far.
- Full members. Where possible pupils are member of a working group and participate fully in all the activities. Especially when the school has an elected 'pupils committee' or something like that, it is very useful to ask these representatives to take part in as much working groups as possible.
- Interviews. On a regular basis there are pupils interviewed on matters of teaching and learning (mostly in groups of 4) by especially trained outsiders. Sometimes it is possible to have these interviews conducted by competent staff members, but we do not recommend this. The results are put together in a summary and provide a basis for discussions in the teaching staff. A very important and powerful instrument in starting reflective activities among teachers.

Learning practice

This is a technique, useful for teachers and students. It is based upon important (written) questions on educational affairs from the participants and has the form of a 'game'. In a very structured discussion in which each of the participants sometimes is chairman, mostly discussion partner and always team member, can intuition and free thought be fully expressed.

After one of the questions is chosen (by the president-of-the-moment) and is read out, each of the group members writes down his first associations, regarding the question. The president asks 3 members to read their associations and starts a dialogue.

The purpose of this process is developing ideas about a suitable action, given the question posed. A the end of the discussion, one or two of the members get the task to develop an action plan, based on the suggestions for action. This plan will be presented in the next session (mostly 1 week later).

The group has 8 to 15 members and is guided by a coach. The coach is only the guard on game-rules and can order a 'time out': a short period just to make some 'meta remarks' (observations about the process).

The action plans developed, will be really carried out in the school, or at least brought to the management of the school as a serious proposition.

There are many more ways in which teachers can be active to change the situation in schools. To the benefit of the pupils, to their own benefit. Essential is always to bring people together and take them seriously in their current practice. The present is always the starting point for any change ('What's going on, here?'). The problems and anxieties that exist in schools, are possible opportunities for reflection, for change. (Jones, 2002)

Management and reflection

Making a school change, requires some kind of motion in every part, at every level of the school. Do not think that schools need a 'quiet' situation in order to move on, to develop better ways of teaching and learning. The management, the teachers, the pupils, the support staff: all have to play their own part in the development of the school. (Hopkins, 2001).

The headteacher is an important 'agent' in the educational development of the school. Headteachers are the managers of the teaching and support staff, but they are also responsible for financial and other resources. With the growing autonomy of schools, the responsibility of the school manager is increasing. This creates some pressure: can the necessary educational leadership by the headteacher be carried out to its full extent?

In our opinion, it is a central task of the management of the school to identify the direction of change in educational affairs. This can lead to some insecurity among the teacher colleagues: the classroom was always purely their responsibility. And now they have to deal with the headteacher and his/her assistants. And more, because the headteacher brings in some new players: the pupils, the parents, even sometimes experts from outside.

New ways of teaching and learning can only be developed when all these groups in the school take part in the process of change. Real change always means changes in the primary process: the interaction between teachers and pupils. How can we manage the ways in which pupils and teachers interact? Top down or bottom up?

Principals can only influence the primary process indirectly. This does not mean that the school management does not have much impact in the school. Maybe in a direct sense not so very much at the primary process, but very much at the organisational level (school level, meso level). (Hopkins and Ainscow, 1994)

Reflection means: stand still at your own actions. And move on from their on. In our own words: have the courage to bring into discussion your work, your own actions. Open up and find out that you can learn from your own experiences. A real professional uses 'reflection' as an integral part of his profession. This gives the management the task to bring in reflection into the school in order to make teachers (and pupils) more and more responsible, more and more *professionals* (Hopkins and Ainscow, ibid). The headteacher has to engage himself/herself in reflective practice: for his/her own benefit, but especially in being a 'role model' for the other participants.

There are no easy ways of bringing in reflection. It has to be organised: mostly by the management of the school. Promoting, stimulating and organizing activities that contribute to professional development. The principal and his or her assistants have the authority and the position to facilitate these activities. (Hopkins and Ainscow, ibid). They set the stage for the 'reflective practitioner', the pupils and teachers who can make the difference, who really are the 'change agents' in the school.

Their school.

References

Hopkins, D. & Ainscow, M. (1994). *School Improvement in An Era of Change.* London: Cassel.
Hopkins, D. (26 april 2001). www.nottingham.ac.uk/education/Hopkins/ inaugural.html
Jones, J. (April 2002). *Practitioner Research: An opportunity for teachers to improve the quality of schooling.* Lecture The Treasure Within Conference, Prague. Londen: King's College University.
Leenheer, P. (April 2002). *Thoughts on the partnermeeting.* Lecture The Treasure Within Conference, Prague. The Netherlands: SOPO.
Morse D. & Mazor E. (1999). *Reflection and resistance.* Israel: Gordon College.
Schollaert, R. (April 2002). *The Treasure Within: some assumptions about quality in education.* Lecture The Treasure Within Conference, Prague. Belgium: VSKO.
Schon, D. (1987). *Educating the reflective practitioner.* San Francisco: Jossey-Bass.
Sentocnik, S. (April 2002). *Critical reflection as a means of teacher empowerment.* Workshop The Treasure Within Conference, Prague MEd, National Education Institute Slovenia.
van Thienen, K. (April 2002) *Why are teachers so unwilling to change?* Workshop The Treasure Within Conference, Prague. Belgium: VSKO.
Vigotsky, L. S. (1962). *Thought and language.* Cambridge, Massachusetts: M.I.T.

Thea Prinsen is Vice Principal of 2©ollege, Tilburg, The Netherlands
Harry Verkoulen is Principal of 2©ollege, Tilburg, The Netherlands

---

[1] April 1976, Twickel College Hengelo, The Netherlands (VWO 4). *Harry Verkoulen.*

PART 3
TEAM BUILDING

CHAPTER 7

SCHOOL TEAMS MAKE THE CHANGE

Magnus Persson

Abstract

Since 1992 Sweden has had a decentralised educational system. Education is managed by goals and objectives put forward in the National Curricula. Based upon the separate but corresponding pre-school, primary school and secondary school curricula, each school has the responsibility of striving towards the national objectives and achieving the goals for each stage of education. Each individual school is free to choose methods and decide how to organise learning and teaching, but is also clearly responsible for its results. On behalf of the Ministry for Education and Science, the National Agency for Education is supporting schools, promoting school development activities and supervising the quality within and the results of schools.

As the goal-based educational system was introduced and actual decentralisation was made possible, Karlstads kommun (the Municipality of Karlstad) was one of the municipalities in Sweden eager to launch extensive school development activities at an early stage. Decisions were taken by the Directorate and Board of Education for pre-schools and primary schools to form an organisation of self-administrative and self-governing schools, to a high extent being autonomous as to decision-making and financial management. The aim was to make possible each individual school analysing and developing its own school development path and thereby enhancing school change; the strategy formed by each school was related not to top-down perspectives but to the specific conditions under which each school was working. In general this concept has shown to be an excellent framework for promoting diverse and intense local school development activities, opening up for creativity and increased staff responsibility.

In Karlstads kommun the schools were organised into school districts, including both pre-schools and primary schools, in order to promote the concept of lifelong learning and to support the perspective of learning from the age of one to fifteen.

During the last ten years integration, such as mixed-age groups and mixed-profession teams, has been a key strategy to form a new and modern learning environment for children/pupils. The after-school centres and their personnel have been integrated with the primary schools, not only as to facilities but also regarding the pedagogical discussion, including the planning and the shaping of learning for children from a whole-day perspective. The six-year old children have been integrated in primary school, thus by the accompanying pre-school teachers also bringing the competence of pre-school teaching into primary school.

Based upon these pre-requisites, the primary schools in Karlstad have created school teams of professionals, by building teams of pre-schools teachers, after-school centre teachers and primary school teachers (the earlier school years) and teams of various subject teachers (the later school years). These teams have been given the role of organising the teaching/learning, professionally improving learning methods, forming interaction with the pupils and acting as agents of change, carrying school development in their hands.

School Teams as Agents of Change

The problems that gave rise to this action were mainly a lack of school development, where improvement could not be traced in the classrooms. The overall objective for education in Karlstad has been formulated as the need for a strong development of the learning processes. A number of school development activities during several years had been carried out, resulting in changes of organisation, the forming of school action plans, diverse teacher and school performances. However, very seldom this could be shown having any effects on teaching methods, pupils' influence or innovations in the learning processes.

In order to create a dialogue on classrooms as a reflective and prosperous learning venue, and to attain noticeable results, the head teachers of the schools - in dialogue with and with support of a majority of teachers - implemented a model of organising the staff into school teams. Simultaneously, the effect would be a support to professionals with different educational backgrounds to form a pedagogical dialogue. By giving the teams freedom in forming their organisation and the set-up, decentralisation would take another step forward. Expected outcomes were the forming of a reflective, cross-professional and cross-curricular learning environment and to see teams with the ability of taking full daily responsibility for all aspects of their professional and organisational tasks.

This measure was aiming to promote visible improvement and changes of pupils' learning methods and results. The professionals were clearly given the task of co-operation and of pedagogical discussion as well as displaying new teaching/learning methods, and the issue of school development as classroom improvement was put in the hands of teams.

These school teams were given venues for maturing, such as in-service training on professional issues and on teamwork, regular follow-up and feedback meetings with school leaders, and in many cases external tutoring from University professionals and/or psychological expertise. The teams were given opportunities to benefit from – and were expected to incorporate – academic theory and research. In daily work – in order to enhance self-ruling teams - they were also given the tools for performance, such as

1   full decision-making on how to organise the teaching and learning; which methods that would be preferred and chosen to be used for teaching/learning; and within the working hours being able to set aside time for school team planning and evaluation meetings;

2   self-governed budget means/resources for deciding on and purchasing pupils' teaching and learning materials; means for their own team and individual in-service training activities; and means for team activities both with and without pupils. Hereby the school teams were able to form the professional discussion related to their own needs and wishes, and at the same time they independently were able to take necessary decisions and to fund these priorities without asking superiors.

To a great extent the school teams control their time, their money and their set-up of teaching and learning school activities.

The Role of Teams in a Wider Context

The reasons for the creation of school teams of professionals were ideological and pedagogical. The main objective for the teams was to promote and bring about school development, to improve teaching and learning in order to fulfill curricular goals.

From ideological point of view this above can only be achieved by school professionals themselves - and in their daily practice. There is a strong faith in the belief that results can be achieved only within the schools themselves and in the classrooms; that change is a matter of changing teacher attitudes, developing teaching/learning methods and sharing good examples to promote a change of behaviour. Change can never be forced from outside, it has to grow from inside and from each professional as a process over time. Competence is a question of structured growth from a beginner to a master, and where each one is on this path at a given time. Changes and growth of competence occur in an environment that promotes open thinking, open debate and where professionalism shows as a structured dialogue to enhance and improve teaching/learning skills, preferably by combining theory with daily practice which for example characterises a research-based reflective practician.

At the same time there is a strong belief that schools need pedagogical freedom to adapt to local needs, problems and opportunities. But at the same time there has to be a clear local school and staff responsibility for school and pupils' results.

From a pedagogical point of view, modern teaching and learning has to be based upon holistic and cross-curricular perspectives. The world is not divided up into fragments, neither is the pupil. The understanding of context, concepts and how matters are connected is vital knowledge for the future, as well as the ability to draw conclusions from a wide flow of information. Knowledge is not only facts, it is also skills, understanding and familiarity – altogether forming the concept of knowledge.

To reach this educational objective for the future different professionals have to closely interact and to meet in daily practice to discuss views on values, knowledge, lifelong learning etc.. School development aiming to reach curricular and educational objectives must take place in interaction between professionals given full responsibility for achieving the goals but also answering to results. By interacting, exchanging and testing ideas and methods a process of development can be seen. Through interaction in a team of professionals with different knowledge, backgrounds, experiences and professions the dialogue is widely extended and gets strongly fruitful. Such a necessary and most interesting dialogue is found within school teams and is the main reason for the forming of such teams.

School teams working as professional improvers and agents of school development has been part of a wider educational process in Karlstad. Parallel to the development of school teams focus is put on lifelong learning, where pupils' learning and involvement in school and learning processes is one of the key issues. However, it is not enough to focus on pupils' learning; equal attention has to be put on teachers' own learning. In order to be a satisfactory tutor, mentor, guide and teacher for pupils, also the teacher him/herself has to be in the process of continuous learning. This approach is emphasised in national documentation as well as in the Karlstad Education Plan 1998-2002.

The Swedish national teacher agreement 2000, followed up by local agreements for a five-year school development process, is backing up the efforts in trying to reach increased efficiency and target achievement. Additionally, several national and municipality projects such as "Attractive School", "ICT in schools" and "Schools without Timetables" surround the core of school development within the classrooms. In these agreements and projects the existence of school teams are stressed and presumed to play a key role.

Outcomes, Conclusions and Future Steps

So far the outcomes of this action have been diverse. In general, more or less everyone is satisfied with the organisation of school teams and a vast majority of head teachers and professional pedagogues are confident in the fact that this has been a correct set-up for working, for responsibility and for school development. This shows in the fact that the employer and the trade unions in Karlstad in 2001 formed a new local agreement FOU 01 based upon these principles. Achievements were seen to have clearly been reached as to benefits for professional co-operation, as to understanding of the strength of and possibilities within teamwork, and regarding joint efforts in a holistic view on the pupils. From teacher perspective the school team concept has been successful, and most teams appreciate having been given budget and instruments for their own development.

Schools document evaluations of the process and the results differently. A wide range of written documentation is produced at the individual school, such as summaries of questionnaires, documented dialogues, annual "pedagogical school team balance sheets" etc., but also oral evaluation such as follow-up feedback and presenting good examples.

By now there is extensive evidence that teachers are in favour of the system and see the benefits within this. The question of debate within groups of upper primary teachers tends to be however teachers have the time to take full responsibility also for practical, organisational tasks such as forming the full timetable for pupils, or not. For subject teachers there also have been some difficulties in finding proper areas of co-operation between theoretical subject teachers and the practical and artistic subject teachers.

Results as to activities in the classrooms, noticeable to the pupils, have been a slower process. When looking at the results of national test for school year 7 and marks for school year 9 only a minor rise of performance can be seen, as shown by statistics in Karlstads kommun for the years 1999-2001. Processes of change in the classrooms have been qualitatively evaluated by Directorate of Education inspectors' reports but the measuring and figures has deliberately neither been focused on nor collated on a municipality scale. Evidence has to been found at each school district independently.

Regarding the earlier school years the teams on-going develop a range of innovative learning activities for the pupils, usually in a professional way combining different teacher competencies into a holistic approach. At a number of schools in Karlstad work teams have tried new methods out and tried to organise the pupils' learning in more differentiated ways than before. There are now several examples of innovatively good practice, for example in the area of individualisation and pupils' self-planning. New forms for target-setting and more focused work plans from the teams have been found at many schools during the recent years. Some schools have developed structured collaboration with university researchers on specific themes such as literacy or music, or on methods such as action research, portfolio, storyline, and project working etc.. Some schools have started parent and pupil boards connected to the work team in order to increase expertise, participation and new thinking. Others have developed the feedback instruments connected to questionnaires or to the regular personal development dialogues (pupils).

In these cases, to a high extent professionals and pupils as well as parents are involved in a continuous search for optimal and adapted methods for learning. For these teams school development in- and outside of the classrooms is on the agenda regularly. When analysed, the outcomes of the work by these teams are good and improving, this seen from personnel and leadership perspective. Also from the pupils' perspective, a stimulating and improved daily learning venue can be seen.

Regarding the later primary school years, the changes of learning venue for pupils have so far been small; more traditional subject teaching is dominating, and when asked in questionnaires or interviews, these pupils do not experience much of a change. However, development work is taking place in various ways, mostly within the work teams at the local schools but also on a common ground.

For example, between the schools in Karlstad have been formed networks of subject teachers, discussing perspectives of the achievement of standards, the bridging from primary to secondary schools but also issues on teaching and learning strategies in connection to school development.

However, in all cases, there is not yet evidence compiled that the results in pupils' knowledge and skills are different from before, this related to new or different working methods, or to the existence of work teams. But reports show that the activities connected to actual classroom change are in strong process at the majority of schools in Karlstad.

For the short-term future, the process of developing the schools teams into highly professional agents for change will continue. More focus will be put on involving the pupils in the classroom activities and to let pupils' views more influence the planning processes and the team activities. More effort will be put to streamline the important elements of change, and from these to demand visible results to show in the classrooms. The objectives of emphasising on learning issues will be more explicit in order to make the discussion more to be a question of learning than of irrelevant issues, which sometimes tend to take over. More will also be done to support proper and defined working conditions for the school teams.

School teams have shown to be a way of organising and performing that will stay, which is shown by explicit decisions on national level and at local level in Karlstad. For the professional pedagogue the working team is supportive in most cases, even if teamwork and co-operation is experienced to take more effort, time and commitment than being a single-acting teacher. Regarding school development the teams are seen as valuable and necessary when to achieve a professional, cross-curricular dialogue in daily practice. Clarity may vanish when the teams are instructed too various tasks, concluding that the leadership and team focus always has to be that teams in the first place have a pedagogical task.

The conclusion is furthermore that having school teams make the change at school: teaching and learning get new impulses. And, showing being beneficial for the schools, it actually takes school teams to make the real change in schools – but it is a process that needs time to fully penetrate into the classrooms.

Magnus Persson is International Education Manager at Barn- och ungdomsförvaltningen, Karlstads kommun, Sweden.

CHAPTER 8

TEAM BUILDING AMONG EDUCATIONAL STAFF

A WAY TO INDIVIDUALISE LEARNING

Stefan Petterson

Abstract

For the last 10 years we have been working as a teacher-team at Oskarslund-school in Karlstad/Sweden. As a result of this, we have had the opportunity to develop a way to individualise the learning for children aged 6 to 9 years. Our experiences have enabled us to introduce the same style of learning to our senior pupils.

We will in our presentation make a brief description of the underlying philosophy and of the decisions at the central and local political level.

Then the teacher-team at Oskarslund-school will describe a case study, in which they describe how they understand their mission and how they work with their children during an ordinary week. They will also show a videotape in Prague to make their work even more concrete. The paper ends with a summary and thoughts about our future.

Background

The government started an inquiry in 1970 which ended in a report in 1974 "The internal functioning of the school" (SIA). One of the conclusions was that the responsibility of the school should be extended, so that the school also had to work with the 'leisure home' which had worked alongside the school under the auspices of the local authority. A leisure home is a child minding centre that operates after school hours. The fact that leisure homes come under a different department of the local authority has complicated the system a little.

We then had a new director of education in Karlstad 1988 and one of his first projects was to contact the director of the leisure-home (Social Department) to create some kind of co-operation. After they had had their first contact, an invitation to start co-operation between the school and the leisure-home was sent to certain schools and leisure-homes. Oskarslund-school was one of the schools that started the project because there was the leisure-home in the building next door and they had the same playground. We started our co-operation project insofar as we shared the same children and the same building.

Up until 1991 schools in Sweden were governed by two 'masters', the government which controlled the teachers (their work and salaries) and the local authority which controlled everything else (other staff and buildings etc.).

This was changed in 1991, when the local authority was given responsibility for the school system. The responsibility of the government is to formulate the curriculum and set goals for the various subjects. They also pay the local authority to take care of the school with a government grant.

The responsibility for leisure-homes was moved from the Social Department in the local authority to the School Department in 1992. These two decisions made it easier for us to create teacher-teams with teachers and leisure-home teachers.

At the beginning of the 90s the government was sending signals to us that there would be compulsory schooling for 10 years (we have compulsory schooling for 9 years). The School Department in Karlstad was convinced that it would be like that in a very short time. Given this background ,we started a project called "small-school" to where 6 year old children were moved from the nursery school to compulsory school. We started mixed-age groups and let the 6-year-old children work in the same classroom as the 7/9-year-olds.

The Government did not decide to insist on compulsory schooling for 10 years after all, but rather all 6-year-old children were to have the right to go to a "pre-school-class" in the same building as those pupils undertaking the 9 years of compulsory schooling.

This way it was possible to start and to maintain teacher-teams comprising nursery-teachers, leisure-home teachers and teachers in the compulsory school together.

We have worked in a teacher-team with a nursery teacher, a leisure-home teacher and an ordinary teacher at Oskarslund-school since 1993. The team has the responsibility for taking care of the children from 6.30 a.m. to 6.00 p.m. The group of children is mixed-age, from 6 to 9 years old.

Case study: "Junibacken"

We are a team of 3 persons. We all have different educational expertise. One of us is a nursery-school teacher, one is a leisure-home teacher and the third one is a school teacher. Right now we have 24 pupils in our class, who are between 6 and 9 years old. The children and we three are together in the same house all day from 8.10 a.m. to 4.30 p. Because we have a shared understanding of the children and their development we have found this organization to be terrific. The advantage of a working team is that we are many people who can follow the children and also support each other if problems arise. We also have different competences depending on our own education and interests. This, we think, gives the children a better start.

The children's school-time is between 8.10 a.m. and 1.30 a.m. Should any child need supervision before the start of school in the morning, the nursery teacher and the leisure-home teacher take care of the children. The after-school centre closes at 6 p.m.

We have different areas of responsibility. The nursery teacher is responsible for the 6-year-old children and their adjustment period and development in the group. The leisure-home pedagogue takes care of the activities in the afternoon and the teacher takes the pupils in class 1 and 2.

We have chosen to have different ages among the children because we are convinced that the advantages are so many:
– social interplay is important
– being helpful and the art of companionship can be developed
– the younger ones learn and are stimulated by the older ones e.g. working through their maths, English...
– fewer conflicts
– benefits from the differences in ages e.g. ideas, spontaneity, knowledge, experiences
– parents can learn from parents who have already had children in the class
– the friend a child left in the nursery school will be a classmate again in a few years' time
– brothers and sisters can attend the same class

Since we are three pedagogues that work with the children in all subjects all day, we can easily link subjects together Swedish – Maths – art- P.E. – music etc and also leisure-time activities with each other. We have lunch together, we have one meeting a day, outdoor days, sports, music, English, religion, class-meetings, theme-work, fun lessons and a lot more in mixed-age groups.

"One week in the school life of a 6-year-old child."

We start every day with a meeting where we go through what we will do during the day. We have some kind of games in language and Maths. Sometimes the "fairy tale lady" comes and tells the children a fairy tale.

Then the children "work" with something in common or with something from their individual planning. The 6-year-old children have art and physical education at least twice a week and music and some English. They get motor skills training by sewing, weaving, working with pearls, with different kind of dough etc. In Sweden it is frequently said that children and youngsters move about too little. We try to stimulate our pupils to be more nimble by having physical education twice a week and by going out in the forest once a week. We also have whole days out a couple of times a term. All pupils go to our Community library every third week to borrow books.

Every Friday all pupils compose a "weekly report". This is to train them to consider that they really have achieved a great deal in a week. It is also important to think about what they've learnt during the week and how they learnt it. The pupils will also have training in writing. This is shown at home later on so the parents get to know what happens at school. The 6-year-old children do not write themselves; I write on the whiteboard what they say and then I type it out on the computer and paste it into their books. In this way they are exposed to writing continuously.

The first lesson starts every day at 8.10 a.m. The older children always start their day by reading; sometimes to a grown-up, sometimes to a friend. After that their individual work starts.
All the children have a schedule that is very individualised. Thus they change from Maths to Swedish, technology, art and play time. This first lesson ends with an assembly, where they eat fruit and discuss important things or listen when the teacher is reading aloud from an exciting book. It's outdoor play or break between 9.30 to 10.00.

Our schoolyard is wonderful. There is a beautiful forest, where the children can build huts and climb trees, or go sledging and build snow huts if there is snow. We have a climbing frame and sandpits. We have large areas for football, tennis and other games.
After the break individual programmes continue. At about 10.30 a.m. we stop a while for common activities. There you can do English, music, theme-work, reading aloud, maths or other activities.

We have our lunch in the classroom. Some of the pupils are hosts at the tables and help to prepare for lunch. The food is made in another school and is sent to us by taxi. We have our lunch at 11.10 a.m. After lunch the children have a break until twenty past twelve.

In the afternoon we are always together in mixed-age groups. Some days we go outdoors and learn about nature and we play. Other days we have sports, dancing or art. On Fridays we always have a cleaning up day and a class meeting. The week always ends with the children making up their own lesson. This is when 3 or 4 pupils plan what is going to happen. It can be drama, games, dancing, quizzes, treasure hunting or other things.

The Treasure Within

Our working team and the group of pupils, "Junibacken", have a house of their own at their disposal. In the house there is a kitchen, which is rather spacious, two smaller rooms and a very large room. In the large room there is a corner where you can paint, and a big carpet, where we have our assemblies. In that room we have our lunch and we also sit and work there.

All grown-ups and pupils have a place of their own at lunch. When it's time to work, you choose your own place to do your work. Perhaps you need to sit on the carpet to have room for all your materials; perhaps you need a little table of your own in quiet corner to be able to concentrate. If you are experimenting with something, the kitchen may be a good place to work in.

Your own work

From our curriculum you can infer that every pupil must learn to take responsibility and that the pupils gradually will have a greater influence on their education.

In "Junibacken" we work according to a work-schedule. No work-schedule looks the same.

Each pupil is in the centre for the activities at school. The development of knowledge is a part of the development of the personality and education therefore starts from every child's conditions and it demands substantial individualisation. I, as a teacher, sit together with every child and discuss a new work-schedule. I draw on my "professionalism" and give every child suggestions for suitable exercises just for that child. I try to be "a good guide" in the jungle of knowledge. I try to encourage the pupils to consider their own proposals and ideas that they can work with. It is after all the pupils themselves who know in what way they learn best.

When they take part in the decisions and have influence on their own work, they find their work much more amusing. The pupils get more involved, are creative and active and discipline problems become fewer.

Every Friday the pupils write a weekly report, a kind of evaluation. There you can read what they have done during the week, how they've succeeded and their comments about the work and their efforts. Then they bring their report home and read it to their parents.
This particular way of working has given us a changed role concerning both the pupils and the teachers.

Their eagerness to learn is clearly visible, the pupils are more active, creative and take more responsibility. The pupils take part and make their own decisions and learn to be more critically reflexive. The pupils are involved and take more responsibility. The teacher has become some kind of manager, organizer and instructor. The teacher must show his or her proficiency to be able to give every pupil what he/she really needs.

Thanks to this we now have *happier and more interested pupils and an exciting place to work in.*

Summary

We have discovered that the children feel better and get more individualised learning if we organize ourselves in teacher-teams. The staff also feel more comfortable and the working environment is better and it is easier to do good work with the children.

The children also participate more in their learning since they undertake their own planning and work-schedules. This will in the end give them more understanding about their own way of learning.

The goal of our work in the whole school-area is that this kind of working-model can be introduced to the senior children.
The 10/11-year-old children work in mixed-age groups and they do their own work-schedules.
The teachers have to develop teamwork and work more like managers, organisers and instructors instead of old style teachers.

In the lower secondary school (12/16-year-old children) the teachers work in teacher-teams, but here we need even more to change the way we educate the pupils. We have to move from teaching facts to a coaching style of teaching and learning. The only area where the children plan their own work is for their homework. There is scope for much more based on our experiences with younger pupils.

Stefan Petterson is Head Teacher of Gruvlyckan's Skolomrade in Karlstad, Sweden

CHAPTER 9

TEAM BUILDING AND TEAM WORK IN PRIMARY SCHOOL LUCIJA

Jelka Pečar, Jezeka Beškovnik

Abstract

Since the introduction of the nine-year primary school in 1999, and in some cases even before, team work has become part of our everyday life at school. Teaching practice and learning processes have changed visibly especially in the first three grades of primary education. Choosing the appropriate course books, preparing syllabus and daily or weekly lesson plans, organizing sports and cultural days, taking part in international projects or normal everyday school life have become regular activities performed by teams of primary and subject teachers.

This contribution will start with describing team work in the first grade of the new nine-year primary school, continue with the co-operation between primary and subject teachers, and finish with team work in physical education and language learning.

In the following contributions, a primary teacher, a pre-teacher, the Slovenian language teacher and the team of physical education teachers have shared their experiences with us.

Franka Pilipovi□ and Tanja Vincelj are sharing with us their experiences about working in a two-teacher class, Liza Romih is talking about the co-operation between primary and subject teachers, the physical education teachers are informing us about their team work and the language teachers' team about their experiences in language teaching.

Co-operation between primary and pre-school teachers in the first grade of the new nine-year primary school

Franka Pilipovi□ is a preschool teacher in the 1st grade. Before she decided to apply for a job in our primary school she had worked in a kindergarten for ten long years. Three years ago she started working in the 1st grade. She was very enthusiastic about her new job despite the problems she encountered at the very beginning - working in tandem in class and being an active part of a 1st grade teachers' team which she had never experienced before. She has managed to solve the initial problems by taking part in the regular team meetings and communication with her team colleagues.

Now she has been working as a pre-school teacher in the first grade for the third year. The programme is very similar to the one in pre-school which means it is much more adapted to the age level of the pupils. The classrooms are equipped with small colourful corners where pupils work and learn in groups. Math and Slovene classes are combined with music, creative art, physical education and in one of the corners there is even a computer that all the pupils enjoy using.

Planning and performing the educational work depends on all those who take part in this process: teachers, pre-teachers and the Italian language teacher. In the first grade the teacher and pre -teacher in a way superstructure and complement each other and in this way facilitate the work in class. One of the weaknesses of pre-teachers' work is that they are present in class only a limited time of the day.

In order to plan weekly activities, the 1st grade teachers' team meets once a week. The topics and contents of each subject are discussed, the objectives are set and methods defined. In the same way parents meetings are organized.

As the team leader Franka is also responsible for sharing and exchanging her team's problems and experiences with other team leaders at school. This is one of the ways that enables the teams to improve the quality of teaching and relationship between them. It takes a lot of time, good will and energy but it is worth trying for the sake of the pupils, the teachers and the school as a whole.

Working as a team

The first time Tanja Vincelj encountered team work was when she started teaching in the eight-year elementary school. Their professional team was built of teachers teaching in the same school levels. Physical education teachers, school counsellors and external collaborators (pedagogues) were also part of the team.

They met once a week to discuss and plan their work for the following week. Each of them transferred the planned objectives to the class and adapted them to the pupils. In the same way the team planned objectives for other parallel activities necessary for the better and more successful learning process such as sports days, cultural days, science days, etc

It was only with the school reform and the introduction of the nine-year primary school that she came to realize what team work really meant.

Now, their professional team has more members, the pre-school teachers have joined the team and they help the primary teachers with planning and realization of the learning process.

To improve the quality of team work, all the team members have attended seminars with the topic 'How successful a team works'.
The newly acquired knowledge helps them a lot in planning the future work throughout the year.

The teachers meet once a week and plan the whole learning process while the pre-teachers, as they have more experience with six-year old children, complete the learning plan by adding methods that are suitable for children entering school one year younger. The difference between a six and a seven-year old is obvious and we need quite some time to adapt to the pupils' "tempo".

After having created the yearly plan, each teacher and pre-teacher have to plan their own work taking into consideration that the pre-teacher is present in the classroom only two teaching hours per day.

Of course, the objectives of the team meetings are not only planning the weekly or daily programmes. Evaluation is even more important. The evaluation is only verbal and the most common questions the teachers ask themselves are if the pupils are happy, pleased and relaxed in their work and if there is anything to be changed or improved. Such evaluation also enables an external observer, teacher or pre-teacher to better follow the learning process.

Experiences of each team are discussed during professional teachers' teams conferences. They are re-evaluated and positive and negative aspects are pointed out. Such evaluations are of utmost importance to all the teachers who are experiencing this kind of work for the first time and even to the more experienced teachers.

In the 1st grade a lot of energy has been spent in team work to improve the quality of the educational process but the efforts have not been in vain. The teams are now more successful in:

- finding more and better ideas,
- planning activities,
- bringing more dynamics into the everyday work,
- creating more interesting activities,
- organizing simultaneous activities,
- organizing more individual and differentiated work,
- providing better safety (physical and psychological),
- sharing responsibilities,
- reciprocal support,

- acceptability and tolerance,
- positive confirmation.

Co-operation between primary and subject teachers

All the teachers, from the 1st to the 9th grade, want to make their work more consistent and more connected. The reasons for wanting to improve the co-operation are the following:
- by knowing each other's work better and more in depth there is more respect for each other's work,
- by knowing each other's work more profoundly teachers can help each other much more easily,
- the progress of the pupils can be followed more effectively.

One of the possibilities for more consistent work presents itself by connecting teams of teachers.

There is a team of teachers in each grade at school and subject teachers' teams.

As our mother tongue, the Slovenian language is a subject by itself and also the language in which we teach, we try to connect the teachers of lower grades and the teacher of the Slovenian language in order to improve the quality of teaching of the mother tongue.

There are regular meetings on which the teachers share their experiences. They talk about the books read by the students, share experiences on how to make them more interested in reading, suggest what help tools are useful and how to use them, share news from the educational seminars and conferences, in short, they discuss what works and what does not work in class as well as good and bad practices.

As an example of good practice, let me mention the cultural day that was organized at the beginning of this year. The title was "Let's play theatre". The primary and subject teachers jointly agreed on the content of the workshops and on how to organize them so that they would be interesting, lively and that the students would be happy.

It was very rewarding to see the pupils of the higher grades acting and creating role plays together with the younger pupils.

This is also one of the ways of promoting quality coexistence among younger and older pupils.

Physical Education Teachers' Team

Active involvement of students and quality are two aims of our school sports teachers' team. Active involvement means that the students are not only spectators of different matches and games, but they take part in most school and after-school activities. Quality means that their planning is aimed to improve the students' physical condition and safety.

At our school physical education (PE) is taught by primary teachers in the lower grades and PE teachers in the higher grades. To improve the quality of teaching PE in lower grades, extra funds were necessary and were provided by the municipality. Now, both primary and PE teachers are involved in planning and carrying out the lessons. All the planning is done in teams and is adapted to the abilities and age level of the students.

In the same way the lessons are planned for the higher grade students, all the work is done in team and all the responsibilities are shared. The team also organizes five sports days every school year for each of the grades at school, the activities are usually swimming, running, hiking tours, athletics, diving, beach volley and many others.

The school PE team is also concerned about how students spend their free time. For this purpose quite a lot of after-school activities are organized, such as volleyball, football, basketball, athletics, twirling, table tennis, karate, mountaineering, etc. The team invites all interested students to join the activities and spend quality free time in the afternoons. There is a lot of interest for such organized activities which has proved to be very positive.

The PE team also organizes all school and regional competitions.

They are very successful in providing students with quality programmes, teaching them to have a positive attitude towards sports and at the same time to aim to a healthy way of living.

Teams in Foreign Language Teaching

Context

Apart from our mother tongue, **Slovenian** three foreign languages are taught at our school. The first foreign language that has to be pointed out is **Italian,** which has a special significance to all of us as, in the region where we live, it is not regarded as a foreign language but our second language. Why? We live in an area with a large Italian minority so Italian language is taught at schools from the first grade on. Subsequently, Slovenian language is taught in schools with Italian as their mother tongue. The minority has their own schools and learn Slovenian from the beginning of their primary education. I could say we are all bilingual.

The second language is **German** which is an optional subject in higher grades. **English** is the language we learn as a foreign language and is a compulsory subject in our schools. In the nine-year primary school it is taught from grade 4 to grade 9.

Language teachers' teams

In order to reach more quality in language education teams of teachers are formed. They are quite autonomous in choosing the appropriate coursebooks, teaching material and designing yearly, weekly or daily lesson plans.

Regular meetings permit the teams to discuss and solve different problems, improve quality of language education, create materials and plan extra activities such as taking part in competitions, research projects, and international projects. During the regular meetings remedial lessons (for the slower students) and extra lessons (for the brighter students who want to learn more) are planned.

Students' teams

To teach a foreign language is quite a difficult task if we want our students to learn a language in such a way that they will be able to understand foreigners, communicate with them, read and write. That is why in language teaching there is and must be a lot of team or group work. Groups are formed according to different factors for different purposes and they are an essential part of our everyday teaching and learning process.

Groups are formed in order to perform different tasks, from doing vocabulary and grammar exercises to creating dialogues, interviews, and short guided compositions. As all our classes are mixed ability, it is never easy to form teams that would function well. That is why the teams are never the same, but they are formed according to the task they have to accomplish. Sometimes slower students are put together to do the exercises that are not too difficult for them and the better ones are given more demanding tasks. Sometimes the teams are mixed, so that the better students can help the slower ones to do the work they have been assigned. If the students know what they are doing and why they are doing it, the results of such a team work are always good and the atmosphere in the team positive and challenging.

What has to be known to the teams to accomplish their work well and be more successful?

- They have to know the purpose of the activity. It means they have to know what they are practising.
- They have to know the objectives of the activity and exactly what is expected as the final result of the activity.
- They have to know what their role in the team is and everyone in the team must have a role and a task to accomplish.
- All the members of the team must be active.
- They must know what the teacher is doing and why.
- They must be aware that team work is connected with other activities going on in class.
- They must share all the responsibilities.

Teams must also be connected with each other and dependant on each other. Each team has to perform a task that is connected to the other teams' tasks.

At the end of the activity all the teams have to present the work they have done and evaluate it – in teams again.

Such work has proved to be very effective and the students have got used to working in teams and enjoy such activities very much. There are always individual students who prefer working alone or others that have special needs or other 'ideas' of what learning is. But the teachers are also a kind of magicians and we always find the way to make them do ... at least something.

This is what our students have written about an English lesson and published in the school magazine.

Our English lessons

Our English lessons are very interesting, we do a lot of different things and we have lots of fun. In one of the lessons of English we sell and buy things. We work in groups.

One student is selling and the others are buying. We create dialogues. Then we take the clothes and other things, and we act the dialogues. We present the work to the teacher and other students in the class. The teacher listens attentively and the school friends too. Then the teacher corrects our mistakes ... If she finds any...

Grade 6 students

Jelka Pečar is Head Teacher of Lucija Primary School in Portoroz, Slovenia
Jezerka Beškovnik is a language teacher at Lucija Primary School in Portoroz, Slovenia

PART 4

THE TEACHER AS CHANGE AGENT

CHAPTER 10

GIVE CHANGE
A BETTER CHANCE

A CHECK LIST FOR CHANGE AGENTS

Danuta Elsner, Phil Whitehead, Felix Claus

Abstract

Dealing with change has become an every day challenge for teachers and
headteachers. Accepting the need for change and then sustaining change can
pose a range of further problems for schools. How can change agents in schools
help colleagues to work through the difficult process of change? How can
schools sustain and build on successful changes?

In order to answer these key questions and provide practical support for schools,
a group of support organisations have devised a checklist for change agents.
Working through the checklist will ensure that colleagues charged with the job
of instigating change are thoroughly prepared and confident in their role. The list
will serve as a tool for reflection and an aide-memoire for change agents within
schools and also provide key links to existing research. Further supportive
documentation is planned and a database of colleagues within the network who
can offer advice and practical support established.

The checklist is at an early stage in development and constitutes the collective
thinking of a small group of school support organisations. This thinking is
presented here as a discussion paper with the intention of collecting the views for
development and improvement.

Rationale

Dealing with constant and often radical change instigated both from within
school and by external agencies is an every day challenge for all involved in
primary and secondary education. All partners involved in education may, at
some point, be required to take the role of change agent. Change agents may be:
teachers, headteachers, teacher advisers, teacher trainers, local education

authority officers, ministry of education officials, parents, pupils and other members of the school and wider educational community.

Being a change agent involves:
– identifying and managing numerous aspects of the change process;
– making difficult decisions;
– dealing with contradictory expectations of various stakeholders;
– acting under the pressure of time;
– coping with stress
– helping to evaluate and sustain the changes

The journey through change, that is the process of change itself, is a difficult and challenging one whether you are the instigator, the nominated agent or a stakeholder. Specific challenges and difficulties when considering this process may be expressed as key questions:
– 'How do we introduce change when personnel do not see the need and are actively resistant?'
– 'We have introduced successful changes into our school but how do we sustain this over time in the face of both expected and unexpected challenges, such as key staff leaving?'

In response to these challenges, a checklist has been devised as a practical tool for change agents to help guide them through the change process in various school settings. Using this simple and logical tool in the first instance would enable change agents to fully explore the groundwork – the reasons, influences and tensions behind the proposed changes. Understanding the process and seeing it holistically, we suggest, would be an empowering first step in managing change and ensuring that it is effective.

Aims of the checklist for change agents

The overall aim of the checklist is to give change agents and those involved in change at any level of an educational system a useful instrument for reflection and an aide-memoire.

The specific purposes of the checklist are as follows:
1 To raise awareness of the numerous aspects of the change process.
2 To ensure key information is available, enabling change agents to present a powerful and persuasive argument to colleagues and interested stakeholders.
3 To help them to be more pro-active, be better organised and consequently less stressed.
4 Finally - to be more effective in bringing about successful and sustained change in their schools.

The structure of the checklist for change agents

The checklist consists of the following elements:
– Issues which describe elements of change;
– Self-reflecting questions connected with each element;

- Examples of possible answers;
- Glossary of the technical terminology related to change;
- Links into further readings.

Self-reflecting questions are the essence of the checklist (column C). They should inspire thinking and if necessary lead to creating further questions that may have direct connections to the specific context of the particular school. Possible solutions (column D) should act in the same way.

An English education system glossary of change terminology will be produced (column E) as well as links into further readings (column F - international research on the given topic, relevant case studies, suggestions for dealing with the main issues, examples of a good practice). The glossary should not only help colleagues to understand the "technical" language of change but also inspire the search for an equivalent in the native language of the reader. The further readings are suggestions of relevant literature to broaden knowledge on various aspects of the change process.

The checklist could easily be turned into a pro-forma document, that is one that could be completed as a record sheet by the change agent.

These are initial only suggestions and are designed as prompts to guide the search for relevant solutions.

The checklist for change agents

Italicized words were added after the Prague conference

No	*Elements* of change	Self-reflecting questions	Examples of possible answers	Links to glossary	Links to further readings
A.	B.	C.	D.	E.	F.
1	Deciding on the change agents	• Who should the change agents be for this specific issue?	• Internal agent- External agent • Practitioner-Theorist • *Persons with managerial position* • *Teachers* • *Pupils* • *Members of the wider education community* • Everybody involved in change process • *Individuals – teams* • *Teams of change agents*	Change agent	Ford, M (1992) Fullan, M. (1993, 1995, 1999, 2000) Gunter, H. (1999) Wray, D. & Medwell, J. (1999)
		• What are the skills and characteristics required of successful change agents?	• Credibility • Excellent communicators • Skilled negotiators • Problem identifiers/solvers • *Politically astute* • *Managerial skills*		
2	Identification of the need for change	• What kind of change are we dealing with?	• Whole system/school • Structures within the whole • Programmes • Content • *People*		Brown, M., Askew, M., Baker, D., Denvir, H. & Millet, A. (1999) DfES (2001) Fullan, M., Earl, L., Leithwood, K & Watson, N. (1999 & 2000) Ofsted (1999b) (website http//www.ofsted.gov.uk) http//www.ngfl.gov.uk (national focal point for learning on the internet) www.standards.gov.uk
		• Who/ Which is the key person/ agency?	• Teachers • *Senior management team* • *Headteacher* • *Governing Body* • Inspectors • Government- local/*national*	Gover- ning Body	
		• How has the need been identified?	• Individual self-review • Collective self-review • School needs assessment • Inspection report • Research	Self- review Needs assess- ment	
		• What techniques can be used?	• SWOT analysis	SWOT	

No	*Elements* of change	Self-reflecting questions	Examples of possible answers	Links to glossary	Links to further readings
3	Involvement of change stakeholders	• How to identify stakeholders?	• School Development	Stake-holder	
4	Choosing the change strategy	• What strategy is appropriate in a given situation? • Who will devise/choose it?	• Top down • Bottom up • Piloting • *Cascading* • Responsible stakeholder • Change Agents	Casca-ding	
5	Creating conditions for change	• How to analyse conditions? • What internal conditions are essential for the successful change? • What external conditions are essential for the successful change?	• Force-field analysis • School climate • Positive relation between staff • High expectations • Curiosity towards novelty • Open-minded staff • Supportive leadership • Suitable resources • Support from parents • Support from LEA	Kurt Lewin's force-field analysis	
6	Planning the change process	• How to set up goals? • What kind of planning is appropriate for the successful change? • How to identify resources? • How to get them?	• SMART • Action planning • Short-term planning • Long-term planning • Strategic planning • Rolling planning • Future-based planning	SMART Strategic planning Rolling planning Future-based planning	

No	*Elements* of change	Self-reflecting questions	Examples of possible answers	Links to glossary	Links to further readings
7	Leadership of change	• Who will manage the change?	• Internal change agents		Gunter, H. (1999)
8	Dealing with resistance to change	• Why are people resistant to change? • How people resist change? • Who are they? Identifying resistant stakeholders • How to deal with active/passive resistance of staff?	• Lack of information/mis-information • Lack of motivation • Poor communication • Rejection • Withdrawal • Conformism • Adaptation • Explain • Incorporate • Support/facilitate adjustment e.g. through training • Negotiate • Co-opt • Coerce • Monitor		
9	Ownership of change	• How to make people feel the owners of change?	• Delegate decision making • *Involve in the change process*		
10	Sustaining change	• How to sustain the momentum? • How to sustain change over time?	• Continuing Training • Follow up	Follow-up	

The Treasure Within

No	Elements of change	Self-reflecting questions	Examples of possible answers	Links to glossary	Links to further readings
11	Consolidation of change	• How to consolidate change?	• Co-operation of all partners • Review • Reflection	Con-solidation	
		• How to institutionalise change?	• Monitor • Celebrate	Institutio-nalisation	
12	Dissemination of change	• Who should disseminate change?			
		• How to disseminate change?	• Piloting • Coaching • Cascading • Networking		
13	Evaluation of change	• Who will be an evaluator?	• A person from the school • Somebody from outside		
		• What kind of evaluation is suitable in given conditions?	• Self-evaluation • External evaluation • Formative evaluation • Summative evaluation	Formative evalua-tion Summa-tive evalua-tion	
14	Success of change	• When can it be said that the change is successful?	• Meets criteria • *Feelings to feature*		
		• Who makes that decision and who confirms it?	• Change agent • Internal manager • External adviser/manager/ inspector		
		• How to celebrate success?	• Event • Reward change agent		

As the Change Agents can get involved at any stage of the change process he/she was placed right at the beginning of the checklist in order to avoid repetitions.

The possible usage of the checklist

The usage of the checklist can be twofold:
- Specific - focus directly on change agents;
- More general – for others involved in the change process.

The change agents could use the checklist before the change is undertaken, during its implementation and after it is completed to compare with previous own and others experiences and to reflect on what is going on in each phase of the process.

Reflection itself is an important factor of the change process. If systematically recorded e.g. in professional diary, it can broaden the insight of the particular person resulting in more effective actions.

On the other hand the checklist may serve as:
- a framework for face-to-face or distance learning training programmes (not only for change agents, but for all interested parties);
- a catalyst for identifying further issues to be added to a printed or electronic version of the manual for change agents;
- the foundation of a research project and be converted into a research tool (questionnaire),
- inspiration to establish the network for all interested in successful change.

Apart from the usage of the whole checklist parts of it can be used separately:
- self-reflecting questions for group discussion during the training of change agents and others involved in the change process;
- issues indicated in the columns B, C, D as themes for short essays, articles, reports, descriptions of a good practice;
- a bibliography as a base for the production of the selected readings on the change process.

The usage of the checklist can be broadened if translated into home languages of the interested parties, completed with the native language bibliography, popularised in the home educational journals or on home language websites.

Questions to stimulate discussion after the presentation of the checklist for the change agents

The questions to stimulate discussion will focus on the following issues:
- Is the checklist a helpful tool to inspire reflection on the change process?
- Is the format of the checklist handy?
- What issues are missing on the checklist?
- What issues should be emphasised?
- What entries should be explained in the glossary of the change terminology?
- In what way can links into further reading be elaborated?

The treasure within

- Is there any other possible use of the checklist than mentioned above?
- Who is interested in getting information on the future developments of the checklist?
- How to keep in touch with all interested parties?
- How can the checklist be tested in different countries?
- How can the checklist be disseminated in the different countries?

Epilogue

During a workshop in which The checklist for change agents was presented, the second part of the workshop was devoted to the discussion of the checklist in three groups. The questions were:
- Is the checklist a helpful tool?
- What issues are missing on the checklist? And what issues should be emphasized?
- Other comments.

The first group commented upon the 1st question as follows:
- The checklist suggests that change is a *linear* process. The point is that – in reality – change is rather a *chaotic* process. Change is not linear but "goes in different directions". So, the lay-out could be improved. The represented checklist is too structured and is a *helpful tool as an analysis of change*. The suggestion is to reshape the list in a *working tool*, e.g. by using the technique of mind-mapping.
- It's more useful to use *elements* in stead of *phases*.
- Overall, the checklist is helpful.

Concerning the 2nd question the group suggested the following additions:
- Regarding point 9 the group stresses the importance of ownership. People should be participating in the process and have ownership. "People have to believe in it": this should be emphasized in the list.
- Regarding 14: when can it be said that the change is successful? The group suggested to add *feelings to feature* or how people can feel about it!
- The group also misses the *opportunity for creativity*, a kind of creative thinking. It's sometimes better to involve people at certain points in the process, rather than to follow a plan too strictly.

The second group first of all raised the question of the meaning of change agents. Are they persons and/or instruments? The group argued change agents should not be instruments but persons, who can play a role in the decision making process, but also in the process of the execution of change.

Another point of discussion was the order of phase 1 (deciding on the change agents) and 2 (identification of the need for change). What should be the first? The group decided that the need comes first. The sort of change agents depends on the sort of change.

With regard to the 1st question, the group stated that the checklist was a "beautiful instrument" because it shows that change is a process and is important. It also gives an insight in the complexity of change. The checklist is of course only one of the possible instruments.

The term 'cascading' should be added to the glossary.

The third group had a "lively but not very structured discussion". The group also discussed the order of phase 1 and 2 and came to the conclusion that the answer depended on the context, on the situation, on the process itself.

The group evaluated the checklist as a "fairly theoretical scheme". An example now or then would make it easier to understand and make it more useful. It could be interesting to have a look at the scheme at various levels, for the use of the inspectorate, of the teachers, of the students…

Regarding the 2nd question the group missed:
– the idea of a *good description* of the change you want to achieve. Before starting the process a good analysis of what you have in mind is important,
– the idea of *support*, although it's mentioned here and there. This support can be different: financial, moral, technological…
– a good definition of the term *stakeholder*. Is it an economical term or has it to do with involvement, or money, or ownership…? This must be cleared up.

The idea of mind-mapping to restructure the checklist will be seriously taken into account. The 'decision of the change agents' was placed on top of the list to suggest that change agents can get involved at any stage of the change process. The following phases (from 2 to 14) concentrate on the change process itself.

References

CfBT (1999). The National Literacy Strategy: Research amongst headteachers of primary schools.

DfEE (1999). Autumn Package (annual statistical analysis of school performance across England and Wales, provided with individual school elements) Sudbury, UK DfEE Publications.

http://www.standards.dfee.gov.uk/performance: this website is a gateway to a range of data and information on schools and school improvement in England and Wales.

Ford, M. (1992). *Motivating humans: Goals, emotion, and personal agency beliefs*. Newbury Park: CA:Sage.

Fullan, M. (1993). *Change Forces: Probing the depths of educational reform*, London: Falmer Press.

Fullan, M. (1999). *Change Forces: The sequel*. Philadelphia, PA: Falmer Press, Taylor & Francis Inc.

Fullan, M. (2000). The return of large-scale reform. *Journal of Educational Change*, Spring

Earl, L., Fullan, M., Leithwood, K., & Watson, N. (1999). *Implementation of the National Literacy and Numeracy Strategies: First interim report*. Toronto: OISE, University of Toronto.

Earl, L., Fullan, M., Leithwood, K. & Watson, N. (2000). *Watching and Learning: Evaluation of the Implementation of the National Literacy and Numeracy Strategies: First Annual Report*. Toronto: OISE, University of Toronto.

Gunter, H. (1999). Contracting headteachers as leaders: an analysis of NPQH. *Cambridge Journal of Education*, 29(2) 251-264.

Leithwood, K., Begley, P. & Cousins, J.B. (1992). *Developing expert leadership for quality schools*. London: The Falmer Press.

Office for Standards in Education (1999b). *The National Literacy Strategy: An evaluation of the first year of the NLS*. London: OFSTED Publications Centre.

Wray, D. & Medwell, J. (1999). Effective teachers of literacy: Knowledge, beliefs and practices. *International Electronic Journal for Leadership in Learning*.

http://www.ngfl.gov.uk
http://www.standards.gov.uk

Danuta Elsner is Senior Adviser at Osrodek Doskonalenia i Ksztalcenia Ustawicznego PARTNER, Poland.
Phil Whitehead is principal lecturer in education at Oxford Brookes University, UK.
Felix Claus is Senior Adviser for secondary education at VSKO, Belgium.

CHAPTER 11

WHY ARE TEACHERS SO UNWILLING TO CHANGE?

Karine Van Thienen

Abstract

Most teachers are not very fond of change, even if the innovation could potentially lead to better practice. In that sense they differ from our expectations of those professionals who are very keen to adapt their practice once they have discovered a more effective way to act. Why then are teachers so reluctant to change?

This contribution seeks to highlight a series of factors which inhibit teacher innovation, factors which emerge from action research after some five years of INSET-experience, action research filtered and structured by current literature. From the analysis some attempts at proposed solutions will emerge.

Context

In January 1998 we started to provide INSET training at VSKO in projects financed by the Flemish Board of Catholic Education. They were aimed at disseminating outcomes of Socrates projects. Rudi Schollaert set up a nationwide school focused project, based on the outcomes of the ECCELLENTT[1] ECP which had as its aim to support schools in designing and implementing an assessment policy for foreign language learning, teaching and testing.

Some hundred schools subscribed to the project over four and a half years. We opted for working with a task force of teachers representing all foreign languages and all learner levels. The idea was to take the 'pioneers' out of their isolation and to provide them with support in order to help them introduce the changes at their own pace, in respect of the initial situation in their Foreign Language Department. Each task force was led by a FL-co-ordinator and had received a mission from the School Headteacher: to work towards a consistent language curriculum for the learner. The School Head and the ECCELLENTT-co-ordinator were given support as to how to implement effectively the project outcomes and to integrate them in concordance with the school vision and climate. The outcomes had to be compatible with educational policy, the school culture and the learner population. Twelve staff development interventions were spread over 18 months, aiming at School Heads, co-ordinators, task forces and twice all FL Teachers. Besides some input, an effective coaching strategy was worked out.

Foreign language instruction served as a test case to study how a given innovation could be implemented in different ways, depending on the internal conditions, the micro-politics of the various schools. And various they were! The project was designed in such way that the criteria for effective INSET were met[2]: the focus was on the group process, it was reflective, experience-related, focused on a felt need, co-operative, consultative and integrated. Actually the project was about co-operation, but the focus was on a specific problem occurring in almost all language departments.

Rudi Schollaert, Director of the In-service training and International Relations Unit, conducted a research study to map the impact of the project and to feed the results back into the theory. The case study was published in October 2000 in a specialised journal[3].

Schools which had covered the whole project cycle were invited to continue their development within the frame of networks. Two of the four networks that started in September 2000 are still active. The aim was to empower the task forces by asking them to monitor their own learning processes and by coaching them towards autonomous learning.

As we had discovered that lots of schools were attracted by the networking principles, but very few were really up to it, in September 2001 we started a third local project, also derived from a SOCRATES Lingua A project, TABASCO[4], designed to introduce a task-based approach in the participating schools, 12 at present, and providing a two-year programme.

Although Rudi Schollaert provided us, the actual INSET trainers, with a whole battery of methods and techniques to armour ourselves against teacher reluctance, we suffered a lot; but we also learned a lot. The real question remains: why are teachers so reluctant to change? What features did the action research reveal to us to frame this phenomenon and to understand it? And let us remind ourselves of the fact that resistance is not always a bad thing.

First we will give an overview of teachers' complaints and problems. From there we will consider a few aspects of what resistance is likely to be about. And from there look for possible actions to take.

Why are teachers so reluctant to change?

As a starting point, we want to focus on the questions which remains after years of experience with INSET provision: Why don't some teachers apply the new insights in their daily practice? And behind this question: did or do we fail? Don't they trust us? Can we help them? But most of all: What can we do?

Let us start very negatively, by listing the problems we had to deal with. Of course these problems were the problems of our "unwilling" or rather "uncertain" teachers, who wanted to get around the innovation, rather than taking a dive into the deep end. Here we are not talking about our valuable pioneers, the ones who dared and thanks to whom lots of practices changed. And between those two extremes we have the critical mass. The actual focus of our project work. Those who will guarantee the actual change at school level. The impact on these people constitutes our major concern. We want them to follow the pioneers. Not the reluctant teachers, those who strongly resist, the 3% hard core which will never follow the stream of improvement and which reminds us throughout the whole process that changing hurts.

What were the complaints which prevented the resistors from improving their practice? In this survey we collected two kinds of data: those coming from the teachers, and the ones that were identified by us, the INSET trainers. This survey is followed by some interpretations of what we thought was going wrong.

What problem areas complicate the educational picture by impeding the development of a climate conducive to change? In order to organise the features in a structured way, we tried to group them at three levels. The macro-level is concerned with society. At the meso-level we consider the school as an organisation. The micro-level is the level of everyday practice. It is the level of the classroom and of actual teaching. Let us take a look at issues that constitute or contour the 'growing pains' of the field workers. Some of them are reasons for resistance, whilst others are symptoms.

Due to the feminisation of the job, we'll refer to the teachers in the feminine. In order not to be regarded as sexist, the learner will be referred to as "he". We want to emphasise that it is not our intention to generalise when we speak about "the teachers". Our outcomes draw on particular action research. From there we tried to pinpoint major tendencies without therefore implying the conclusions refer to all teachers. Furthermore we really want to add that "all similarities with persons you happen to know are accidental".

- **At Micro-Level**

The most tangible is of course the micro-level, the field of the individual teacher, the one of the practitioner himself.

Teachers' complaints

– Nothing new!

One of the most frustrating reactions to training of innovation is that disbelievers react in terms of "there is nothing new, we have been doing this for years!" Frustrating because that utterance is a perfect alibi for not changing because one can't say one doesn't believe them.

– Additional work?

Some teachers say at the end of a session that it was all very interesting, but that actually they have no time to do this in their daily practice. Imagine you are working towards more effective instruction based on findings from acquisition and learning theories. You have designed training according to the Kolb-cycle: a shared experience by means of a demo, a period of reflection, conceptualisation in a structured frame and then implementation strategies for the daily practice; and a teacher is complaining that she lacks time to give efficient instruction...

This kind of reaction deals with the actual interpretation of change. One of the reasons is that many teachers build upon the wrong schemata. They associate everything new with additional work, rather than with improvement of existing practice. In the same way, they interpret the change as being cumulative rather than as something to be integrated into the actual teaching and learning facilitating process. So for instance in our current project, we deal with approach and methodology rather than with content, which is hard to understand 'on the other side of the dale'. Most of the teachers relate the project insights to other types of tasks they need to undertake. When we ask them to try something out, sceptical practitioners explain at the next occasion that unfortunately they ran out of time, and they didn't have the opportunity to experience it with their learners.

– Give us models!

In our programme evaluations we regularly received the same comment: "Too theoretical! Give us models! Give us materials to try out..." And when we gave the exemplary materials, we received complaints about the situation being different from theirs... "With my level of learners I could never use that! It's too difficult for them".

Whereas we want them to learn how to fish, handing out from the start some fish in order to satisfy their worst hunger and to keep them on track, they want nothing but more fish... fish, that will have to wait until these fish become stale and old, or that will sink into oblivion. The tension between the learning process and the products we are going for, is an ongoing problem. We would surely be amazed to see how some teachers deal with such processes in their own lessons, but just like their learners, they don't actually make the link.

The treasure within

Although they experienced lots of techniques due to the looping principles of our sessions, our disbelievers appeared not to notice it and did not make any connections to their own class management concerns.

- Our learners are not motivated!

Even if the motivation of some teachers – most of the time those who were sent by their School Head, sometimes also the ones who wanted to take the lead in their department because of their "authority" as senior teachers – was rather poor, some of them tried to get around the innovation by claiming that their learners were not motivated to learn languages. "They don't show any involvement", "They are too lazy", "What about discipline when they think that they can speak or move freely around the classroom?"... "It won't work in my classes!" and there goes the self - fulfilling prophecy!

The funny thing is that indicators of success in the changes we facilitated and supported suggested that the learners were more eager to actively improve their languages, that the change resulted in more actively participating... motivated learners. It seemed almost as if the traditional approach was a kind of punishment: we'll first wash the dishes, and then we'll eat what I prepared for you – whether you like it or not.... Here we have a tension between boring courses and "Spielerei"...

- We don't have enough time!

A significant aspect of the 'lack of time' factor, or let's call it feasibility, is the work load and pressure which interferes with teachers' potential enthusiasm for 'more' work. But sceptical teachers also complain about lack of "teaching time" to implement innovations. The "curriculum demands" come first... As if these demands would not imply an approach based on best practice...

One of the essential practices in learning is to reflect in order to get below the surface level and to result in actual change of beliefs, and from there to real change. But many teachers claim that they don't have time to spend on reflection... This is of course is related to the interpretation of the desired change... "Too time-consuming", "Loss of teaching time" – even if it results in better quality learning time.

When we consider that adaptive learning only affects a surface level, the observable behaviour, and that generative learning needs reflection because this is the only way to ensure a stretching of the personal interpretation frame, the perception and representation of what learning is about, time management in one's daily practice needs to be revised.

- Give us the conditions!

Lots of teachers complain about a whole range of deficient conditions and facilities which have hampered them from implementing the innovation.

First of all there is the domain of 'didactic comfort'. Teachers claim a need for an adapted infrastructure in terms of subject classrooms, computers, audio and video tools and materials, textbooks, reference works, notwithstanding a well-provided library, …

They are not eager to experiment with large classes, sometimes in cramped rooms, mixed ability groups, factors which they perceive as genuinely obtrusive, as indeed they are.

The absence of these facilitating conditions results in a huge burden and in a perceived 'inhuman' workload at the teachers' end.

Many teachers do not see how working in a new way affects learner progression, not assuming that they would know what their colleagues from the year before or since have done with the learners. Vertical tuning-in is rather exceptional in our schools, although the curricular goals are always of two-years duration.

Underlying problems

As we already suggested, these problems are not straightforward, but are rather to be situated on a continuum.

– Professional or executive

A teacher can act as a professional who has control over her own learning and development. The field independent teacher. The expert who is eager to learn and to improve her daily practice. Or she can act as an executive. She is neither creative nor critical, and doesn't reflect. She just acts and builds upon routines. This shows of course a very narrow view of the profession.

We saw lots of product-oriented teachers in our projects, asking for fish rather than wanting to learn how to fish. It is the prototype of the textbook-centred teacher, who explains five times in a row the same thing in the same way to the learners. And if the learners don't understand, the teacher is astonished by the apparent unwillingness of the youngsters.

It's the type of teacher who complains from the start of the training session to the end that she just needs some models, that she's not willing to learn how to fish because that's another task too many, and of course because that's the job of the textbook designer, who has to deliver pre-chewed materials, ready for consumption!

Some of these teachers claim they don't want to read the curricula. "I've been teaching for years! I know what's best for my learners!" Actually they talk about pupils, et pour cause… Others follow the textbook, page after page "because learners need structure", "Learners need a grip, you know". It's like in traditional villages where the butcher doesn't sell lambs chops because on Monday three quarters of the village eats sausages, on Tuesday chicken, and so on, week after week, until eternity will put an end to their habits.

– Conditioned by a cognitive model

Lots of teachers are willing to change, but they don't know how to deal with it. They have been conditioned towards a cognitive model where the teacher is the one who knows. As for language teachers for example, they come from the era where grammar was to be beaten into learners' brains and endless lists of words poured into the poor learner. They have even forgotten how they taught their own children how to speak. They even have no grip on their own learning.

– Reluctant to theorise

One of the most amazing things is how many teachers are reluctant to theorise. Knowing that theory is a shortcut to articulating what works well and why, knowing that "for the sake of control" they prefer teaching the subject related knowledge (the language system for instance) rather than teaching learners how to use the knowledge or how to solve subject related problems, this strikes us as rather weird.

All professionals share a metalanguage which enables them to discuss work-related matters in a technical and efficient way, without falling into the trap of emotionally charged discussions. We ascertained that some of the problems could be resolved by 'clarifying' concepts so that at the end of our ECCELLENTT project, the term "validity" was well anchored in our schools.

We have two categories of teachers in Flanders: those with and those without a university degree and it is not only the latter category that stumbles over theoretical concerns.

One of the causes of the dualism between theory and practice may be found in pre-service education, where the trainees on the one hand have the theoretical backgrounds in their curriculum, and on the other hand the – sometimes opposite – models or requirements of the practical training tutors, who "know" what works on the shop floor, and who have to assess the trainees in this regard as well. Our graduate teachers have the additional problem that they have very little time for teacher education and practice, because of finances, of course. How could the transfer possibly occur in that narrow time frame? It's only one of the factors, of course. We all know that stressful situations – because of anxiety for instance – also lead to regression.

– Poor teaching repertoire

Generally speaking, we experienced that many teachers lack certain teaching dimensions. Most of all they lack agogic skills, thinking skills and ways to convey and to provide training in such skills.

The teachers who have insight in learning strategies or in other than cognitive intelligence are not particularly numerous. Additionally most of them have a rather restricted repertoire of methods and techniques which most of the time lack depth. They have their preferred style, with little variation. They have their own emphasis in their classes, which can be confusing towards learners because the latter have to conform to consecutive approaches and views on the same subject from other teachers... On the other hand this diversity can provide young people with a fresh start and with a strategy which is more adapted to their learning style.

Time constraints often lead to short-term solutions and lack of depth. Our teachers struggle with time and class management, but also with management of learning opportunities. Some of them run like a Eurostar train through the curriculum instead of focusing on the actual learner. They see their subject as a sausage which can be sliced. By putting one slice upon the other they think they have dealt with the whole curriculum. "They should know that! We dealt with it last year just before Christmas! O, did they forget it again?" As if each course item 'delivered' by the teacher would stay for ever as a stigma in learners brains... reconstructing this way the sausage as a whole. And that's it!

They don't always know how to cope with prioritising, evaluating efficiency and effectiveness, and then prefer to follow the book from page 1 to the end, confident that textbook and guidelines are conceived by professionals, by those who should know. Lack of self-direction... Teachers as executives...

– Low self-esteem, lack of appraisal, fear of disapproval

One of the worst problems is teachers' lack of self-esteem, self-confidence. We became fully aware of it during the Lingua B or Comenius courses we organised or taught. Our teachers asked for regular appraisal, which they deserve of course, after all the investments they make. "Am I doing it right?" That was one of the most common questions we were asked when they requested feedback!

And just like the learners, the teachers decide for themselves which are the criteria for being acknowledged or becoming appraised. Everything takes a turn downwards when at the end-of-year deliberation, a particular subject appears not to be "important" enough to be taken into consideration for decision making[5]. When the decision to let the learner pass successfully is not impeded or at least put into question in case of a "failure" in a certain subject.

One of the problems with learner-centredness is that many teachers are uncomfortable at not being at the centre of the process anymore. They fear suffocation, getting lost and start drawing on survival skills. One thing is sure however; a learner-oriented approach demands more expertise, competence and skills than a traditional one; and the less well performing learners need to have the best teachers, which clashes with the former 'privilege oriented' tradition, but here we are already at the meso-level.

• **At Meso-Level**

All factors at the meso-level are related in one way or another to the school climate. As already pointed out, people need a safe environment if they are expected to learn, and certainly the teachers do, since learning is the trade of the school. The social climate is affected by all stakeholders, inside and outside of the campus.

On the homepage of his personal web site, David Hopkins[6] defines the ideal 'classroom' or 'powerful learning' in the following way: "A school teaches in three ways – by what it teaches, by how it teaches, and by the kind of place it is. (…) The best learning occurs in classrooms where content is conceptual rather than particular, where learning is constructive enquiry not passive reception and where the social climate is expansive instead of restrictive". And he continues: "such classrooms exist in schools whose organisational conditions and cultures are characterised by high expectations, collaboration and innovation."

Teachers' complaints

–   Our School Head wants to keep everything under control

In our project on Task-Based Learning, teachers are experimenting with giving more responsibilities to the learners. But then, some School Heads want to keep everything under control - actually they prefer their teachers to be executives, rather than professionals... In some schools teachers are even asked to plan in detail their lessons from the beginning of the year, and not to deviate from the plans. The autonomy of the school can clash with the autonomy, the need for flexibility of the teacher.

–   It wouldn't work with our colleagues!

Power versus Authority. Once they were used to play the pioneer part, some task force members had forgotten that their colleagues rely on their own beliefs, and that they would only adapt their practice if they felt the change is really beneficial to them. One of the complaints which came back was the lack of impact on – some of - their colleagues. And even if people learn more from their peers than from "superiors", having a colleague in their own school who knows "better" is often a bit harder to digest…

–   All those meetings… an organised waste of time

First of all most teachers don't like to participate in formal meetings organised from above. Secondly they often lack meeting skills and techniques. Thirdly, discussing practical issues is less threatening and therefore it was common practice in lots of schools, rather than tuning in horizontally, let stand vertically.

In our projects teachers had to set up decision making procedures in order to benefit from those meetings lots of them are allergic to. They experienced that with or without mandate from the Head, they didn't have the power over their colleagues. So they had to set up consultation rounds, negotiation time and to come up with a well documented file in order to get the "authority" to impose a new practice. It's very hard when after all, teachers are used to going back to their classrooms, to closing the door and to doing their own thing… It was also hard to experience that some teachers didn't follow up the decisions which had been made within their department. In this way they hampered those who wanted to go further.

Openness is a major condition, but unfreezing teachers was rather problematic, and in some schools it took more than a year. From there, some of them needed continuous support to keep the staff on the right track; others felt able to take the helm.

– All that paperwork...

One of the management demands is to keep track of what happens within the school by means of paper work, and this for the sake of documentation and controllability which is the basis for reflection, or follow-up, but also for accountability towards externally positioned people. Most externals just pop in for a few hours, they are overloaded with work and the School Head feels always more comfortable with a nice file to show how well the school is doing.

When we attempted to formalise peer consultation and teacher meetings in our project work, by asking our task forces to document their action plan, we were confronted with a wall of complaints because most teachers are resistant to paper work on account of its negative connotations. They felt confronted with externals pretending they wanted to support and to facilitate innovation in their school which would lead to becoming better teachers. It is our belief that targets to be met need success indicators to prove the impact of the change, but many teachers complained about all additional paperwork they needed to provide. They felt controlled again.

Generally speaking, teachers get the impression that they have to account for their work to too many people: learners, parents, school management, external assessors. They get the impression that it doesn't leave them the time to do their actual job, which is teaching and – in the best of worlds - learner coaching. As INSET providers we were confronted with reporting problems as well: with schools which delivered reports of the two-years' work at the end of the project-period, under pressure from the School Head, hastily drafted pages, just in order to receive the ECCELLENTT label, because it would be nice to hang it somewhere visibly on the wall.

– We have to do it on our own!

In one of our schools, the teachers who had to come to the sessions, had to look for a colleague who wanted to take over their lessons, on a voluntary basis. It did not work for very long...

Teachers who wanted to experiment with the innovations sometimes asked to be given parallel classes. The benefit would have been twofold: less preparation time and more monitoring opportunities. They were disappointed when it appeared to be impossible to timetable.

Some teachers became frustrated when they heard about colleagues in another school who received extra hours for their project work, or a separate departmental meeting and working room; when they heard about School Heads who planned meeting opportunities within the teacher timetables; when they

The treasure within

were told that a School Head praised its team in public; when they heard that some task forces were accomplishing real mandatory work, made official by the School Head after discussion time, for instance in a new school-wide reporting system; when they heard about School Heads who participated in the task force meetings and even drafted the report – a considerable administrative burden, to be sure... And some task forces fell apart when their co-ordinator received a management position because she had grown so much professionally.

A school task force knowing that their work doesn't matter, that it will not change anything, needs a large degree of idealism in order to maintain the interest to continue investing in the project, which includes having to keep the rank and file of the party on track. Sometimes they felt as if they were being used to make a good impression upon the external environment, and most of all they resented being used to keep up appearances in the case of an external audit by Inspectors from the Ministry of Education. The question is of course what longer term benefit this sort of situation can produce. Their conclusions from this experience are not so hard to imagine...

Underlying problems

–   For free...

One of our problems was that we offered our services for free. We had finances coming from other sources than the school. This resulted in a less strict attendance and participation in the activities from some agents. What's the added value of participating in all sessions if there is nothing to pay? People don't always respect what is not expensive for them. There is less real ownership, real choice. Consuming free shareware.

–   Inefficient consultation

Previous changes have been accompanied by lots of information meetings where all requirements were poured over their heads. It resulted in a huge allergy to consultation: most teachers see that word as a trap... If they are to give their opinion, nobody from above will listen to them: they will have the opportunity to voice their concerns, and that's it!

As to peer consultation there is the eternal area of tension between one's own identity, autonomy and collegiality, co-operation. Lots of teachers see themselves as entities rather than as a part of the chain... This is partially due to the "them and us" phenomenon, the management versus the classroom practitioner, which do not always share views, goals or frames of good practice. And when they co-operate, they prefer to do so informally, losing in this way opportunities for setting structured common targets and celebrating their milestones. But generally speaking there is not sufficient tuning-in at school level.

Most of the schools plan meetings on a subject basis. Teachers are invited to consult each other and to tune in to the discussion. Even if our project work led to a real improvement in that respect, some teachers struggle with the institutional need for working agreements and commitments. Co-operation can be very hard for the average teacher, even if they are supposed to help their learners to work co-operatively.

As our projects were targeted at foreign languages in general, we were also confronted with clashing language culture and traditions. In most schools the depth of the implementation differed from one language to another and the teachers always explained that difference by referring to more or less involved or reluctant 'individuals'. At that point, as INSET trainers, we were asked to act as a referee…

This is also linked to the power teachers asked us to assume because they were convinced we had that power… Because they have a wrong view on the role of external agents. And we were external agents as well, even if our agenda was to act as scaffolders for growth, confederates or partners within the school setting. We were sometimes expected to play God, and to say what should be done and what might certainly not be done, a role we did not want to play. We provided stimuli, we made people reflect, we confronted them with their own beliefs, and created for them opportunities to grow from there. We were moderators, but not policy–makers or mandated control agents.

–   Control of teachers by the Head, control of the learner by the teacher

Teachers whose freedom of movement and experience was blocked by the School Head for the sake of controllability almost automatically restrain the freedom of experience of their learners, as it has become a characteristic feature of the school climate.

–   Lack of systemic thinking

Some of the teachers don't see beyond the walls of their classroom. Furthermore, they see all formal interaction as well as reporting as a burden because they don't see the need for transparency and for supporting each other to stay on track, for working towards the same mission. They don't see themselves as a part of the system which results in the whole 'school profile'. Some of them have even never thought about what learning is about, let alone that they would share a view on the primary process.

That our staff development module was effective in that respect has been proven by a number of co-ordinators who became integrated into the middle management of their school because of the developmental processes they had gone through successfully. They had learned to work in a pro-active, consultative way instead of complaining. They had learned to take initiatives.

–   The crucial role of the School Head

If an innovation is to take place, it must be because of the benefits it can result in according to the School Management. To us this means that it meets the institutional targets and priorities, written out in the school improvement plan, and that it can be expected to be worth active management support. Some teachers complain about a lack of didactic support, or lack of communication channels and consultancy structures.

In our ECCELLENTT project on the implementation of a school-based assessment policy, Rudi Schollaert insisted on making the School Heads agree on their supportive role. They had to sign a written commitment. This was meant as a guarantee that the changes which would be introduced would matter, and would be supported actively by the management. School Heads and internal MFL co-ordinators received training sessions in implementation strategies and successful schools were those where the School Heads kept their promises, fulfilled their role.

Nevertheless we had to support language teacher teams in negotiating their rights and to comfort those who didn't succeed in doing so. What could we possibly expect from professional development when teachers' wants or needs do not meet the institutional ones? When teachers have the impression that they are kept busy without any significance for the school system?

Of course there were also the managers who offered to draft the reports of the task force meetings. The one who conducted a research study on the feelings of learners with new assessment styles. Those who created a budget for the task force in order to plan the purchasing of new materials or resources. The one who facilitated the edition of a Language Teacher Newsletter. Those who provided the language teachers with meeting rooms, with classrooms specially equipped for language teachers, or with new video recorders or computers. And they got better teachers as a result of their efforts. The support of School Heads can work miracles.

Teachers expect active support from the School Head. They are entitled to. It is their right, and it is the duty of a School Head to do so.

- **At Macro-Level**

There are of course a number of factors which impede practitioners from implementing changes that derive from the broader context in which teachers have to work, the macro-level.

Complaints

– We know what's best for our learners!

Lots of our language teachers express their dissatisfaction about instructions coming from above. They explain it as "directions from people who don't know or who have forgotten what teaching is about, what a classroom looks like or the way present-day learners behave..." And some teachers go rather far in their opposition. They refuse to carry out the instructions. So for instance there is that local regulation in modern languages requiring that at least 60 % of the assessment has to be on skills. Well, there are still teachers who don't know how to cope with that, some of them because they don't believe in it, others because they don't know how to do so.

The other way around, there are also teachers who take the School Head as a kind of hostage, for instance one Chemistry teacher who said he couldn't work with classes of more than 20 learners because the curriculum requires that the learners work hands -on, and there are only 20 places in the laboratory...

And our most recent curriculum change providing fewer hours for languages will not have a beneficial impact on our Flemish language teachers, those with the heaviest amount of marking to do... They see it as a disregard of their work but of course they don't lobby at the top in the same way for example that the computer business does.

– It's always us they blame, so why bother?

AIDS, drugs, alcohol and tobacco addictions and prevention programmes, traffic casualties, ... all problems affecting our modern lifestyle are to be dealt with in the school, because it is there that young people are readily grouped and can be reached. All teachers who care are gathered in working parties and try to cope with all problems of society. They are so busy with all kinds of extra project work that they feel happy whenever they stand in front or beside their learners, when they can concentrate on their actual job. Thus all the demands are concentrated on the same shoulders.

If society were only grateful for all the work teachers are doing... but no, in the newspapers we only read that teachers are lazy, they have too many holidays, they are unwilling to work. Schools are taken to court because learners fail. Education is more and more rule restricted in order to prevent legal reprisals. People feel as if they have to act in a defensive way all the time. This keeps them away from more valuable activities and takes up a lot of energy.

It is hard to work without recognition. One can wonder how on earth parents can bring themselves to leave their children – their pride and joy – with such bad people.

Underlying problems

- Our language teachers are fed up with all changes they have had to go through

A first finding which is voiced by a majority of teachers is that lots of innovations have affected Belgian schools, and most of all the language teaching landscape. So our disbelievers live in the hope that some of these changes will be undone. Furthermore the fear of additional structural changes makes them feel extremely uncomfortable. Like the Gaul, they are afraid that the sky will fall upon their heads... In that respect we conceived the plan to get language teachers to work with colleagues whose discipline has been less subject to changes, more towards content-based instruction...

- Lack of support when educational structures change

Even in the third millennium, even if our national authorities feel very strongly about school autonomy, public finances do not stretch far enough to provide the schools with enough money to implement the desired changes, most of the time structural changes.

When the concept of the Study House, the famous Dutch Open Learning Centres, was introduced in the Netherlands schools were able to benefit from financial support for the implementation. They were encouraged, also financially, to make connections by means of networks. When curricula change, support organisations create textbooks or materials to go with it. Our teachers are envious of Dutch colleagues in that respect.

- No ownership

Changes are felt as requirements from above which lead to uncertainty, problems, ... Actually most of the teachers don't feel involved – and certainly not when opposite ideologies are fighting again for more impact on education -, they don't see the benefits of most changes, also because they are always presented as in a very theoretic way or they refer to structures instead of to classroom and learning issues.

Educational changes are felt as administrative burdens, because teachers have to document more and more without seeing any benefit in it. Lack of ownership drives people to executing tasks which are considered absurd.

- Open debate culture

Parents have become more and more demanding. Our Minister of Education is "favourable to public debate and consultation". She imposes it on teachers but some parents don't play by the rules. They would do anything to avoid their children having to repeat a year. A lot of the paper work requested in the schools deals with accountability towards parents who might want to sue a school in court and it must be said that the legal discourse is not helping the learner, because teachers have to keep records on them in case the parents ever attack the validity of their decisions.

– Societal recognition

Societal recognition is certainly not proportional to the needs and expectations of teachers. They feel threatened by the society they are serving. A society that provides them with a long list of duties without appropriate remuneration, and who blames them for all problems which occur nowadays. A society that seems not to be really interested in the first mission of the school, in the primary process of learning.

What is teacher resistance to change about?

If we want to remain positive we could interpret a large part of the resistance as evidence of teachers' actual involvement. The idea that teachers want to behave badly is untenable. It is reasonable to believe that 99% of our colleagues want to do a good job and love their work, even though it is demanding. But first of all: how do they perceive change? And how do they learn? And from there: what is the link between learning and resistance?

Teachers' perception of change

How do teachers perceive change? What are the most common features they have to cope with, and which impede the actual professional improvement? Here are some of them we recognised during our project work.

First of all – and this is one of the main features for their reluctance to change - they want to have full control of what happens in the classroom… Amongst others because they are held accountable for all kinds of things happening to the learners. But also because they feel it as being a part of their job to keep everything under control. Most of the teachers have been trained to become people-who-know. And they have problems to be those-who-don't-know-yet, let alone those who give control to the learner.

Secondly they get a feeling of imperfectness, of deficiency during the process of change. It's like a lobster that changes shell. While it loses its shell to let the new one grow, it is very vulnerable and uncomfortable. In order to acquire new insights, one must first be aware of a lack, which is often referred to as to 'deficiency', rather than as opportunity for growth. Besides, new competence goes through a temporary stage of conscious incompetence, which hurts, of course the one-who-used-know…

Imperfectness is a difficult situation to cope with by the teacher. She forgets to link it with positive growth by trial and error, and instead, links it with deficiency or not performing well.

Thirdly there is a need for a larger tool box: how to achieve or to transfer the newly acquired beliefs and approaches to daily practice. New procedures, new routines have to be settled, new ways of creating learning opportunities. Although change doesn't mean that people should start again from scratch… The whole repertoire has to be revised in order to sort out what still can be useful, and what should be adapted.

And finally we want to stress the time problem in growing. It's not just like buying a new pair of shoes. It needs time, and nobody would benefit from rushing it… People have to do it at their own pace. Support however and positive impulses do help.

Beliefs on teachers' practice and frame for learning

As change, or call it innovation, requires a changing or learning process, we have to ask ourselves how we believe teachers learn. And how do they know what they think they know? A kind of framework for stored knowledge and learning which resulted from our own background, experiences and beliefs.

– Subjective teaching theory

Teachers act from what we can call their subjective educational theory, their inner judgmental frames or content structures. Everything they do is related to conclusions they have made from previous experience, guided by positive experiences as well as by fear of getting egg on their face.

It is the development of that subjective educational theory which will lead to better practice or improvement, once all bias or prejudices have been sorted out. Our personal understanding of teacher learning has been derived from a theory on subject learning, more precisely on a theory on language learning. The Interlanguage theory which explains how the acquisition of language works. From there we will transfer to the professional growth of the teacher: how does she acquire new insights?

This will lead us to what we call in a more unfortunate way the teacher's "Interteaching Theory". An open concept, less threatening than just "expertise", and which allows for ongoing professional development. Life Long Learning, you know.

– The Interlanguage Theory

As a language teacher, we compare the teachers' subjective learning and teaching theory with learner interlanguage. In a nutshell, this means that the learner who tries to acquire a new language, only has a view on what he already discovered from the system, which is not necessarily the same as what he has been taught. His understanding of the target language system is comparable to a Gruyere, but then with more holes than cheese. As some holes are difficult to work with, he fills them up – consciously or unconsciously, or let's say explicitly or implicitly – either with features of his mother tongue, or with overgeneralization or oversimplification of patterns or rules. And what dictates his findings on the system is based on his own logic. Actually this is a plea for inductive learning with thinking aloud on how to induce or how to discover patterns within the system… The personal logic of the learner deals with his representation of the world, not necessarily with 'reality'… As Pirandello said: à chacun sa vérité. And those representations are stored in the brain as what we call mental schemata and scripts.

Schemata are some kind of abstract associations, based on a sort of prejudice. So for instance a bus crashing into a precipice is associated with a tired driver who hasn't slept the whole night, and so on. Scripts are a kind of scenario which represents logical or chronological sequences which make sense. So when one goes to a restaurant, the man has to go in first - in order to check if it's safe, a feature which perhaps has its origin in the Cowboy and Indians era – and then they have to wait for a table, then, depending on the cultural climate it takes more or less time before a waiters shows up with the menu, but they can already ask for an appetiser, and so on. All these features have developed from previous experiences in the world and are compiled in a script.

– Teachers' schemata and scripts

This schemata and script theory on storage of knowledge of the world is actually a theory of learning, of how to integrate new knowledge.

Here is an example of teacher schemata or associations. When the teacher has just reprimanded a learner, most of the time the youngster doesn't know how to behave towards the teacher nor towards his mates, and starts grinning. Well, lots of teachers misinterpret this attitude as laughing in their face because they associate the reaction with was has happened before, that is the reprimand, and not with the whole – survival – climate for the learner.

In the same way the teacher has scenarios in mind, for instance a doomsday scenario on group work, dictating amongst others that group work means for the learner that he wants to be with his mates, to rush through the task, wasting time in social chat. And when the teacher goes around to take "control", the youngsters disturb the whole classroom organisation by pretending to talk because they have already finished the work. That work turns out later to be a very slipshod piece of work. Enough to complain and to voice reluctance about group work, and at the same time about collaborative learning, to voice this opinion all over the school, and even beyond. "Pupils are not like they used to be", because in the meantime the teacher has replaced her own school experience of learning with her current expectations of what being a good learner is like.

One of the problems arising from giving control and responsibility to the learner after the Copernican revolution which put him at the centre of the process, is to be out of control, not being the *deus ex machina* any more, coming up with all correct answers, wisdom and model behaviour. The growing pains of the teacher who has to evolve from the sage on the stage to the guide on the side are quite problematic, all the more since the teacher is accountable for the group to the school management and the authorities.

The consequence of all this is that in the best case an INSET-lecture falls into the scenario of a nice fairy tale. Again, if we want to stretch teachers' teaching repertoires, thinking skills have to be addressed gradually, spiced up occasionally with experiential learning cycles. There goes again the plea for inductive work. It takes more time but as the Italians say: chi va piano va sano e lontano. This is also what we experience through feedback with some of our project schools: as our projects are limited for time for reasons of funding – even if we always have received positive support – the time needed by teacher task forces, let alone by those who didn't choose the pioneer role, clashes with the project expectations.

– Interteaching Theory

Actually when we compare Interlanguage and what we called ironically the "Interteaching" system, we come to another field of tension. Interlanguage means intermediate system between language one and target language for reason of imperfection, but without any negative connotation. When we call the actual teaching repertoire "Interteaching" we see the monkey again coming out of the sleeve: imperfection, a situation difficult to cope with by the traditional teacher, but growing opportunities for those who want to evolve.

It's from there that learning starts. New items get restructured and if they have to stay in the brain, they have to match the existing representation of the world, and the whole is to be restructured into a comprehensive substance. In other words, learning is not a simple process, and should be seen as organic, reflective... but most of all as time consuming. And not all issues which are taught are internalised by the learner.

Gerard Westhoff compared learning to a pinball machine, where the provider of new theory has placed pins all around. The consumer of learning is the ball, following its own route, and every time he hits a pin, it's a new item which has been learned or acquired.

Learning and resistance

– Professional growth: how to cope with change

Actually resistance is also a regular stage in professional growth, which develops in four stages.
First there is resistance, the fear of losing autonomy or control. At this first stage, the teachers ask themselves if all they did before was wrong. Then there are the questions about what they should do, about the instructions. The third stage is the how: how to do it? This stage deals with concepts behind the instructions, the stage of the concrete translation of the prescriptions. Here there is more depth. The fourth stage is that of autonomy, of self-direction.

– Traceability of resistance: Le dit et le non-dit

If resistance is a good sign, we should be able to trace its path and pre-empt it. How to interpret teachers' reactions to an Inset session? What you see isn't always what you get! Teachers' utterances cannot always be taken literally. It is impossible to have a clear view on what's going on in their brain! Le dit et le non-dit... with all consequent interpretations and misinterpretations from both sides. One could not expect a teacher to say: "Hey, actually I'm willing to learn but I'm not that comfortable with the implications it will have on my well being and self-perception. And what if I can't cope with the transfer to daily practice?"

At the beginning of an INSET-session, some people start complaining vociferously. It makes the trainer feel uncomfortable. But most of the time it's just to say "hello! I'm here". Other participants are acting in a problematic way because they were just sent by their School Head but most signs of resistance are indicators of involvement, of growth, of trying to cope.

Actually we can consider ourselves lucky if we have reactions. What would we do if they had nothing to say and stayed silent the whole time? That would be problematic!

–   Importance of reflection in the learning process

In their paper on how resistance affects the ability to reflect, Deborah Morse and Ella Mazor (1999) consider resistance as a step in the reflective process. They start from the widely accepted principle that reflection is one of the essential forces leading to teacher development and progress and is the basis for the construction of a bridge between theory and practice. Reflection which requires three basic conditions: distance – both emotional and over time; we need to move from the personal to the academic level; we also have to redefine the very nature of the experience.

Morse and Mazor distinguish two types of learning. Adaptive learning and coping, closing the gap of what is needed and not present, on one hand; generative learning, also called double loop learning or learning how to learn, on the other hand.

Generative learning comes into play when we discover that the identification of the problem or gap is itself contingent on learning new ways of perceiving and thinking about our problems. It is this type of learning which produces a tremendous amount of anxiety, both survivor anxiety – the uncomfortable realization that in order to survive and thrive, I must change - and learning anxiety – the fear of learning something new, showing that we are wrong or imperfect or we will lose our effectiveness, our self-esteem and maybe even our identity. We feel the need to embrace what we are presently doing rather than facing the unknown. As change comes from some disconfirmation which leads to disequilibrium, we can either ignore them, blame it on others or deny its validity. But once the disequilibrium is acknowledged, the need for change has to be accepted. This can happen either by increasing the first type of anxiety or decreasing the second. It is at this stage that resistance to change begins to surface.

Resistance does not often appear in a straightforward way. It can take many different forms including apparent passivity, a recurring old-fashioned credo or misunderstanding or confusion, stalling or attacks on any new ideas. The cognitive unfreezing and redefinition must occur before any real change - refreezing - takes place and needs to happen in safe environment.

How to deal with resistance?

Resistance to change is not easy to negotiate, neither by a colleague, nor by the management, and certainly not by an INSET trainer. The process of what they think is happening is not always the only process that is going on. And misinterpretations lead to erroneous reactions towards teachers in the field. All births are painful, but they lead to a new entity. Sharing ideas, risk taking and support can help and as soon as one begins to change, a shift of perception takes place. Learning involves a degree of uncertainty. Uncertainty is painful for some people, uncomfortable for other and challenging for others still.

If we anticipate anxiety and resistance, however, we can meet it with a more supportive and directed environment and acknowledge it as a natural part of the process.

At VSKO, the INSET providers are able to attend expert training on particular skills. Dealing with resistance was one of them. From there we derived a few strategies that work.

So we learned concentrating on asking questions. We experienced it ourselves. The issue is to continue asking in order to let the trainee express his own view. A Socratic treatment is a longer, but a more efficient way to reflect upon a new insight. By advancing an opposite thesis, by arguing, the trainer will enhance or trigger off useless resistance.

A second technique consists of first giving confirmation to the person, and afterwards to deal with the content. And not to take the resistance personally.

We also experienced the danger of role playing. In a skills training activity, people who acted in their own name, who didn't 'play a role' felt a lack of approval or even misappraisal when feedback from peers was expressed.

The safety and openness of the climate is again one of the major conditions for success. This environment is often facilitated by a positive identification with a role model or by creating a more learner-centred environment, including coaching, encouragement, support, developing a positive vision, providing a practice field in order to learn and make mistakes, providing direction, sharing in groups, rewarding small steps and embracing errors, learning through a trial and error process based on scanning the environment for new concepts by reading, talking to people, exposure to lots of new information that might reveal a solution to the problem.

And of course, if we really want to go for change, we have to give the people time.

Conclusion

Change has a major impact on teachers' daily functioning. It is all about ownership, being involved in decision- making, respect, recognition, self-esteem, social climate, atmosphere, having the opportunity to see the full picture, to see where the change leads to, what will be the benefits for all stakeholders... About fear, controllability, not willing to fall flat on one's face, about growing pains. It's all about being a learner. Wouldn't it be easier to conclude that teachers do not really want to change? That would be an expression of our own resistance...

Towards a comprehensive solution: A Teacher Portfolio to provide ownership of the own professional development.

As INSET is most of the time a free and individual business, maybe getting ownership of the own professional development could bring some light into teachers' dark areas... Teachers who have to guide their learners towards autonomy could be given autonomy in that respect as well, within the frame of the school mission of course. Maybe a teacher portfolio with regular appraisal interviews could help them to find their own identity, to build up their confidence with a document that would give some sense to paper work?

The idea is to turn factors which lead to teacher resistance or uncertainty into goals to be achieved gradually, and to provide the desired supporting conditions as a rewarding system from the management side in order to encompass and to praise actively teacher development in a way that working on one's own development is felt as something which matters, as something that narrows the gap between them (management) and us (teachers), as something initiated by the teachers. The list of teacher goals can be drawn from the responses of all kinds of stakeholders to the question: to me, a good teacher is someone who can, does, and so on. There could be a gradation from starter competencies to basic competencies and from there to an advanced level. The overall aim is to reach a win-win situation that both, institution and members of staff , can benefit from.

Even physicians have a system to enable them to continue updating their practice… and we are most grateful that they do!

Desired knowledge, skills or behaviour (attitudes)	Conditions	Success Indicators	Comments		
			Teacher	School Head	Externals
By Teacher					
By School Head					
By Externals					

Such a portfolio derived from essential behaviour, skills and knowledge within the frame of the educational policy and mission statement of the school can support the professional improvement and will echo in all sections of the school, but most of all in the classroom where it may well result in a consistent, school focused and powerful learning climate. And the learner, that's why we are here, isn't it?

Epilogue

What Teacher complaints and underlying problems did we recognise in our own environment?

During the presentation of the problems which impede practitioners to adapt their practice, most of the participants at the Prague Conference were nodding the whole time. A few School Heads said after the workshop that they had the impression that it was their school which had been analysed.

In a first discussion-round the 28 participants who attended the workshop discussed the complaints and teacher problems they recognised in their own home situation.

From all those presented, "Nothing new…" was the one which seemed to be on top of the list. Apparently this reaction is well known all over the countries represented. "I have already been doing this for ages!"

Other complaints at micro-level listed in the group discussions were the following ones. Teachers feel that they lack curricular time to "play new games", or to work on innovation. They feel bent by the heavy workload – preparing lesson plans, marking, looking for suitable materials...-, but also by additional working parties. Lots of practitioners don't see any benefit in change: things seem all right according to them. Or they hardly try to apply the innovation, and rush to the conclusion that it doesn't work in their situation, without giving it a real chance.

Another reaction shows they don't feel involved at all when it comes to improving their practice: "You don't know what you are talking about!" This way they separate the providers of "good news", the theorists, from the fieldworkers, those who have to carry it out. Furthermore, either they don't see how to cope with learner variables or with mixes ability classes or they hide themselves behind that argument, knowing that in order to deal with this remark the Trainer will be kept busy for a while.

Lack of control is a general complaint which impedes teachers to change easily. Even when a concept is clear, and worthwhile giving a chance, so much practical and administrative burdens come up, that people give it up rather quickly. If only there was some appraisal to make self-esteem increase...

At meso-level, the problems are still comparable with those present in the action research in Flemish schools. Poor communication, no open consultation, too many formalised meetings. And even if there is room for consultation, lack of real openness impedes people to deal with it seriously. Hidden agendas in school politics result in hiding games. Emotional reaction between the pros and the cons or between INSET-providers and trainees. Feeling of being threatened. Anxiety. These features make the whole picture more complex.

People feel also betrayed by the authorities who don't provide enough support. How to focus on ICT when there is no money for computers? How to continue filling the schools' shopping list when additional funding of education is out of line? Innovations are dictated from above, not negotiated by the actual fieldworkers, who are not hindered by any ownership. At the content side they feel that the Curricula are far too heavy. They complain about curricular changes which are not supported while they are implemented; at least in most countries they are not. This makes teachers complain about injustice.

Towards possible solutions

During the second discussion-round the participants were invited to think about possible solutions or hints to evolve in the opposite direction, starting from scratch and building upon positive measures and settings which can prevent them from falling into the negative patterns again.

Actually teachers want to change, but they feel imprisoned by the curriculum, or by the learners who come into a certain grade and who are not ready to cope with the required level of abstraction or complexity. Better groups "always move faster". Heterogeneous classes however are always more difficult to deal with. In other words: techniques are needed to deal with poorly performing learners or with mixed ability classes should be integrated in the innovation programmes. In Ireland for instance people feel supported in working with mixed ability groups.

We heard a plea for respecting and trusting the teacher, who has her own beliefs in learning, her schemata which are built up from interpretation of learner behaviour. School Heads should show more support towards the teachers they take on board. Also because of the complexity of change. It is not just an approach or new contents that innovation is to be focused on, there are also the learners who require attention, and other aspects that the teacher has to keep in mind.

One of the subgroups suggested just putting more pressure on people to make them co-operate, to consult each other in an open climate, providing efficient communication channels and procedures.

Another group listed up a series of basic principles from where to start. As a main point they argued that managing teachers' emotions would be an imperative perspective to end up in positive action. Therefore they suggested a school setting where the School Head acts as a colleague, as an agent who shares the same concerns. Not as the one in his ivory tower. A second point would be to accept as a FACT that the first reflex is always one of self-defense. Thirdly to accept that new things ARE indeed threatening. But from there they suggest to having new things based upon positive points in the actual presentation of the challenge. If new things are presented from examples of good practice which already exist within the agenda for change, those who provided the examples will feel confirmed and esteemed because of the involvement they show. Other people could be invited to discover the added value of the home-made example, and from there, step by step approach the model. A fourth suggestion is to let innovation grow out of needs felt by the fieldworkers within the school, not out of needs mentioned by others for whatever reason. Starting from the problems as perceived by the staff, would have more chances to result in teachers developing school programmes together on the basis of mutual involvement and consultation.

References

Bruce, J., Calhoun, E. & Hopkins, D. (1997). *Models of Learning – Tools for Teaching*. Buckhingham – Philadelphia: Open University Press.
Hopkins, D. (2001). *Personalpage. Professor David Hopkins. Dean of the Faculty of Education.* University of Nottingham: School of Education. http://www.nottingham.ac.uk/education/Hopkins/inaugural.html [08/01/2002].
Morse, D. & Mazor, E. (1999). *Reflection and resistance.* Gordon College. Haifa. Paper from the TRTR4 Conference September 2-4. Leuven.
Pemberton, R., Li, E.S.L., Or, W.W.F. & Pierson, H.D. eds (1996). *Taking Control. Autonomy in Language Learning*. Hong Kong: Hong Kong University Press.
Schollaert, R. (1993). *An Internal evaluation of a School Focused INSET Project*

for Flemish Teachers of English as a Foreign Language. Dissertation submitted for the degree of MATEFL, Centre for Applied Language Studies. University of Reading.

Schollaert, R., Peeters, K., Van Cauwenberghe, A. (1996). *Spiegeleffecten. De Vlaamse decretale navorming doorgelicht.* Leuven: Garant.

Schollaert, R. ed. (2000). *Effective Staff Development. An evaluation manual.* (Syllabus serie nr. 2). Leuven: Garant.

Schollaert, R. (2000). Nascholing als aanzet tot vernieuwing op school. ECCELLENTT, een case study. *Tijdschrift voor Onderwijsrecht & Onderwijsbeleid.* 1. September - October 2000–2001. Diegem: Kluwer.

Van Looy, L. & Vrijsen, M. (1999). *Development of an Analytical Tool to Measure the "Profundity of Reflection" Based on Reflection Reports.* IDLO – VUB. Paper from the TRTR4 Conference September 2-4. Leuven.

Van Thienen, K. & Schollaert, R. (2000). *Gewikt en gewogen. Evaluatie van Communicatieve Vaardigheden in het Vreemdetalenonderwijs.* (Syllabus serie nr. 3). Leuven: Garant.

Verkoulen, H. (2001). "Door ondervinding wordt men wijs." In Leenheer, P. – Kaldewaij, J. – Westhoff, G. (eds). 2001. *Meso Focus 40. Wat werkt en waarom. Beschouwingen over de didactiek van gestuurde professionele ontwikkeling in scholen.* Houten: EPN.

Courses for INSET providers organised by Rudi Schollaert, Director of the In-service Training and International Relations Unit, VSKO, Brussels.

Karine Van Thienen is Project Manager at the INSET and International Relations Unit, VSKO, Belgium.

---

[1] ECCELLENTT is an acronym of Evaluation of Communicative Competence in European Language Learning Encompassing New Testing Technologies. ECCELLENTT is a three-year Socrates Lingua a project (39719-CP-1-97-BE-LINGUA-LA). Partnership: VSKO (BE), University of Potsdam (DE), University of Grenoble (CUEF - FR), University of Lisbon (PT), University of Hull (UK) and National Teacher Development Centre of Tampere (FI)

[2] These criteria were set out by the Socrates Comenius project EVINSET, Evaluation of effectiveness and efficiency of In-service Training. Partnership: VSKO (BE), Hellenic-American Union (GR), University of Hull (UK) and National Teacher Development Centre of Tampere (FI)

[3] SCHOLLAERT: 2000 b

[4] TABASCO stands for Task Based School Organisation for the Acquisition of Languages in Europe. TABASCO is a three-years Socrates project (87228-CP-1-2000-BE-LINGUA-LA)

[5] In our Belgian educational system there are no central examinations. Teachers

The treasure within

design their own tests, and two or three times a year there are "deliberations". These are assessment meetings, in which all teachers discuss the learners' progress. At the end of the year, they decide from the overall outcomes if a learner can pass. Teachers become frustrated when the results on their own subject hasn't enough weight in the final decision.

[6] http://www.nottingham.ac.uk/education/Hopkins/inaugural.html

PART 5

SCHOOL NETWORKS AS VEHICLES FOR PROFESSIONAL DEVELOPMENT

CHAPTER 12

NETWORKS OF SECONDARY SCHOOLS IN THE NETHERLANDS

LEARNING COMMUNITIES IN THE CONTEXT OF INNOVATIONS

Pieter Leenheer

Abstract

In 1994 the Dutch Department of Education decided to stimulate networks of secondary schools. At that time a large-scale innovation of pre-university and senior general secondary education was in an initial phase[1]. In the innovation process a national steering group (or, as it was called later on: *process management*) played an important role as an intermediary between department and schools, support organizations, teacher training institutes, pupils' organisations and so on. One of the leading figures of that group, a school leader of considerable renown in the secondary field, proved to be a strong advocate of involving schools in the process. In the past she herself had experienced how helpful networks of schools could be, and she thought it a waste not to profit from the expertise schools had at their disposal. Thanks to her drive the department provided a budget to stimulate networks of schools for a period of roughly 6 years[2].

Looking back, one might consider this course of events as rather predictable, and nicely fitting into the developments that showed up at that time. A full picture is not necessary, I think; so just a few words about two important ones of these developments:
–   In the Netherlands, exactly like in some other European countries, the government was increasingly doubting the effectiveness of central steering and on the contrary more and more inclining to give greater autonomy to

organizations that so far functioned under its direct responsibility. And although the transition unmistakeably involves some or even a lot of problems, the direction intended still seems no ephemeral phenomenon.

- From the eighties on experts and in-service trainers gradually began to doubt the effectiveness of the traditional top down, research-and-development based approach of innovation as it became increasingly clear that despite all efforts little or nothing was achieved. One of the main reasons for that seemed to be that the target groups (teachers, school leaders) didn't feel the innovation as something of their own. Apart from common sense, in the search for more effective approaches constructivist learning psychology played an important role, at least in the nineties. As more adequate ideas about the ways we should organize - or rather: support – the learning of pupils found their way into public consciousness, most of us began to realize that what holds for pupils might also hold for teachers.

As I wrote above, with hindsight the decision to stimulate networks of secondary schools might seem a rational, predictable one. But in fact the process was more haphazard, more a matter of trial and error, of mixing old and new. For instance, a considerable number of policy makers and people from support organizations doubted whether schools would be capable of bearing more responsibility than they were used to, or whether they could do this without the beneficial support of experts from support organizations. And likewise, the steering group and some experts consulted about it, had some difficulty in saying farewell to the research-and-development model. For instance, the first ideas that emerged proposed the funding of some 20 networks of leading, innovative schools that should develop ideas, materials, and resources from which subsequently the rest of the schools would benefit. However (and luckily), in no time reality turned out to be stronger than theory. Reading the applications for grants, talking with schools and/or intended network co-ordinators, and thinking about how learning of organizations proceeds, we realized that spending the limited budget only on networks of leading, innovative schools was wrong. Rather than focusing on the development of examples, materials, resources and what not, plus the transfer of these to other schools, we saw that we could better use the budget to stimulate school development in as many schools as possible. Thanks to that change, between 1994 and 1999 some 400 schools participated in networks aiming at the innovation of pre-university and senior general secondary education, and so far some 300 schools participate in networks aiming at the recently started innovation of pre-vocational secondary education[3].

Of course the decision to stimulate school development didn't mean that all plans for would-be-networks submitted would be acceptable. Obviously their plans needed to bear on the innovation of pre-university and senior general secondary education. But out of the full range of possible themes and sub themes the applicants themselves had to choose the goals and objectives that fitted best in the development phase and culture of their own schools. In fact we formulated as few requirements as possible in order to prevent networks simply writing plans they hoped would be completely in the spirit of things: plans had to be their own thinking. Likewise we didn't prescribe an organization model: networks had to organize themselves according to their own needs and tastes.

And in assessing the plans, we tried to act more as critical friends than as officials strictly adhering to regulations, and we often decided to give a network the benefit of the doubt supposing that things would more or less automatically crystallize in the course of the first year. Of course, this inductive approach was partly due to the fact that virtually no research into the functioning of networks was available. But also – and I like to think: perhaps even more – owing to the nature of the approach I just described, this was a consequence of our conviction that given the opportunity – and provided we succeeded in sticking to a process - oriented form of monitoring - schools would prove to be capable organizations.

In the course of the last 7 or 8 years however, we have learned that certain ways of organising and/or running a network are more productive than others. What I present below is a summary of the lessons we have learned, with problems highlighted here and there that we have met and questions we are still considering. Actually, one of the problems of the following exposition is that I had to resort to a relatively short, linear description of a multidimensional, very complex phenomenon. I'm afraid I haven't succeeded in all respects in solving that problem.

Some definitions

Before describing the network model we have learned to be the most effective, at least in all likelihood, I have to define two crucial terms: *network* and *school*.

Networks as such are as old as mankind. You always have had the *informal networks* of individuals, for instance the old boys (and increasingly: old girls) networks aiming at helping each other, but also the informal networks of professionals aiming at sharing knowledge and gossip. These last ones sometimes develop into more *formal networks* of individuals like professional organizations, for instance teacher associations. And finally there are the *formal networks of organizations*, aiming at some form of co-operation. These networks pursue such different aims as:
– serving common interests
– co-operation, resulting in a consortium or even a merger
– development and innovation.

In this context I'm talking about networks of the very last type: formal networks in which a number of organizations co-operate with a view to development and innovation. To be more precise, our networks of schools are:
– temporary structures
– consisting of on average 7 schools (plus or minus 1)
– having between them no hierarchical relationship
– and co-operating with respect to certain aspects of a national innovation by learning from each other's experiences.

Apart from the meaning of 'school' in 'school of thought', in Dutch the word *school* has a double meaning: an organizational one and a more physical one (i.e. building or relatively autonomous unit). In general a secondary school in the organizational sense consists of several schools in the more physical sense. For instance: a secondary school (or as we say: a community of schools) might consist of a school (or unit) for pre-university and higher general secondary education, one or more prevocational schools, a junior college, and sometimes schools of the same type in different districts or towns and so on. Communities of schools roughly count between 1000 and 4000 pupils, divided over several schools. In our networks participated (and still participate) mostly schools in the physical sense, and the management involved was (and is) the management of these.

A network model

NETWORK OF SCHOOLS

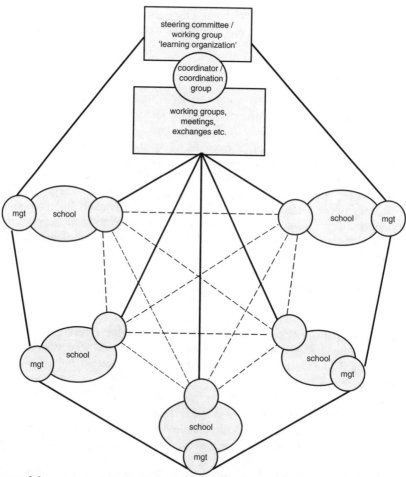

The model we use to describe the ins and outs of networks consist of two parts: the network in the strict sense (steering group, co-ordinator or co-ordination group, network activities like working groups, meetings, conferences and so on), and circling around that core the schools that participate (5 in this example). The uninterrupted lines indicate the regular network contacts, the interrupted ones the more incidental, mostly bi-lateral contacts that frequently come to life thanks to the network.

Participation in networks of course doesn't mean that complete teams participate: apart from the occasional grand scale meeting or network conference, it's always only a relatively limited number of persons that participate directly in network activities. It may be self-evident that the exact number of people involved and the intensity of the involvement depend on how the network is organized, what type of activities it offers (working groups, meetings and so on).

Most of the model speaks for itself, I hope; I only dwell on a few important details of the model, intertwined with some remarks about the functioning of networks.

Initiative and ownership

Crucial for the functioning of networks is the degree to which the participants feel the network as their own. So one important thing is: who takes the initiative.

In the first years the schools for pre-university and senior general secondary education we worked with, were not used to this type of networking. That explains why frequently the initiative was taken by support organizations, such as teacher training institutes or in-service training institutes. In cases like these the goals and objectives hadn't arisen inside the participating schools, but had been proposed by an outsider, and that quite often caused problems. For in several cases, when it came to the point, it appeared that basically the real priorities of the schools lay elsewhere. Even if – which more than once has been the case - the participating schools at first had judged the network goals plausible or even attractive and urgent.

On the other hand, most schools are, to put it mildly, rather internally oriented. They easily let themselves be absorbed by all the pressures of the daily work and they often have difficulty allowing themselves time to seek network partners, even if they declare networking one of the most fruitful learning activities. So, sometimes there is no other way than that an external person or organization or one of the schools takes the initiative, with all the problems resulting from this course of action.

We have learned to live with that problem. The best solution, however, would be to split the grant in two parts: a small one for a short preliminary period and a far bigger one for the actual network period. In the preliminary period the intended partners should intensively deliberate about the goals in order to procure the necessary ownership and to prepare a well-based agreement about what to do and realize during the network period. Unfortunately, so far we never have had the opportunity to try out this solution.

Composition of the network

The preliminary period mentioned above would also serve to solve a closely related problem: in this way schools have time to get sufficiently acquainted with each other before deciding to co-operate during a period of 2 or even 3 years, instead of afterwards gradually detecting that some partners can't get along. Obviously, participating schools should differ from each other in certain crucial respects, otherwise there is nothing to learn from each other. However, the differences should not be too big. For example, despite certain differences school cultures and stages of development should be sufficiently recognizable for the partners so as to make communication possible and prevent dependent behaviour on one side and/or irritations on the other. In other words, networks should aim at a fruitful balance between bringing something in and getting something out of it.

A preliminary period might help to sort out whether the intended schools might successfully co-operate. Of course that can't prevent all problems. In the first place, it's not easy for any outsider to get a clear, reliable picture of the strengths and weaknesses of a specific school. Besides, in most cases only by working together can you really find out what your partners are worth. But all that doesn't alter the fact that by taking some time to get acquainted, you can make a better start than depending only on good luck at the start.

I conclude this section on the composition of networks with two points of quite a different nature:
First: *can competing schools participate in one and the same network?* The answer is: yes. If competitors in the automobile industry can co-operate in the development of new engines, or corn cultivators in the improvement of corn, why shouldn't schools be able to do something similar? In fact, we have seen it happen. Of course most of the times a network consisting of competing schools started like the mating of hedgehogs (i.e. very, very carefully), but after some time nearly always the mutual behaviour of competitors concerned became increasingly normal and adult.
Second: *is there a limit to the number of participating schools and to the geographical distance between them?* Again, the answer is: yes. As for the number: less than 5 schools is risky because if one drops out, there might remain too little to learn from each other or too few people to do the work agreed upon, while more than 7 or 8 schools usually entails a certain form of bureaucracy, a more or less parliamentary type of consultations and sometimes even the taking a back seat by at least some of the participating schools.
As for the geographical distance: managers often like to travel a lot, but teachers seldom do; we have learned that a circle with a radius of some 30 kilometres is more or less the maximum.

Involvement of school management

Of course a network is only effective in so far it sustains the development process of the participating schools. The point is certainly not to keep some enthusiastic people busy. However, things don't happen automatically, for instance by letting forerunners of a school participate and for the rest hoping for the best. This type of out-sourcing the school development process puts the innovation burden nearly completely on the shoulders of forerunners who on returning from network activities seldom have the necessary qualifications to involve their colleagues[4]. We have learned that to a high extent the effectiveness of a network depends upon the commitment of the school management, on their ability to really coach their networkers and look after continuity in participation, on their willingness to show real interest in the learning of the participants, and on their capacities to organize the transfer of what was learned or developed in the network to the rest of the school.

An interesting question is whether Dutch school management is up to the tasks I mentioned in the last paragraph. The answer is: yes and no. Unmistakeably Dutch school managers are trying to get less control oriented and more process oriented; in that some succeed fairly well, others still are more on the control than on the process side[5]. Interestingly enough networks can help school managers to develop themselves in the desired direction. In other words, sometimes networks themselves help to create the conditions that are necessary for the network to be effective.

In the first years we were inclined to neglect this factor (i.e. the involvement of the management) and thought it sufficed to ask for commitment in the sense of facilitating participants in time. Gradually we have learned that that is not enough as it leaves too much room for leaning back. You have to make the (relevant part of the) school management actively responsible for the functioning of the network, something we made into a prerequisite for the recently started networks aiming at the innovation of prevocational secondary education. The model above allows for that prerequisite: in each school you find a small circle with *mgt* for management in it, and uninterrupted lines linking these *mgt's* to the steering group).

Something we haven't made into a prerequisite, but just strongly recommend nowadays, is: try to turn the network steering group into a 'learning organization' working group in which school managers think and talk about how their schools can be developed into learning organizations. So far only a few networks have implemented this recommendation.

Network co-ordination

Every network needs an agency responsible for the agenda, the planning, the organization of meetings, the monitoring of the progress and so on. The downside is to burden one person with a great many, sometimes conflicting tasks, roughly varying from secretarial work via providing content input to keeping schools to their obligations and taking measures if they don't. The more tasks you confide to one person the greater the chance that the others lean back (and prove difficult to satisfy!), of course especially in the case that the co-ordinator is an external expert from a support organization. Moreover, roles concerning the undertaking of services (taking minutes, organizing a meeting) don't agree very well with more managerial like roles such as holding people to their obligations or trying to correct their behaviour, especially when the latter have to be performed in a non-hierarchical environment. In recent years we have learnt to recommend that one of the school managers acts as president of the steering group while the (external) co-ordination acts as a sort of secretary.

But even if the range of duties of the network co-ordinator is reduced to something more feasible, it is evident that this function asks for considerable skills. A good network co-ordinator is a good organizer who is able to coach participants and is well-informed enough to be able to ask the right questions. A combination not given to everyone.

Transfer activities

As I said above effects of networks don't happen automatically. There are quite a few conditions to be met on the side of the participating schools. Apart from the commitment of the management, one of the essential conditions is that the participants have at their disposal a sustaining environment in their own school, something like a project group or at least a sounding-board. But even then nothing happens automatically; the transfer has to be explicitly organized and sustained. As far as that is concerned, one of the pitfalls is to revert to the research and development model we don't believe in anymore, and let the participants provide internal trainings and/or lectures, let them write papers and distribute these by internal post and so on. Real transfer can only be brought about by involving one way or another the rest of the organization in the thinking and development process. In other words, not when the thinking and developing is done, but when it is still going on. Otherwise no ownership will develop.

The life cycle of networks

The networks I write about in this article are temporary structures. In every one of them there comes a moment when the mutual benefits begin to decrease, although not for everybody at the same pace. The pattern we have most frequently met is the following:
- a first year in which the participating schools got used to each other, tried to get a grip on the central issues and essential concepts, agreed on objectives and planning and so on
- second year: a harvest year
- third year: rounding off the network activities, writing publications, deciding whether to go on with each other or not, or perhaps with a smaller group or with a mix of old and new schools.

As a matter of fact, this pattern is not always experienced as smoothly as this description suggests. Often at the end of the first year or in the beginning of the second year some sort of crisis occurs, when participants begin to ask themselves, whether what they do is worth all the efforts. We have learnt that such a crisis is more or less unavoidable, and in any case more often than not proves to be very helpful in the end. Sometimes it leads to a sensible shake-out amongst the participants, and nearly always to a rephrasing of plans and goals, resulting in a sounder and broader basis amongst the participants. However, a crisis requires from network co-ordinators and members of the steering group the ability to cope with stress, not get alarmed but to stay calm and confident. As a matter of fact, you might realize that such an event occurs in a non-hierarchical environment, so the type and number of measures that can be taken is fairly limited. All in all, coping with a crisis in a network is not easy, and that is, amongst other, a reason why it deserves recommendation for offering opportunities for network co-ordinators to exchange experiences. We have done so at least once a year.

Outcomes

In professional organizations the true capital is stored in the minds of the professionals themselves. So in the first instance it's the participating individual who should profit from participation in a network. He or she might for instance be consoled by detecting that colleagues in other schools meet the same problems (and equally have no answer to them). The greater part of their working time teachers work alone, without ample time for reflection, and as a consequence they easily tend to think they are the only ones who meet certain problems. It often is a great relief to perceive that that is certainly not the case. Furthermore, they might get inspired by the ideas of colleagues or the feedback they provide, and they might see in the classroom of colleagues how a so far unknown method works (or even thàt it works at all). Their self-confidence might also be strengthened by experiencing that others learn something from them. And all in all they might develop the external orientation that is indispensable for innovation as well as improvement.

The point is, however, that a sound balance has to be established between personal and organizational goals and profits. No school can profit from participating in a network if its teachers, co-ordinators or managers don't benefit from it as individuals. But as a schools' reason for existence is providing learning opportunities for pupils, what counts in the end are the outcomes for the school as a whole. These outcomes might be divided in two categories:
- support for the implementation of a specific innovation or action for improvement
- support for the process of becoming a learning organization.

The first category includes in the first place more or less tangible outcomes as I mentioned before: ideas, materials, new methods, resources; I think this type of outcomes needs no further explanation[6]. Next, on a more abstract level, the networks helps schools to develop a vision, to choose a course of action, to come to grips with central concepts concerning a certain innovation or the learning of pupils and so on.

Support for the process of becoming a learning organization occurs when participants, while working on the implementation of a specific innovation or improvement action, reflect on the process, try to envisage how processes develop and what conditions are to be met, provide feedback to each other and so on. In Argyris' terms: when they do not stop at single loop learning, but as an extension of that embark on double loop learning. This sequence (i.e. double learning as a by-product of single loop learning) somehow seems to me not unnatural. It often so happens that you start with the obvious things, the things directly at hand, and only after that, when it's no longer inevitable, you begin to dig deeper.

As a matter of fact, outcomes in this area often are not very evident or spectacular, and most of the times they resemble tender hothouseplants, but on the other hand, they are certainly not negligible. What we have seen is that networks contribute to outcomes such as:

- improvement of communication, of exchange of information in the participating schools
- development of a more collegial culture, and related to that: development of a learning policy for the organization (instead of the usual planning of in-service training events)
- development of a more external orientation (or: greater responsivity), i.e. a greater sensibility for external impulses, and curiosity for what is going on in the outside world.

The first two need no further explanation. As for the last one: in business and industry external orientation is seen by researchers as one of the main indicators for 'innovativity', and I think this indicator also holds for education. Most schools still behave as closed systems, without a strong, broadly felt need for adaptation and change. On the contrary, in the organization of work in schools, in procedures and allocation of duties the emphasis often lies on control, order and predictability, and that is fatal for curiosity.

This might, to conclude, be the best point to make a few remarks about networks of schools in comparison with two types of interventions schools often resort to in the context of innovation or improvement actions: in-service training (i.e. courses, training sessions or conferences, provided by an external expert) and projects (i.e. the step by step, more or less well-structured development of certain things). In terms of knowledge management the differences between these three are:

- the core of networks is the creation of knowledge and new competences by sharing experiences and knowledge
- in in-service training the point is the transfer of knowledge from an expert to a certain group
- in projects everything turns around the development of a new product, no matter whether it is materials or a new approach or method.

In comparison with the other two, networks have more a sense of a voyage of discovery undertaken by equals. But I have to admit that due to the pressures of daily work networks sometimes lose their character of learning communities and begin to show traits of courses and projects. For a short time there is no harm in that, and in some cases it might even be a necessary stage. But in the long term actions should be undertaken to restore the intended character.

Why do networks work?

So far I have never come across research in the strict sense of the word into the effects of networks of schools, or the factors that explain their successes and failures. What we have at our disposal is a series of books and articles – in Dutch of course - with descriptions of outcomes of specific networks, and some of these also contain reflections on processes, and on the use of networking. Furthermore, we have some reports – equally only in Dutch – about a few surveys we have conducted with the help of questionnaires we ourselves had designed. And I myself have written some book chapters and articles like this one, based on the materials I just mentioned, and on lengthy discussions with network co-ordinators, experts and schoolleaders, and – of course – my own observations in the field. All in all, however, the rather widespread common understanding between Dutch teachers and school leaders and members of support organizations that networks are useful or even desirable, so far is more a matter of perceptions and convictions, than something based on hard evidence.

The lack of empirical research might partly be due to the fact that this type of network is relatively new and perhaps still finds itself somewhat outside the researchers' field of vision. But more important might be that the way educational research is funded in The Netherlands doesn't stimulate this type of research. What we need in the case of networks is long term research, but most educational research today is as a consequence of the funding unique, synchronic, and mainly focusing on making inventories of perceptions. However, a third reason, and for me perhaps the most pressing one, might well be that networks are too complex for the possibilities of educational research. Effects post hoc in a school that has participated in a network might of course be ascribed to the participation, but often with equal right to other activities or combination of activities. And to complicate that, you might justly claim that the more a certain outcome is integrated in the daily life of a school and the less it can be distinguished from its environment, the more effective the network activity concerned has been. But that of course makes the chance of ever providing hard empirical evidence almost nil.

In view of this state of the art, the best thing we have found to do is to compare our perceptions, ideas and experiences with what in other contexts is stated about the learning of teachers and the development of learning organizations. Or, reversely, let us ourselves be inspired by the latter in the search for explanations why networks do work or do show certain problems. Overviewing educational research literature ànd management literature of the last 10 years, to us it seems that what we do and think, is quite in line with insights in vogue at the moment. Below I restrict myself to some central concepts explaining success and failure of networks, that we derived from or recognized in recent research literature.

Learning

The classical staff development activity is the one day or one afternoon study day, with the odd lecture by some expert, flooded with transparencies, and some workshops that turn out to be lectures, equally flooded with transparencies, leaving only 10 minutes at the end for questions. This manner is diametrically opposed to what we know about the learning of adults (and pupils). Although I think the principles of constructivist learning psychology are well known, for the sake of comprehensiveness, I shortly enumerate the most important characteristics:

- Learning is a matter of active construction of knowledge, of actively handling information by comparing and eventually hooking new to existing information and so on. And it is certainly not a matter of passively absorbing information, as if you were a pot into which some expert pours his knowledge.
- Learning is a social process: you need others to try out or develop ideas, to get feedback.
- Learning is not only an intellectual, but also – and that is often neglected in adult learning – an emotional process.
- In the first instance learning is context and content related: you proceed from the concrete to the abstract, more general things.
- It is important that the learner has possibilities for self-regulation and that he feels the learning objectives to be his own.

After the preceding exposé about the functioning of networks, it goes, I hope, practically without saying that participating in networks closely resembles learning in the sense I just described. Provided, however, that in the schools the participants come from, the conditions are met I mentioned earlier in this article. For expectations about the applicability in the daily work of what is learned in the network, and about the reactions of colleagues and management, strongly influence the learning process.

Tacit knowledge and peer learning

The most important type of knowledge of a teacher is his tacit, or practical knowledge. That is: the partly conscious, but mainly hardly conscious complex of knowledge, skills and attitudes a teacher develops on the job. That type of knowledge is essential for adequate functioning, for reacting and deciding as quickly as the course of events in the classroom asks for. But at the same time, this type is difficult to reach and influence. So, it is not easy to change less effective or even counter- productive ideas, approaches and attitudes a person has developed in the course of the years. The classical staff development course usually addresses the explicit, more formal and conscious part of knowledge, and that's why it seldom proves to be very effective. On the contrary, all forms of learning on the job and peer learning are usually far more effective – provided, of course, sufficient time for reflection is built in - for they connect more easily, more naturally to the tacit knowledge of the participants. What teachers tell or advise each other, smells as it were of the classroom, and that is what establishes the necessary contact, makes expositions credible. Moreover, teachers tell each other how things work, not like experts often do, telling how things shóuld work; teachers usually experience the last type as depressing or too far from reality, but the first as comforting or inspiring.

Most schools so far offer insufficient opportunities for learning on the job. Networks can help them to develop such opportunities. As a matter of fact, even if schools offer opportunities for learning on the job and peer learning within their own walls, it goes without saying that even then networks might act as a useful supplement.

Learning organization

What I have so far reported, however briefly, about the learning of professionals (teachers, school managers) boils down to one thing: their learning looks like a pin-ball machine. We know, at least in rough lines, what factors might play a role (i.e. where the pins of the machine are) but the exact course a ball takes is always unpredictable. In other words, learning processes differ from person to person, and even on an intra-personal level, dependent on subject, phase of life, personal conditions on a certain moment and so on. So the only conclusion can be that it is important to offer school teams a wide range of learning opportunities, and not (or rather: not only) the odd yearly study day. A more promising perspective is to try to develop a learning organisation in which learning is an integral part of the daily goings on.

For the sake of clarity I briefly mention the most important characteristics of a learning organization:
– a learning organization tries to establish a good balance between personal and organizational objectives
– a culture of learning is seen as more important than structure and control; mistakes are not something to avoid, but seen as opportunities for learning; members of the organization can cope with a certain degree of chaos, and although there exists a certain sense of direction, there is no blueprint that decides the behaviour of the team
– information and feedback are seen as vital; asking the opinion of panels of pupils and working in multi-disciplinary teams are as much perfectly common procedures as looking over the border of the organization; the organization as a whole is focused on issues of quality and evaluation
– learning processes are not out-sourced to external experts and advisors, but kept in one's own hands
– there is no staff development policy in the traditional sense (focusing on planning, allocation of funds and time and so on) but a learning policy that sees in-service training as just one of the instruments for school development.

At least in our country this perspective is still a far cry. Notwithstanding promising developments here and there, and notwithstanding the widespread feeling that this is a very desirable perspective. To me this state of affairs doesn't come as a surprise. Until recently schools could function rather well as, let's say, an addition sum of subjects and courses. Or to use a more contemporary metaphor, as a shopping mall where within the boundaries of the building every shopkeeper as much as possible went his own way, except perhaps for things like the Christmas decorations. Increasingly, however, fragmentation like this becomes a problem as mutual adjustment and multidisciplinary cooperation prove essential to solve the problems education is confronted with. However, realizing what is asked of you is one thing, trying to do so is quite another. Help from colleagues seems indispensable. In several cases we have established that networks can help schools to get a clear picture of what a learning organization is and make a start with the development in that direction.

Coaching networks

Are networks of schools as I described above a temporary phenomenon or can't they be thought away anymore? Or are they just an artifact of the subsidies we provided and still provide? Of course, I myself firmly believe this type of network is here to stay. Any innovative organization, and that is what we want schools to be, keeps a permanent external orientation, wants to co-operate with others, is curious how others perform. So, the ultimate proof of my conviction is, whether in a few years time innovative schools will spontaneously emerge.

One of the conditions to make that possible is the degree to which schools are in a position to act as relatively independent, grown-up organizations, with the necessary qualifications to regulate their own work. To be sure, this certainly is no plea to privatize schools and to make them market organizations like any other business, striving for profit and competing as much as possible. What I have in mind are relatively independent public organizations: relatively independent for any healthy organization ought to have the possibility to regulate its own work and prepare for the future in its own way – but at the same time fully aware of its eminent public mission. Most schools I know want to go for that. Policymakers, politicians and society as a whole, however, are – to say the least - not always helpful in promoting this development. Often they see education mainly as a garbage can in which to drop as many problems as society meets, while at the same time tolerating or even promoting a gap between private wealth and public poverty. Apart from that, we see in our country a growing tension between the pursuit of efficiency of the government (i.e. the attempt to realize an educational system that delivers as much value as possible, mainly meaning less pupil drop-out, for a minimum of money), and the constructivist views of learning with an accent on trial and error and learning of mistakes that is almost contrary to efficiency.

In any case, so far it seems that as a rule of thumb, an external impetus is needed to stimulate schools to form networks. Though we firmly believe in the principles stated above, in practice schools and professionals do not always live up to them. Most schools easily turn inwards as they, unlike business and industry, do not permanently experience the urge to watch what happens outside and if necessary to adjust to their environment. That happens to be the consequence of the fact that changes in their environment go slowly. So, little or nothing prevents schools behaving like closed systems in which bureaucratic control prevails over receptiveness and external orientation for the importance of the latter is not directly evident. The more so where the daily pressures during certain periods in the year often are enormous, as the workload is very unevenly divided over the year, leaving little time for learning on the job[7].

Under these circumstances a task force as the co-ordination point I am a member of, seems very useful and perhaps even more or less indispensable. What we do may be just the modest impetus needed.

Apart from regularly reporting to the Ministry of Education how the work proceeds, we do the following:
- from time to time we call for applications (depending on the budget the government provides) and confer with the applicants about their plans
- the subsidies we provide, are relatively small, i.e. not so much an amount that is really cost-effective, as an incentive that reminds the networks of the obligations they have mutually agreed to
- during the network period we regularly visit the network steering group and some network activities, and try to provide support and coaching where possible
- we organize national meetings for network co-ordinators and try to promote communication between networks
- we support and promote network publications and other transfer activities.

At the moment we perform our work with 5 persons, most of them part-timers and (ex-) school leaders. And to conclude, this is the type of work I have done during the past seven or eight years. And I have never had a more inspiring working environment before. It's such a pleasure to see people develop. A long time ago, when I was an in-service trainer, I was inclined to let myself go in designing models or approaches or in explaining to people what they should do. In the course of the years I gradually learnt how counter-productive that was, at least in quite some cases. It's a blessing to have had the chance to start the other way round. I hope I have made clear what a blessing that is.

Epilogue

Colleagues present at the workshop were interested in the following:
- To what extent networks involve the wider school communities beyond the actual schools. A Swedish colleague described such community involvement.
- What the content focus might be. It was suggested that, for example, networks could be set up on issues such as ICT, new materials, even the development of new subjects such as general literature and social education that had been developed as a result of and within the network.
- What was the role of support organisations? Obviously to advise and to provide a range of support and to assist with co-ordination activities, even - if necessary - do 'the dirty work' on behalf of schools. The background of the advisers would include specialist subject areas, for example.
- A question was asked about how schools began the process. Sometimes this evolved very easily with local schools but sometimes a school might advertise for network partners to join in on a particular focus.
- A colleague was interested in whether schools had a contract. It was explained that this was not the case and that the work involved was based on goodwill. It was felt to be important not to be over organised.

- Goodwill was an issue in another comment about those teachers who did not join in. There was no conscription to the network, only a warm welcome and open invitation.
- The start of the networking process. Sometimes this evolves very easily, for example with local or regional schools that know each other already for a long time. But sometimes a school might – so to speak – advertise for network partners to join in on a particular focus.
- Networks and competition between schools. Several colleagues asked whether competing schools can collaborate in the context of a network. Experience learns they can, but it takes some time before they understand that.
- The geographical distance between network schools. For managers distances seldom are a problem; teachers don't like to travel more than, let's say, 25 or 30 kilometres.
- The presenter himself was interested to know to what extent networking is a transferable strategy and whether the success of our Dutch scheme is an artifact of the funding made available to schools or a reality deriving from innate interest.

References

Below you find references to research publications on networks. I have refrained from providing a full-length bibliography of relevant research publications concerning the learning of teachers and the learning of organizations. Of course a list of references would include such well-known Anglo-Saxon experts and researchers as Fullan, Hargreaves and Hopkins. But actually those researchers that have influenced me most have written in Dutch and references to their work are as a consequence not very informative in this context. Of course, it's a pity that nearly nobody outside the Dutch borders knows names like Kitty Kwakman, Sanneke Bolhuis, Femke Geijsel or Peter Sleegers, but that is how it is. Perhaps a literature survey in English would solve this problem.

General

Godfroij, A.J.A. (1992). Dynamische netwerken. M&O. *Tijdschrift voor organisatiekunde en sociaal beleid*. Vol. 46, July/August 1992, 365-375.
Krogt, F.J. van der (1995). *Leren in netwerken. Veelzijdig organiseren van leernetwerken met het oog op humaniteit en arbeidsrelevantie*. Utrecht: Lemma.
Mast, W. & ten Brummeler L. (1994). *Organisatienetwerken in de non-profitsector. De dynamiek van netwerken aan de hand van vijf relevante dimensies*. Teksten beleid & management. Utrecht: uitgeverij SWP.
Oosterwijk, H. (1995). *Netwerken voor organisaties. Hulpmiddelen bij het bestuderen en ontwerpen van netwerken in een inter-organisationele omgeving*. Utrecht: Lemma.
Wielinga, E. (2001). *Netwerken als levend weefsel. Een studie naar kennis, leiderschap en de rol van de overheid in de Nederlandse landbouw sinds 1945*. 's-Hertogenbosch: uitgeverij Uilenreef.

Networks of schools

Daale, H. & van Asselt, R. (1996). *Netwerken havo hbo. Hoe werken ze?* Enschede: LICA.

Galesloot, L. (1994). *Collegiale netwerken van ervaren docenten en schoolleiders.* ABC De Lier.

Jansen, A.J. (1996). *Docenten netwerken begeleiden.* Leuven/Apeldoorn: Garant.

Leenheer, P. (red.) (1995). *Ervaringen in netwerken.* Studiehuisreeks nr. 5. Tilburg: MesoConsult.

Leenheer, P. (1995). *Geen babbelboxen maar werkplaatsen.* Meso Magazine 82, 16-22.

Leenheer, P. (1999). *De ontelbare effecten van zes-en-zestig netwerken. Terugblik op vijf jaar netwerken havo -vwo.* Meso magazine 107.

Liebermann, A. & McLaughlin, M.W. (1992). *Networks for Educational Change: Powerful and Problematic.* Phi Delta Kappan, May 1992, 673-677.

Liebermann, A. (1996). *Creating Intentional Learning Communities. Educational Leadership.* 54(3) november 1996, 51-55

PMVO (ProcesManagement Voortgezet Onderwijs) (2000). *Netwerken in Nederland. Een panorama van 72 netwerken havo-vwo. PMVO.* Den Haag

Veugelers, W. & Zijlstra, H. (1995). Learning together: in-service education in networks of schools. *British Journal of In-Service Education.* 21(1), 1-13

Veugelers, W. & Zijlstra, H. (1998). Learning together in networks of schools and university. *International Journal Leadership in Education.* I(2), 169-180

Vrieze, G. & Van Kuijk, J. (1998). *Leernetwerken: alternatief voor dure cursussen? Praktijkvoorbeelden uit het basisonderwijs.* Meso Magazine 103, 28 e.v.

In preparation:

Kwakman, C.H.E. (2000) *Leernetwerken in onderwijs.* This article will be published in an up-date of 'Netwerken in Nederland. Een panorama van 72 netwerken havo-vwo' Den Haag.

Voncken, E. *Netwerken po-vo als verbeterinstrument?*

Pieter Leenheer is national network co-ordinator in The Netherlands.

---

[1] The first reconnaissances of what should be done to update pre-university and senior general secondary education and what could be done to solve the problems in the connection between secondary and higher education (dropout, delays in study careers), started as early as 1991. The necessary legal framework was completed in 1997.

[2] The regulation for the networks of pre-university and senior general secondary schools provided subsidies for a period of 2 years of networking. It was a system of matched funding: per school something like 700 euro was available, to be matched by the same amount by the school. In exchange for the subsidies the networks committed an obligation to transfer the outcomes by writing publications, providing workshops and so on. The yearly budget sufficed for the formation of roughly 15 networks, each consisting of at average 7-8 schools.

Later on, in 1999, a more or less similar set of regulations was fixed in order to stimulate the formation of networks of schools in the context of the innovation of pre-vocational secondary education.

[3] In Dutch the term school is ambiguous, as explained in the text.

[4] An interesting variant is the following. Some school managers deliberately choose to delegate stragglers or sceptics to the network. They did so because they saw themselves not able to 'convert' these persons and hoped the network would have a salutary effect on them. As a matter of fact in most cases participants of this type only caused problems, annoyance and delay.

[5] It goes without saying that what matters is a good balance: a purely process oriented approach doesn't work either.

[6] Perhaps a warning is advisable. At first sight pooling of capacities seems efficient and profitable for all parties. But experience learns that the more complete the product developed in the network is, the less people in participating schools think them fit for their use.

[7] Some people tend to think that turning inwards is typical for educational institutions. I doubt that. Reading for instance publications about quality care and control in the commercial sector, one cannot but conclude that in quite a few market organisations, comparable problems occur. Otherwise one cannot explain the huge flow of publications in this field, let alone the nearly endless series of seminars where quality gurus preach their quality gospel.

CHAPTER 13

TEACHERS' LEARNING IN A SCHOOL NETWORK

A CASE STUDY: AVIMES PROJECT

Daniela Bachi, Silvana Mosca

Foreword

The AVIMES network is a network of 40 primary schools and lower secondary schools (6-14 years of age) that voluntarily collaborate in activities concerning school self evaluation. Experts in evaluation methodology and in the didactics of Mathematics and the Italian language give their support and advice to the network, which is sustained by the Regional Inspector's Office.

The aims of the network can be summarised in four fundamental points:
- discussing and developing issues about school self-evaluation;
- gathering data on pupil attainment, quality of leadership and the perception of the school on the part of parents and students;
- constructing tools for the self evaluation of school quality;
- designing staff development plans.

Abstract

This paper describes the context, purpose and content of the research activity, which is being carried out, alongside other investigations into school functioning, in the schools participating in the AVIMES network, on one crucial issue in the evaluation of the quality of education: the teacher/learner dynamic and the investigation of how it affects the effectiveness of the teaching/learning process. It describes the tools used for a survey on teacher reflection on his/her own professional attitudes and teaching practices, and on feedback from the children. It also describes how the findings of the survey result in the production of teachers' professional development in a co-operative way.

Context

In the last few years, within the framework of the Italian educational system, schools have become more autonomous for their decisions on education policy and the control of their expenditure. The whole system is going through a process of radical change which will see headteachers and local authorities become more accountable for elaborating the concept of school quality, gathering and analysing data and making decisions. So far there is no national evaluation system of school quality. The national curriculum sets the guidelines for pupil achievement, but a system of standardised tests is in the process of being piloted for the first time this year.

It is in this context that the schools participating in the network have undertaken a process of self-review of the various aspects of their functioning: quality of teaching, student performance, quality of leadership and management, school reputation.

The aim of the survey programme

The rationale which gave rise to our survey is that the dynamic of the teaching/learning process is the core issue of the school quality and that the feedback from examination of the teachers' perception of their own attitudes, conduct, and knowledge of the subject matter can be productively confronted with the pupils' attainment and perception of their own learning process. This confrontation can offer a starting point for spreading the culture of schools as learning organisations and motivating the teachers to engage in the development of their own professional practice. The network offers the necessary survey field and the resources that would otherwise not be available to individual schools.

The tools and the findings

The first step we took in 1999 was to find out what was going well and what was going wrong with students' achievements. We therefore submitted Italian and Maths standardised tests to 1,960 students of Grade Four (10 years of age). Achievement tests may not be the only way to assess pupils' results, but they are the only objective instrument we have to evaluate and compare school quality in terms of learning achievement. The test results were compared among the various schools of the network with the aim of revealing strong and weak areas and investigating the reasons for both.

We asked the teachers whose classes had been tested to answer a questionnaire on the self-evaluation of their teaching. The aim of the questionnaire was not an attempt to single out individual teachers or to make judgements. As a matter of fact in Italy we do not have a system of teacher appraisal carried out by head teachers or any other school authorities. The questionnaire was aimed at evaluating teaching: its purpose is to discover whether there is a general lack of expertise in an area of the curriculum which can be helped by further training, to provide a means for spreading good practice and to generate professional discussion about teaching strategies.

The questions were aimed at gathering data on the professional attitude of teachers, their planning of activities, the time they devote to teaching different areas of their subject matters (Italian and Maths), the difficulties that they encounter in special areas of the curriculum.

Here are a few examples of the questions related to Maths:

"What are the abilities in Maths that you think students of the fourth grade should achieve at the end of the school year?"
"Which of them do you consider the most important?"
        1…….2………3..…...4..…..5…….
–   How much time per week do you devote to problem solving activities?
–   In which areas of maths do you encounter the most teaching difficulties?
–   In which areas of maths do the children encounter the most learning difficulties?

These questions were meant to focus the teachers' attention not so much on the standard of their teaching practices, but rather on issues related to their perspective on teaching in general, with a special focus on their attitude towards children's errors.

The information thus collected was reported to Headteachers and to groups of staff members trained in evaluation issues who participate actively in the network programme and are in charge of organising and developing self evaluation activities in their own schools. It was then presented during school staff meetings and discussed within groups of teachers of the same subject matter. The questionnaire has proved an effective instrument in enhancing self reflection, increasing awareness and stimulating the desire to learn.

The answers to the questions provided the basis for discussion within each school on choices regarding lesson planning and evaluation activities and for sharing teaching strategies. On the other hand, they also revealed problems and incoherence.

For instance, with regard to Maths, the 120 teachers that answered the questionnaire indicated as the most problematic areas the teaching of logic and statistics and the solution of mathematical problems.

While the first topic shows a higher value as a teaching difficulty, the second is mainly perceived as a learning difficulty. This means that in the first case there must be a general lack of expertise on the part of teachers, together with an objective teaching difficulty; the second topic, which is perceived as a learning difficulty, shows a real cognitive obstacle. These topics undoubtedly represent didactic obstacles.

Unexpectedly, when we came to look at how much time teachers devoted to these "critical points" it appeared that only 6.9% of the teachers that had indicated problems as a "difficult matter" devoted 60 to 90 minutes per week to activities related to problem solving, while the others devoted even less time than this.

The same teachers were asked to analyse the test results achieved by their pupils - with the assistance of teachers experienced in self-evaluation - and to compare them with other classes and schools of the network. During this analysis reflection was concentrated on the fact that there must be reasons that account for better or worse results, other than those that can be attributed to socio-cultural background. These reasons presumably lie in the relationship between the teacher's method of teaching and the children's learning strategies.

Therefore experts in the teaching of Mathematics have suggested a change in part of the curriculum, starting from problem solving, cognitive obstacles and pupils' errors. This process, which has been called "retroactive planning"[1], develops in three phases:
- analysis of teaching
- analysis of learning errors
- feedback from self-evaluation
- change of planning

Another aspect of the question was that, up to that moment, the pupil component had not been taken into consideration. We knew roughly what the teachers' point of view was. But what did the pupils think of their learning?

Last May we piloted another instrument for getting information about the children's perception of their own learning. The research was conducted on 1.835 children in Grade Four. At the end of a Maths test we asked them to put a coloured sticker by the items they felt confident they had done correctly. They had to choose five items.

ϑ   ϑ   ϑ   ϑ   ϑ

The results showed that in some cases pupils think they know something that they actually do know, in other cases they think they know something that they don't know, and - which is more amazing - there are cases where children think they don't know something which in fact they do know.

Here is an example of how we tried to interpret the data.
Over 90% of the children put their stickers by the items which were meant to evaluate the skill of reading and writing numbers. In fact, 2/3 of them had given the right answer; on the contrary only 33% of the children that thought they had answered correctly an item which required the ability to write decimal numbers had actually given the right answer.

Another piece of information is significant: some items considered difficult by Maths teachers were easily answered by a good percentage of the children, especially those items concerning non-stereotyped problems.

The interpretation might be that something which does not look "too mathematical" may be considered by the children as a challenge, while in more traditional mathematical problems the children think they know but many do not.

The items that the children chose most were those related to computing. Is this because computing is considered to be easy or because children have the perception that computing is very important and so, they thought they should show they were capable of doing it? The question raises a problem which is very relevant to teaching. The difficulties encountered in the teaching/learning process have a double aspect: one aspect is related to the difficulties of some areas of the subject itself; other difficulties depend on the views that teachers and learners have on these aspects. It is not just a question of a good relationship between teachers and learners - which, as we all know, is basic to any learning process - but the perception, concepts or misconceptions that they have of the subject, and it is thus located in the field of the meta-cognitive.

Action plan

It is on the basis of these reflections on their own professional attitudes and on errors produced by children that a staff development programme was started. It involves three/four teachers from each school who have started to meet regularly in work groups. With the help of and continuous confrontation with experts on the subject, they develop and experiment new approaches to some of the crucial teaching difficulties and learn how to take into consideration aspects they had not considered before. These teachers act as change agents in their own schools, bringing forward new ideas and assisting their colleagues in the planning of lessons and in improving their teaching practices.

In this process, the function of the school network is determinant. Teachers do not only exchange experiences and materials, but create co-operative learning through confrontation and dialogue with colleagues, thereby building together new strategies on a larger scale than a single school.

Difficulties

There is a difficulty in establishing criteria and protocols for the evaluation of pupil attainment, which, as it has been noted above, is not an institutional practice in our country.

A second problem is resource availability. This process absorbs time, demands extra work from teachers and requires expertise in interpersonal skills and professional evaluation. These resources are not easy to find and are subject to instability.

The greatest difficulty is how to involve a great number of teachers within the schools and extend the change in some teaching practices to colleagues who are often reluctant or feel threatened by the process. It takes time and it works only where the school climate is co-operative, the leadership supportive and a consensual agreement is strategically built.

Conclusions

We do not have enough evidence to confirm whether these new approaches to some areas of the curriculum have produced positive effects on the actual learning of students. It is certain that "key skills" and "thinking skills" are being gradually introduced into teaching and that are becoming an important part of the subject content.

Changes take time and do not only consist of new equipment or technical innovation. They require reconceptualizing teacher's knowledge of the subject matter and considering the meta-cognitive aspects of the complexity of the learning process that may so far have not been sufficiently considered.

We shall need data banks and different instruments for investigating meta-cognitive competence.

The test prepared for this May will present open answer items, according to the international PISA, TIMMS and IEA models. A group of teachers experienced in self-evaluation will take part in the correction of the tests and will receive practical training in the evaluation of student production.

Schools' expect to benefit greatly from the implementation of scientific methodologies which are often the prerogative of theoreticians and specialised institutions.

Epilogue

During a workshop in which the AVIMES project was presented a lively debate ensued and included the following comments and questions:

- What about teachers who are not or do not want to be involved? It was replied that it is certainly not easy to include all teachers, and the culture of some schools is more inclined towards collaboration but that ultimately teachers become involved because they want to be involved.
- A colleague was concerned about what he considered to be a narrow perception of attainment. Daniela replied that Maths and Italian are considered important core subject in which basic competence is expected of all pupils and thus they are subjects that have research credibility in the school community. Furthermore, this research served only as a case study and a case study needs a well-defined focus. There was broad agreement.
- The role of the inspector was inquired about. The function of an Italian inspector was explained (very broadly advisory, supportive and expertise-based). Silvana, the Inspector, explained that she had the role of pedagogical advisor and worked alongside and not top-down in any way to the teachers. She is able to provide a catalogue of, for example, mathematical instruments to use. She also supports the testing procedures and the data analysis.
- Daniela re-iterated that Italian and Maths are a solid learning foundation that can provide a basis for testing procedures, the generation of valid data and thus a basis for comparability. She also stressed that the supply of good Maths teachers is now a European wide supply problem and that it was thus

timely that research should be focused on a high profile subject area in an effort to join in the debate in a very positive way.

- It was reported that teachers had become very adept at quite sophisticated techniques of error analysis, a higher order skill that provided intellectual learning for teachers
- A Swedish colleague briefly described his school networking experiences and expressed concern at the obsession with test results. He asked how we could, for example, measure values education. He also suggested that school autonomy generated a new range of problems and that single teachers in single schools could not by themselves solve major problems, not even in small networks. He agreed, however, that developing networks of learning schools was the way forward.

In conclusion, it was pointed out that AVIMES was a good example of practitioner research and of schools trying to make a difference. The presenters thought that the willingness of teacher colleagues to co-operate and to collaborate, to discuss problems and to seek solutions amongst themselves and to think critically was a very important outcome of the project.

References

Barzanò, G., Mosca, S. & Scheerens, J. (2000). *L'autovalutazione nella scuola.* Milano: Mondadori.

M.I.U.R. Torino, *VALMAT project - Professional development and self-evaluation in school as a learning organisation: mathematics case study,* Comenius 2.1 Action, 2001-2003.

Silvana Mosca is an inspector of the Ministry of Education in Piedmont, Italy Daniela Bachi is a teacher trainer for the AVIMES School Network in Turin, Italy.

---

[1] Jaap Scheerens, paper for internal AVIMES circulation, 1999.

PART 6

QUALITY MANAGEMENT IN SCHOOLS: STRATEGIES AND INSTRUMENTS

CHAPTER 14

THE STRESA SCHOOL QUALITY PROJECT

A CASE STUDY

Francesco Tadini

Abstract

What is school quality? What works well in starting a school quality project? What are the best procedures in setting up the process and what are the most appropriate criteria to assess it? This case study is aimed at identifying some features of the Stresa self-evaluation project in the specific national context of Italy. The key tool is a checklist developed by Jaap Scheerens (Dutch Professor of Education Management) and Giovanna Barzanò, (Inspector in the Bergamo region) and filled in by 14 schools during April-May 1999, about eight months after the beginning of the project. It covers four main questions: Why are we doing it? How can we do it? Is our school organisation ready for it? What are we going to do with the ensuing data information?
A parallel between the international survey that the school quality group is going to carry out in *The Treasure Within* project and this case study should give some further opportunities for reflecting about school quality criteria and processes.

The national context

The Italian educational system is involved in a phase of major reforms with inevitable problems due to the change of the governments' school policy. Some of the reforms have already started:

- school autonomy,
- equal opportunities for state schools and for private schools,
- real headship power given to the head teachers,
- the creating of comprehensive schools: comprising nursery school (pupils aged 3-6), primary school (pupils aged 6-11) and lower secondary school (pupils aged 11-14).

The reform of the learning cycles, on the contrary, developed and started by the former Education Ministry, was halted by the current government, which has developed another reform, based on quite different lines and which has just been approved by the Ministers' Council. A more fundamental reform is expected to be initiated with the "Devolution Act", which should give very strong powers to regional authorities, within an overall state settings reform towards a federal republic.

Decision making within the school is shared between the headteacher and two collegial bodies, the Teachers' Council and the School Board. The former is the main body, voting on all-important issues concerning learning and teaching process; the latter has a more institutional role, but can be seen as a platform for a powerful teachers' and parents' voice.

The teachers' unions still maintain a strong power base in the organisation of their profession in Italy and limit the headteachers' freedom to manage the school. However, headteachers' power is expected to develop, according to the current school policy and the ongoing reforms.

At a higher level, power and decision making can be seen in a triangle comprising schools, local authorities and central government. The Local Authorities (LA: municipalities, provinces and regions) are becoming considerably more powerful than they were; in fact they have more and more responsibility for making local school policy. The central government, and particularly the Education Ministry, is going to redefine itself in a role responsible for constructing only the main guidelines of national school policy, and of monitoring and assessing the educational system.

However, so far in Italy there is no national evaluation system: it is just being set up and it is expected to have more of a support rather then a control function. In such a political, social and cultural context, school evaluation is more likely to come from within and not to be externally imposed by the Education Ministry or by the LA. It is aimed at considering how the school is functioning and how external people (such as parents, public administration ...) see the school, how to establish effective links with the social environment, how to improve school effectiveness.

The project context[1]

In the school year 1998-99 a group of primary and lower secondary schools[2] in the province of Bergamo (Lombardy) set up a network called STRESA aimed at:
- discussing and deepening their understanding of some conceptual issues about school effectiveness and school self-evaluation with the support of an international expert, Jaap Scheerens;
- developing three questionnaires for parents, pupils and teachers on their perceptions about the functioning of the school;
- monitoring pupils' achievement through standardized tests in three subjects: Italian (understanding of a written text), maths and history; and asking for support in analysing data and presenting them in appropriate grids or tables;

The Treasure Within

- giving teachers more opportunities for professional development:
    - developing a training course to introduce the main issues of the project to the teachers of those schools involved in Stresa;
    - starting working groups on some key issues of the project (result-oriented management, retroactive planning, the school as "learning organization", peer observation, testing...);
    - organizing international seminars and meetings on specific issues;
    - getting in contact and sharing practice with other Italian and/or European networks.

The main features of the Stresa project's current organization are illustrated in the following diagram:

STRESA SCHOOLS IN 2001-2002

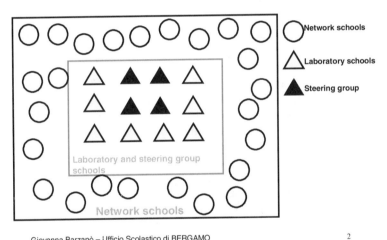

Giovanna Barzanò – Ufficio Scolastico di BERGAMO   2

A major aspect of the STRESA project is the interaction between schools, experts and the network, which gives an added value to schools' reflection and activity. The conceptual development of the experts has to confront the ongoing processes in the schools and to support the activities. So there are three 'actors': the schools as individuals, the schools as network and the experts.

THE ACTORS

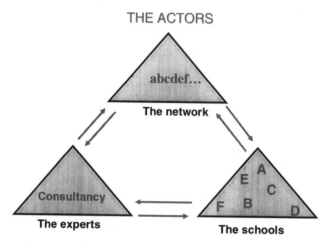

Giovanna Barzanò – Ufficio Scolastico di BERGAMO

3

The School Board and the Teachers' Council are responsible for deciding whether to involve a school in the Stresa network. Within each school a group of experienced teachers is established (the school task force) and is charged with the development and research activities of the network and of organizing improvement activities in their school.

The role of the Headteacher and of the task force is basically to involve the Teachers' Council, to share decisions and to disseminate information on the project. It must be stressed that the network provides the facilities, support and instruments, clarifies the way they are to be used and supports schools in developing their acti⸱   ⸱ on the needs of individual contexts.

Organization

THE SCHOOLS

Sch. Board's
deliberation

Council's
deliberation

**School
Board**

Teachers Council

Task force

Headteacher

tea
ch

teach

tea
ch

tea
ch

Giovanna Barzanò – Ufficio Scolastico di BERGAMO

The development and research activities of the network involve the basic concepts, developing new tools, data analysis and working with expert consultancies. The schools' task forces (about 200 teachers) are engaged in school activities (administering tests and questionnaires, analyzing data, giving back information to teachers and developing new school plans) and in network activities (working in groups, developing training courses, sharing models, ideas and contributions from individual schools).

The checklist: planning and assessment in quality projects.

The checklist contents refer to the first phase of the project and cover four main issues:

1   The key question in the first part is **"Why are we doing it?"**. Its aim is to clarify whether teachers have a clear idea about issues and objectives that will be the main features of self-evaluation and to what degree they are shared and accepted within the teachers' council.

1.0 *Has the school already taken part in a self-evaluation process?*
     Ten out of fourteen schools said they had, but not in a systematic way, that is they had administered some questionnaires and tests, but they had not carried out a planned and structured improvement plan.

1.1 *What were the motives behind taking part in the data collection?*
     –   to know the perceptions of the parents, pupils and teachers about the functioning of the school 8),
     –   to improve the quality of school planning (2),
     –   to know the strengths and weaknesses of the school (1),
     –   to understand the headship style (2),
     –   Nil response (1).

1.2 *Whose initiative was it to take part?*
     –   the headteacher (10),
     –   the headteacher and the task force (3),
     –   the Teachers' Council (1).

1.3 *Is the idea of taking part supported by all the staff, by a considerable number of staff or by only a small group of staff members?*
     Formally it was approved by almost all the teachers, but in actuality:
     –   most of them were not involved in the discussion about the project;
     –   a considerable number of them had doubts about some key concepts of the project: the school products, result- oriented management etc.;
     –   the project was not a "strongly shared issue" with the Teachers' Council.

1.4 *Was there any debate or even conflict before the decision was taken to use the instruments?*
     Discussion, but not conflict. However, many teachers were worried or not completely convinced because the project:
     –   was aimed at assessing the outcomes and not the processes,
     –   was aimed at assessing pupils' outcomes only in a few subjects (Italian, maths and history),
     –   was not very clear at the moment about the decision (e.g. concerning tools like questionnaires and achievement tests, the main objectives, the use of data etc.),

       –   was expected to involve more work for the teachers,
       –   was expected to give an assessment on individual teachers.

1.5 *Is the subject of the chosen instruments among the core areas of interest concerning the way the school is functioning?*
Yes, all the subjects are important (13).
They might touch on some core issues and be a reason for disagreement among the actors of the school (1).

1.6 *Please put in rank order the five key issues in the functioning of your school on which you would like information gathered.*
    –   Pupils' achievement outcomes as a school product (5).
    –   The functioning of the school (1).
    –   The effectiveness of school planning (2).
    –   The learning opportunities for pupils (2).
    –   The school climate (1).
    –   The school's communication with parents (1).
    –   The perception of pupils about their school (2).

1.7 *To what degree can your motives to use a self-evaluation procedure be considered internal or external?*
They are more internally oriented: 50/50 (1), 60-70/30-40 (7), and 80-90/10-20 (4).
Nil response (2).

1.8 *What expectations about taking part in administering the instruments do you have? To what extent do you think using a data collection procedure like this will ultimately improve the functioning of your school?*
    –   Assessing the strengths and weaknesses of the school (2).
    –   Knowing the perceptions of parents, pupils and teachers about the way the school functions (4).
    –   Data available for quantitative analysis and not qualitative analysis (1).
    –   Analyzing the needs of the school and of the environment (1).
    –   Involving all staff in the ongoing self evaluation process (1).
        –   High expectations about self-evaluation instruments, but teachers are aware they have to become familiar with them in advance (1).
        –   High expectations about improving the school's functioning (2).
        –   Low expectations, because of previous experiences of using tests and questionnaires or because of the lack of a school self-evaluation culture (2).

1.9 *What concrete events led to the final decision to take part in this data collection?*

- The Enhancing of teachers' skills on self-evaluation within the context of the ongoing reforms, particularly of school autonomy (4).
- An opportunity for comparison of self-evaluation data with other network schools (5).
- More awareness about the project, after the confidence the teachers gave to the head teacher at the beginning of the process (1).
- The need to assess the work teachers are carrying out (1).
- An opportunity for discussions with experts (1).
- An opportunity for carrying out the process already started (1).
- A need to change the current school organizational model (1).

1.10 *What conclusions can be drawn about costs/benefits?*

Costs: more work on collecting data procedures, the stress of being assessed, and a shift of methodology from qualitative to the quantitative analysis of data.

Benefits: consultancy with experts, school networking, conceptual knowledge, discussion among teachers, opportunities for improving individual teachers' performance and the school as a whole.

2   The key question of the second part is "**How to do it**?". It is aimed at assessing which specific competences and method awareness are available within the school and which are needed to be acquired with the help of an external support.

2.1 *Do you feel sufficiently aware and knowledgeable about the logic of school self evaluation?*

Most of the teachers have only a limited knowledge and they need training to deepen their understanding. In some schools only the task force has a satisfactory level of knowledge.

2.2 *Do you feel you have sufficient knowledge about the use of the chosen instruments?*

Yes (4).
Only some teachers, only the teachers on the task force (3).
No (7).

2.3 *What practical criteria would data collection instruments have to satisfy, in your opinion?*

Clarity (11), reliability (1), effectiveness (1), nil response (1).

2.4 *Is there clarity about the exact products that administering this self-evaluation instruments would yield?*

Yes (5).
Yes, but the process is still ongoing (1).
Not completely, but teachers have got high expectations (8).

2.5 *Will the required external support be sufficient?*
Yes: conceptual information, concreteness, international perspective, competence (of experts); data input on computer (by secretarial staff). No: there is need of more training time, a need for more meetings with experts; there is a problem of difference of language and of culture with some experts[3].

2.6 *Do you believe that the data collection procedure might be obtrusive with respect to the normal school routine? If yes, say how.*
No (9).
It depends on the instruments and on data collection procedures (2).
Yes: it might overlap with pupil and administrative activities at the end of school year (3).

2.7 *Do you feel there is enough know-how on alternative data collection procedures in your staff-team to make a well-motivated choice of school self-evaluation procedure?*
No (13): they need more information.
Yes (1).

2.8 *Do you feel that there is enough know-how for an analysis and an interpretation of the results (such as tables, cross-breaks, histograms, "box and whisker plots")?*
No/ not enough (10).
Yes (4): teachers can read, but not analyse data; they can however read data supported by experts (2)[4].

2.9 *Are you familiar with the concept of benchmarks (reference point or standard to which school-data could be compared?*
Yes (10): but only in a basic way; only conceptual knowledge, not in terms of putting it into practice.
No (4).

2.10 *Is there a clear concept about the data-records that will be created on the basis of the data analysis?*
Yes (2).
A little (3).
No (9).

3   The key question is "**Is our school organisation ready for it**?". The key words in this part of the checklist are: communication shared information, the way to face resistance. The time necessary to carry out self-evaluation actions is a main feature as well.

3.1 *Is there a regular communication platform where the design, implementation and use of the self-evaluation procedure can be discussed?*
Yes (9): only for the task force (2), not regularly (2).

Occasionally (3): but evaluation procedures are still poor (*1*).
No (2).

3.2 *Are there regular opportunities where school staff members, parents, associations and representatives of the local authorities are consulted and informed about the school self-evaluation study results?*
Yes (7).
Occasionally (3).
No (4).

3.3 *Are the pupils going to be informed about the self-evaluation and data collection? If yes, say how.*
Yes (11): the way is to be defined; only pupils in their last year; only for the individual outcomes as feedback; only through their families.
No (2).
Nil response (1).

3.4 *Please indicate the support you have received at this stage from external facilitators.*
Do you consider this support as sufficient? Which additional support would you need?
Yes, by the experts (13): but the school needs more training (2).
No (1).

3.5 *Are the school and local authorities supportive of the school self-evaluation process?*
Yes (12).
Yes, but not enough (1).
No (1).

3.6 *Is there a specific plan to make the results of the intended study known to external officials or the parents?*
Yes (13): procedures are to be defined; data are to be selected; the ways will be: a booklet put together by the task force, mixed work groups (parents-teachers), meetings.
No (1).

3.7 *Did you experience differences of opinion on the possibility of making the data public to external constituencies and not to school staff alone?*
No (7).
Yes (5): doubts and fears of some teachers; a need for selecting data for different target people.
This issue has not yet been faced (2).

3.8 *Is there any apprehension ("test anxiety") among staff? Do they feel threatened in some way? Do they think they could be judged?*
Yes (8): teachers are afraid of the new evaluation tools; of being assessed personally; of external assessment.
No (4): but only after action aimed at informing and reassuring them,

mainly on a school site (*1*).
No (2).

3.9 *To what extent do you consider that the self-evaluation activities can be used to assess teachers?*
Not at all (2).
Yes (12): as self evaluation, as global evaluation of the staff. The basis of the evaluation should be pupils' achievement, but there are some problems: teachers are afraid of being assessed, of being subsequently limited in their teaching methodologies, of being involved in a kind of competition between school classes.

3.10 *Have work groups been formed among school staff, or have specific tasks been conferred on certain people?*
Yes (10): work groups have been formed, in some schools within the Teachers' Council committees.
No (3): only the task force has specific tasks.
Nil response (1).

3.11 *How much time do you plan to invest in the school self-evaluation procedure as a whole? Do you feel that it is sufficient?*
The planned time is variable (10): 16 h, 30 h, 10 h, 12 h, 25 h, 50 h, 18 h, 12 h, 6 h, 12 h.
Not yet planned (4).

4   The key question of the fourth part is "**How are we going to use the results?**". The main features to be weighed up are: useful data, procedures and ways to give back information, communication planning, exploiting data to develop a school improvement plan.

4.2 *Is the possibility of comparing the results of the study on one or more school processes with the pupils' performances planned?*
Yes (11).
Yes, but only if experts provide tools with which to make comparisons to the schools (1).
It is an issue the teachers are going to take into account (1).
The link between outcomes and processes is important, but teachers have not yet planned for this (1).

4.8 *For what purposes do you plan using the study results?*
To assess and diagnose the school policy as a whole (e. g. the monitoring of the school's timetable to avoid "time loss"); to analyze chosen aspects of class dynamics; other.
To evaluate the school policy (11).
To analyze some aspects of classroom life (3).

4.9 *Will the study results provide feed-back to: the school board; the staff-team as a whole; individual teachers; classes?*
To the School Board, Teachers' Council, classrooms, parents, LEA. The

instruments for feedback will be: training courses for teachers, mixed work groups, meetings of collegial bodies, meetings with parents (12). Teachers have not yet planned the feedback opportunities and have not yet reflected adequately upon this issue (2).

4.13 *Do you plan a comparison with the results of other schools? Will it be done in confidence or publicly?*
Yes, data will be published (8): comparison will be made with data of other network schools, but keeping confidential the name of the schools (2).
Yes, data will be published, but only within the school (3)
This issue is to be decided (3).

4.16 *On a scale of 1 – 5, how useful do you think the study will be, in terms of the following?*
Efficiency, educational quality, professional development, visibility of the school, feasibility (also with respect to doing this on a regular basis)
The scores relating to the scale of points of the single schools are:
–   Education quality (8).
–   Professional development (7).
–   School image in the external environment (6).
–   Efficiency (4)[5].

Some final considerations

A self evaluation project is something more complex and more structured than just administering questionnaires or tests and implies a process: choosing a concept of school quality, gathering data, analyzing and interpreting them, making decisions according to the results of the analysis with the intention of improving the school. In the context of the Stresa project the process is generally initiated by the headteacher and formally approved by nearly all the staff. The concrete problem, however, is to involve all the teachers in the discussion about school quality, to convince them that benefits will be more than the costs of the process, to make them feel secure about the outcomes of the assessment they are afraid of.

This means that starting such a process is not only a management or organisation issue, but essentially an educational leadership issue for the head teacher, because he or she has to propose values, to involve people, to manage knowledge, concepts and technical tools but also consider the expectations, emotions and fears of the main actors of the school. Secondly, the headteacher and the task force can start the process, but they cannot carry it out successfully if they are not able to involve as many teachers as possible. You might say that these two features are connected with the specific Italian context, where there is no national evaluation system and where the Education Ministry does not itself have a formal or clear concept of school quality. It is however interesting to note what Stoll and Fink argue, referring to Canadian and English educational systems, that: "Real improvement comes from within and is not externally imposed or mandated"[6].

The Treasure Within

This overall assumption can explain the responses to the first part of the checklist, some of which appear quite contradictory: respondents say that their project is more internally oriented (item 1.7), but in the following items say that major expectations are "knowing parents, pupils and teachers' perceptions about the school's functioning" and "analyzing the needs of the school and of the environment" (item 1.8) and that they took the concrete decision to start the project "to enhance teachers' skills on self evaluation within the context of the ongoing reforms, particularly of school autonomy" (item 1.9).

The second main question is: "Which specific competences are available within the school and which ones are needed to be acquired with the help of an external support to carry out successfully the quality project?"

The situation of most schools in the Stresa project after around eight months is still difficult: teachers generally have only a limited knowledge about self evaluation concepts (item 2.1) and instruments (item 2.2) and about procedures of collecting, analyzing, interpreting and using data (items 2.7, 2.8, 2.9, 2.10). However, they are confident in the external support: conceptual information, concreteness, international perspective, the competence of experts (item 2.5) and have high expectations about the project (item 2.8).

Making the schools aware of this lack of knowledge in the first instance and strengthening their confidence in the project goals is giving them an opportunity to develop an effective school policy and to plan training courses or other ways to enhance their knowledge.

The third main concern is about school organization: are there meetings to discuss and plan the use of data and how to give information to teachers, to pupils and to external people? How often have these meetings taken place? How many people were involved in them? How many hours per month did the headteacher and the task force spend in the first phase of the project?

Nearly all the school say that the project is supported by experts and by local authorities (items 3.4 and 3.5). However, they seem to be ready for it to different degrees: more than 50% have regular meetings to discuss the project, but they do not specify which teachers are involved, whether only the task force or some others. We can see the same problem as in the first part of the checklist: schools offer opportunities for meetings and discussions. However, concretely, it is important to know how many teachers beyond the task force take part in these meetings and discussions. Some (or many) of them are afraid of being assessed and are mistrustful of the instruments, of quantitative analysis and of statistics in general (item 3.8).

Furthermore (and this point also concerns the fourth part of the checklist), schools say that they want to inform teachers, pupils, parents and collegial bodies (items 3.3, 3.6, 4.9) about the data from tests and questionnaires, but they have no clear idea as to which data and for what purposes: furthermore, it is not known whether data will be published or whether they will be (partly) confidential. In this latter case, what would be the criteria of confidentiality (items 3.7, 4.13)? Will the data be used to assess teachers? If so, in which way (item 3.9)? Schools have not yet faced these issues sufficiently in detail and have not yet taken coherent decisions about using the data or about giving feedback (items 3.7 and 3.9).

In the Italian context, this problem is perhaps more complex because of the lack of a national evaluation system, so schools will have to develop an overall policy for themselves and make clear to everybody, and particularly to the staff, what they are going to do with the information, if they want to overcome teachers' mistrust. The major issues of such a policy, we would suggest, should be:

– Gathering data: which data are expected to be more important or more useful?
– getting them analyzed with the help of an expert;
– asking experts to help design suitable grids, tables and diagrams to pinpoint the crucial features of a school's functioning or of the teaching-learning process;
– involving as many teachers as possible in analysing data and interpreting the crucial points;
– developing sensitive procedures to give feedback to the main actors of the school: pupils, teachers, parents and collegial bodies;
– involving as many people as possible in giving feedback and in developing a coherent school policy.

Once again, headteachers have to combine skills of school management and educational leadership in setting up and sustaining effectively a school improvement and quality project.

Epilogue

During a workshop in which The Stresa project was presented, the discussion evolved around the following key concepts

CLIMATE
What sort of school climate is needed to enable pupils and teachers to work and be educated in an optimal way?

COMMITMENT
We are convinced teachers' commitment and initiative are the only way out. Over-reliance on external experts or authority to organize our job in insufficient. Unwillingness to take internal initiatives is the best way to fail.

COMMUNICATION
It all starts with communication. Communication is an open door to reflection, to individual work. Communication is a tool for conducting projects.

CONFIDENCE
Quality in schools can be improved if you have teachers who can work feeling respected by the headmaster, together in good confidence. Self-evaluation can help to find the (less) good in the school.

EDUCATIONAL RELATIONSHIPS	The relationships between pupils and teachers are a crucial condition for quality education. It is very important to create the right climate, to support learning through it and to support pupils emotionally in the learning process.
EXCHANGE	Are teachers convinced there is always something to learn from pupils, parents, colleagues, headteacher,…,
ORGANISATION	With no money, with no connection with real experts, it seems to me hard to work properly.
	With no really organised support between pupils, parents, teachers and headmasters, it seems to me difficult to agree on practical issues. Teachers, pupils and parents can activate each others abilities.
PARENTS' DEMOCRACY	Why couldn't they take part in their children's learning process? Is it really impossible to organise?
PERSONAL INTEREST	Am I interested in what I am doing?
PUPILS' DEMOCRACY	When the pupils feel and experiment they can take part in the learning process, the quality of the learning grows.
SUPPORT	This words can have two meanings: – the whole staff supporting every single member of the learning community; – the additional support of headmaster, inspectorate, external experts.
TEAMWORK	Teachers are not islands.
TIME	What can we do with inadequate time? Idioms like "in less than no time", "as soon as possible" are definitely not quality friendly in a school process. Any self evaluation needs reflection, analysis and reflection again. Schools and their staff need time, much time to implement activities in class and time to reflect further again. Furthermore, schools and their staff need more time to disseminate to others.

TRUST	Confidence leads to trust and trust leads to "self-learning in and as a team".
WELLNESS	How can we imagine it is possible to run a quality project if everyone in the school, pupils, parents, teachers,... aren't feeling good? The happier they are, the more they can be involved in their school development.
GOODWILL	The most important is to develop a voluntary action with the whole staff.

Francesco Tadini is a headteacher and a member of the steering group of the Stresa Project, Italy.

---

[1] This part of the study is quoted from a paper by the Stresa steering group: "Esperienze di Autovalutazione nella scuola", edited by Emanuela Brumana and Elisabetta Ferrari.

[2] The following schools took part in the Stresa project in the school year 1998-1999: Direzioni Didattiche (primary schools) of Almè, Alzano, Brembate, Caravaggio, Osio Sotto, Ponteranica, Sarnico, Spirano; Scuole Medie (lower secondary schools) of Bottanuco, Caravaggio, Costa Volpino, Curno, Dalmine; Istituto Comprensivo (comprehensive school) of Tavernola.

[3] Most of the schools underline the strengths as well as weaknesses of the external support.

[4] The number in italics means that it is a part of the quantity indicated by the previous number.

[5] Some schools made more than one choice from the 5 points.

[6] Stoll, L. & Fink, D. (1996). *Changing our Schools.* Buckingham: Open University Press, p. 169.

CHAPTER 15

STARTING A SCHOOL QUALITY PROJECT

A QUESTIONNAIRE

André Elleboudt, Joaquim Laplana, Alexandra Schrutz

Abstract

While starting a school quality project, we think it could be useful for new starters to share others' experience. How have schools started a "Quality project"? What materials did they use? What were the obstacles? What were their conclusions that could help those who have just been starting the process? Why is it worth starting such a process? These were questions underlying the questionnaire.

The workshop context

In the context of *internal quality management* a working group has established the objectives of which workshop were defined as follow: *starting from the schools' experience on Quality management, the workgroup will deal with*
– *The outcomes of an inquiry made in schools in all partner countries,*
– *The success & failures of their actions (how, why),*
– *The lessons we can learn from these experiences (good practices and warnings),*
– *Suggestions for those starting.*
We decided to use two tools:
– A series of indicators and criteria developed by the Vienna School Board,
– a questionnaire for schools on how they started a Quality process.

The indicators and criteria

Some two years ago a group of headteachers, school psychologists, school developers and school administrators (& inspectors) began to develop a catalogue of criteria for school quality and their indicators. The catalogue is based on the nationwide programme "QIS = Quality In Schools", developed by the Ministry of Education. We made a draft version. Then we consulted international literature concerning this aspect, then we introduced the preliminary version to "quality facilitators" in Vienna and asked for their feedback. After this we considered their feedback and added or incorporated certain items. After that we introduced the catalogue to headteachers throughout Vienna and asked for their feedback, which we also tried to work into our catalogue. Thus this handbook came into its first version. We went through two discussion sessions with all the headteachers (higher secondary schools) of Vienna (85) and then produced the final version, which we gave to all our schools - both on paper and electronically. We added the electronic version to enable schools to take out certain aspects and concentrate on others. What we required was that every school that engaged in an evaluation process would have to include major parts of the chapter "Teaching and Learning" which seems to be the centre of the whole enterprise." Karl Blüml, Vienna School Board.

The questionnaire

The Vienna School Board offered a draft version questionnaire. The draft version was sent to partners for correction and suggestions. We then got the final version of it that was sent to the schools. The partners decided that the synthesis of the answers would be the contribution of Universitat Politecnica de Catalunya.

The questionnaire has been sent to 25 primary and secondary schools in 8 European countries, members or related to The Treasure. Then, the results were collated and a summary was made (see PowerPoint presentation in the BB).

A. Values: which idea of school quality did we have in our mind when we started the project?
  - Pupils' achievement outcomes   07 schools
  - School climate   10
  - Perceptions of main aspects about school functioning/school 11
    organisation

B. We assessed the various aspects of school quality in the following order (please indicate by numbering from 1 to 10).
  - What came first in importance
    School climate: 13 schools
    School equipment: 05
    Quality teachers: 04
    Quality instruction: 03
    Quality local environment: 01
    Quality parents-school relationship: 04
  - What came second in importance
    School climate: 09 schools
    School equipment: 04
    Quality teachers: 02
    Quality instruction: 09
    Quality local environment: 03
    Quality parents-school relationship: 03

- What came third in importance
  School climate: 07 schools
  School equipment: 04
  Quality teachers: 04
  Quality instruction: 01
  Quality local environment: 04
  Quality parents-school relationship: 04
- What came fourth in importance
  School climate: 02 schools
  School equipment: 04
  Quality teachers: 06
  Quality instruction: 06
  Quality local environment: 06
  Quality parents-school relationship: 06
- What came fifth in importance
  School climate: 01 schools
  School equipment: 02
  Quality teachers: 04
  Quality instruction: 01
  Quality local environment: 02
  Quality parents-school relationship: 03
- What came sixth in importance
  School climate: 03 schools
  School equipment: 02
  Quality teachers: 03
  Quality instruction: 04
  Quality local environment: 04
  Quality parents-school relationship: 02

C. Our project was:
- more internal oriented   03 schools
- more external oriented   33

D. We developed the instruments (tools) for evaluation (questionnaires etc.) ourselves.
- completely   05 schools
- partly (we had an expert from outside who helped us)   09
- partly (we paid for an expert from outside who helped us)   08
- we paid for the expert from our school budget   03

E. The process is
- completed   02 schools
- not completed   23

F. Aspects, events, items that facilitated our endeavour?
Please, name some: see further on

G. Aspects, events, items that hindered our endeavour (stumbling-blocks, obstacles, drawbacks)?
Please, name some: see further on

H. Data analysing
- Who analysed the data?
  - an external expert .... 03 schools
  - a group of expert teachers of the school 14
  - other people (specify) 08
- Who paid for the analysing of the data:
  - the school out of its regular budget .... 16 schools
  - the school form its extra income (from parents, from sponsors ...) ... 02
  - the LEA (local educational authority) 02
  - the state (extraordinary budget) 03
  - no answer 02

I. Data were:
- Published in local newspapers or other easily accessible media ... 03 schools
- Not published 02
- Confidential (partly) 20

J. Who decided about publishing data or keeping them confidential?
- Education Ministry .... 02 schools
- LEA 08
- Head-teacher 10
- School Board 05

K. If data were (partly) confidential, which were the main criteria of selection?
- different targets for different people .... 04 schools
- enhancing the external image of the school 03
- promoting reflection among the staff 18

L. How were data published?
- only data in a booklet .... 03 schools
- data with a written comment 03
- in a meeting with the staff 13
- in a meeting with parents (and pupils) 06

M. Did we get the data we intended to get and could we work on the basis of these data? (open answer)
- yes .... 21 schools
- no 04

N. And then? What did we do with our findings?
- inform the parents and pupils .... 19 schools
- inform the educational authority 09
- discuss the results within the school authorities (e.g. inspectors) ... 06
- change teaching methods 18
- dismiss teachers (only in some countries possible) ... 00
- change application policy 06
- try to raise more money for school development 07

- change teaching programmes   09
- expand your school   05
- change public relation policy   07
- change your complete school programme   01
- shut down the school (in some countries possible, in   00
  most countries not possible)
- increase in-service- training...   17
- start a school development project   16

Questions F and G: the participants gave "open answers". It seemed to us better to present what was written down (see PowerPoint presentation) and comment on it. When referring to schools, we'll use school 1, school 2, …

F. Aspects, events, items that facilitated our endeavour?
- School 1:
  - We became experienced in creating evaluation instruments.
  - Electronic form of data processing was of great help.
  - The commitment of a majority of teachers enriched our work.

- School 2:
  - Facilitators were: the school mission document, a pastoral school programme, the teachers' knowledge of the school inner processes.

- School 3:
  - We realised the necessity of any evaluation in education and this increased the teachers' participation in the process of evaluation.
  - Change in the teaching programmes and of teaching methods.

- School 4:
  - Training of teachers forming the school self evaluation team (courses, seminars, meetings,…)
  - Comparison of own school data with other schools of the network without any ranking.
  - Confidentiality of data.

- School 5:
  - The ground for the quality evaluation project had been prepared by the use of a questionnaire for children, discussion work with teachers on evaluation criteria of pupils' achievements, the training of teachers in administering and correcting assessment tests in the Italian language conducted together with the Regional Institute for Research and Experimentation, the validation of Maths tests.

- School 6:
  - Evaluation of pupils' achievement: staff meetings on planning and evaluation relationships.
  - Reflection on the minimum level of achievement required.
  - Discussion with experts on the construction of evaluation tests.
  - Evaluation of school climate: a questionnaire for parents' representatives on their perceptions of the school.
  - Questionnaire for parents of incoming children of class one (first form) about their expectations.
  - Questionnaire for teachers (prepared by the headteacher) on the strengths and weaknesses of the school.

- Self-evaluation in a school network which has enhanced the school's already existing potential.

- School 7:
  - Open mind teachers groups.
  - Active 'future thinking' headteacher.

- School 8:
  - Staff commitment and loyalty

- School 9:
  - Help of the school Authority.

- School 10:
  - Keep staff ready to work in teams as a new approach.

- School 11:
  - Staff were all interested in raising attainment.

- School 12:
  - Parents were highly motivated and created their own questionnaires.

- School 13:
  - Support came from external facilitator.

- School 14:
  - Visit of British and American school inspectors.

- School 15:
  - Conferences helped the process of developing corporate identity.

- School 16:
  - External support.
  - A majority of the staff interested in school development.

- School 17:
  - External support.

- School 18:
  - Inspection reports.

- School 19:
  - Open school climate.
  - Eagerness to learn in several school partners.

- School 20:
  - Parents' response and involvement.

G. Aspects, events, items that hindered our endeavour (stumbling-blocks, obstacles, drawbacks)?

- School 1:
  - Government financial cuts-down.

- School 2:
  - New government and new measures.

- School 3:
  - Lack of time.

- Resentment of the staff, change for the worse.

- School 4:
  - Lack of reflective practice among teachers.

- School 5:
  - The intercultural and intergenerational gaps.

- School 6:
  - Passive answers, resistance of some teachers.

- School 7:
  - Extra paper-work involved.
  - Real differentiation in lessons requires considerably more extra planning and resources.

- School 8:
  - Lack of money and resources of all kind.
  - Crumbling buildings.
  - Pressures from inspectors.
  - Large number of children with behavioural and learning difficulties.

- School 9:
  - Extra paper-work involved.
  - The need for extra resources and planning.

- School 10:
  - Many poor families in the school population.
  - Diversity of teachers' involvement and practical answers.

- School 11:
  - The cost of the project.
  - The overwork required of teachers and headteacher.

- School 12:
  - Recent enlargement of the school organisation.
  - New school staff.
  - Lack of financial resources.

- School 13:
  - Fear of being "evaluated and judged" on a scale of merit.
  - Financial burden for the school.
  - Additional work for staff.

- School 14:
  - Vague answers from parents.
  - Cost of paper and of printing evaluation instruments.

- School 15:
  - Resistance of some "key" teachers.
  - Restricted collaboration with parents.
  - Inadequate help from the local authorities.

- School 16:
  - Negative attitude towards new ideas.
  - Lack of money.

- Lack of essential facilities at school.
- School 17:
  - Teachers unwilling to change.
- School 18:
  - Difficulty of enabling secondary school teachers with different timings to work together.
- School 19:
  - Too large a number of teachers.
  - Fear of starting something new.
  - Trade Unions' resistance.
- School 20:
  - Time.
- Miscellaneous:
  - Thanks to our contacts with foreign schools we could draw on their experience and expand our knowledge in the field of Quality and share our findings with them.
  - Working in a school network becomes an additional value if schools' data are reliable.
  - Don't hesitate to ask experts for help in creating instruments and deciding together how to use them and interpret them.
  - Keep strictly to the agreed rules.
  - The school needs to be organized in teams with clearly defined goals to which they are committed. There must be practical outcomes.
  - Staff have to be involved in decision-making.
  - All contributions must be recognised and valued.
  - The project worked well because it was clearly perceived by all staff.
  - We involved pupils and parents in the project.

Some comments

After reading these pages, one can no doubt consider that it is a considerable job to start a Quality process in one's own school. It is clear that such a process means a lot of personal involvement, of hard work on one's own and with teams.

There are however many good (convincing) reasons for starting a Quality project. And I'm personally convinced it is here more a matter of enthusiasm, of dynamism, of renewal than simply hard work. I like Roland Barthes, French philosopher and researcher in Sociology and Lexicology when he says, discussing the French travel guide, the Guide Bleu: *"The Guide hardly knows the existence of scenery except under the guise of the picturesque... found any time the ground is uneven... Only mountains, gorges and torrents can have access to the pantheon of travel... Just as hilliness is overstressed to such an extent as to eliminate all other types of scenery, the human life of a country disappears to the exclusive benefit of its monuments' for as he later writes: 'It is every day life which is the main object of travel...rather than an uninhabited world of monuments'.* (p. 76)

I can't prevent myself from changing his words a bit and say that it is everyday school-life that is the main object of education...rather than an uninhabited world of unchanging educational future.

Coming back to our subject I definitely share Jane Jones' comments on the results of the questionnaire. *"An analysis of the responses leads me to suggest that the enabling factors principally concern the attitudes of teachers. This is not surprising since we know that real change only takes place at learner level and thus through the actions of teachers in classrooms. Where there is commitment, interest, open-mindedness, a willingness to learn and loyalty to all that the school represents, then conditions for quality change will be favourable. However these attitudes need to be promoted and sustained by a school culture that is receptive and open. It needs to be a school that has a strong sense of mission lead by what one respondent called ' a futures- thinking' head. This head will provide opportunities such as staff discussions, access to conferences and even international links enabling teachers to engage with the quality debate both at home and cross-nationally. Appropriate resourcing and expert supportive help from outside as well as the internal strengths will ease the extra workload that will invariably be involved in change processes.*

The whole school community will be involved, especially parents and pupils, with the additional help of supportive inspectors and advisers. The school will not be afraid of evaluation, being permanently engaged is self-evaluative processes as part of its school development and improvement planning. This is what the responses indicate.

Unfortunately the evidence also indicates that teachers, those who are resistors, resentful and the easily self-satisfied , hinder improving the quality of schooling. There are teachers who do not wish to change and are unwilling to reflect upon either their performance or that of the whole school. If the 'resistors' are in influential positions or have personal power then they can have a very powerful and controlling influence over other teachers. Some teachers will look for any excuse to avoid self-evaluation and change, claiming lack of resources, lack of time -the perfect excuse! - and will pinpoint all the extra work and the financial implications. There will be no attempt to seek creative solutions to what are certainly real problems but that can be confronted and worked upon with good will. The leadership and the school culture will lack change-readiness.

In these 2 scenarios, representing the responses of questions F and G respectively, it can be seen that the following questions need to be asked:
- *How do some schools manage to find creative solutions to problems and obstacles whereas others do not?*
- *How is loyalty and commitment inspired and maintained?*
- *How do we reward and tangibly value our teachers?*
- *How do we ease the workload and provide the necessary resources?*

Time for the school to 'stop and think' and to take stock."

Taking stock from Alvin Toffler, I will allow him to provide the conclusion: *"Although change is always a little unsettling, that is the pace of change in modern day life that is disorientating and that causes a syndrome he calls ' future shock': to survive, to avert what we have termed future shock, the individual must become infinitely more adaptable and capable than ever before."* Toffler suggests that we need to be aware of the chain of biological events touched off by our efforts to adapt to change *"in order to understand why health and change seem to be inextricably linked to one another. If future shock were a matter of physical illness alone, it might be easier to prevent and treat. But future shock attacks the psyche as well. Just as the body cracks under the strain of environmental over-stimulation, the mind and its decision processes behave erratically when overloaded"*.

With "How we got started", the intention was to share with you the conviction that it is worth starting and running a Quality project. So, start one, tell colleagues about it, share your doubts and strong beliefs, create new ways, imagine undiscovered horizons, stop and think, take stock but above all, start.

References

Barthes, R. (1957). Sociology and Lexicology, translated in 1972, republished in 1993. *Mythologies*. London: Vintage.
Toffler, A. (1970). *Future Shock*. London: Pan Books.

André Elleboudt is Head of the International Relations Unit of SéGEC, Belgium. Joaquim Laplana is a lecturer at the Universitat Polytècnica de Catalunya, Barcelona, Spain. Alexandra Schrutz is a staff Member of the Vienna School Board, Austria.

CHAPTER 16

THE SEEDS OF SUCCESS

SELF EVALUATION AND DEPARTMENTAL SUPPORT

Shân Mullett

'A school that knows and understands itself is well on the way to solving any problems it has. The school that is ignorant of its weaknesses or will not, or cannot, face up to them is not well-managed. Self evaluation provides the key to improvement.'

Abstract

In England schools are expected systematically to review and evaluate their teaching methods and overall performance. This paper describes one school's response which, in addition to the monitoring that is a requirement of subject leaders, is a system whereby senior management conduct a detailed scrutiny of all the work in a specific subject area. This evaluation of performance includes the process of lesson planning, delivery, assessment, pupil attainment and attitudes, and the quality of leadership and management. This process results in the production of an action plan for the department and every teacher within it. This paper outlines the background, purpose and content of the scheme and describes some of the difficulties encountered, the response of teaching staff and the implications for the school's management. It concludes with an assessment of the effectiveness of the strategy and speculates about further development.

Context

For the past decade there has been a general move within English education to make schools more managerially autonomous and more individually accountable. They have to a large extent control of their own expenditure but not income, which is determined largely by pupil numbers. There is a National curriculum which identifies content and sets norms for pupil achievement at four "key stages" in their compulsory education to the age of 16. Schools are compared by the publication of comparative tables of examination results and the key-stage test performance of their students.

There is a national system of inspection. Approximately every four, soon to be six, years there is a week-long visit by a team of independent inspectors (appointed by the National Office for Standards in Education" – OfSTED) who view lessons and appraise every aspect of the school's work. Inspections result in detailed reports which are public documents. A "poor" inspection can result in severe, externally driven action including the introduction of new management. Generally however inspections provide a rigorous analysis of a school's strengths and weaknesses that is crucial to its action planning.

As part of this process of inspection, action planning and improvement, it is expected that every school will have a programme of self-review using the same criteria that are employed by OFSTED inspection teams. This ensures that critical self analysis and consequent action is built into the on-going life of every school and is not confined to the run-up period when an inspection is due.

The Folkestone School for Girls (FSG), in the administrative district of Kent, has approximately 900 pupils aged 11 to 18 years. Kent is unusual in England in that generally its children at the age of eleven go through a selection procedure intended to identify the more able 25% to 30% of the cohort who transfer to "Grammar Schools", of which FSG is one. (The majority of English secondary schools admit pupils of all abilities). FSG admits only girls and this also is unusual.

This atypical character of the school however has little bearing on its general situation. It experiences the same pressures, sanctions and incentives as other schools in the state system. The locality served by the school has a high incidence (for the UK) of adult unemployment, poor housing and up-take of socials benefits.

Purpose of the SEADS programme

At its last inspection (1998) the school was deemed by the OFSTED team to be in the "very good" category and to have strengths in management, student attitudes and conduct, and the quality of the education provided. To raise very good to excellent is demanding and it is also a fact that even in very good schools achieving consistency across the whole curriculum remains a considerable challenge.

The objective of our Self Evaluation and Departmental Support (SEADS) programme is to address these challenges and to bring about improvements in student performance in all areas. This is "self evaluation" in that the process is initiated and carried through by the school itself and is independent of OfSTED , or any other external, process.

The SEADS strategy

We needed to answer the questions:
– How well are we doing?
– What are the key areas for intervention and innovation?

–   What are the instruments by which change will be effected?

–   What are the measurements by which we will judge success or failure?

Our own data and the inspection report provided the basis for the answer to the first and last questions in a general sense. That is, it was possible to identify areas of underperformance that needed particular attention and to establish clear over-all targets for their improvement.

There was a need however to be more specific. There is considerable evidence that generalised improvement programmes are not owned by individuals and there is a marked and rapid diminution in their effectiveness after the conclusion of the intervention. On the other hand programmes that engage individual teachers in the development of their own professional practice, with clearly identified target outcomes, have a much greater chance of long-term success.

"Schools self-evaluation is about diagnosis and change in the way people work, and this is particularly so for teaching and its impact. But it must carry a 'health warning'. It can be a mistake to do a self-evaluation of the whole school, treating it as one event like 'having an inspection'."

With this in mind, and after careful thought and consultation, particularly with senior staff and Governors (lay people charged with the oversight and policies of the school), it was decided that that we would concentrate on individual curriculum areas, one each school term (there are three each year) so that:

–   Scarce resources could be focused

–   Information could be gathered and verified in detail

–   Highly specific teaching objectives could be identified

–   Individuals would have their own targets.

In answer to the third question, concerning the instruments of change, the strategy is to deal with improvements in teaching processes rather than student programmes which are separately addressed. To this end the school adopted a self-review model based upon the criteria used by OfSTED because this approach provides a generally accepted and rigorous framework for this activity based upon a common language which has been developed and accepted on a national basis. This in turn permitted the more general acceptance of the programme by the school's staff and obviated the need for the school's management to devise and pioneer its own evaluation and observation criteria and language.

The SEADS process

Identification

The first step was to decide on the priority departments for scrutiny. In addition to the formal inspection data, account was taken of year by year data on student performance, particularly in the public examinations taken at the end of courses (GCSE and AS and A Level examinations), and other evidence including the response of students to the opportunity to choose courses (usually at age 16).

A key problem is that in a well regarded and stable institution it is sometimes difficult for individual teachers and departments themselves to identify that they have fallen behind. This meant that the decision as to which departments should receive early attention had to be taken by the senior managers. On the other hand it was important that the process should not be, in reality nor appearance, punitive. The process had therefore to be clearly supportive and directed at improving the quality of lessons and not a threat to the status of the staff.

Thus, at the start of the programme, two departments were identified: one with marked under-performance that was seriously affecting the opportunities offered to students and one with relative strengths. The Governing Body took the view that the first of these should take priority.

Investigation

A department is given notice of the intention to carry out a SEADS review in the term prior to that in which the procedure will take place.

Within the department there is a process of close examination of its practices, lasting one half term. This is based on an initial consideration, from the available data, of areas for particular attention which may for example be the way in which the department controls and evaluates the assessment of students' progress. The detailed scrutiny comprises:

- Lesson observation by senior staff using OFSTED protocols for evaluating the effectiveness of the teaching;
- Scrutiny of departmental documentation: lesson plans, schemes of work, homework and marking policies and similar relevant information;
- Monitoring of students' work by sampling and examination of the output of whole groups;
- Student Interviews, by senior staff, with a precise format intended to discover the attitudes of students to the subject and the teaching they receive and to elicit their views as to desirable change.
- A review of the use of resources available to the department, including the deployment of teachers and the use of auxiliary staff such as technicians, learning support assistants and student mentors.

Action planning

There follows a period of consideration of this information leading to a summary document prepared by a lead member of the senior management team. It includes:
- A summary of findings
- Areas for action
- Resource implications

This is discussed in detail with the head of department and every teacher in the department. The document is subject to modification as to fact and action priorities, but key evaluations, about the quality of lessons observed for example, are not open to negotiation.

The department is then invited to prepare a detailed action plan, with the assistance of a senior manager, addressing the issues identified in the report. Support is offered as necessary and the outcome is intended to be a joint programme for the school's management and for the department.

The action plan sets targets, against a timetable, for the department as a whole and also for individual teachers particularly where it identifies ways in which their teaching can be enhanced. A core element is a statement of the areas for earliest attention, lesson planning for example. It details the support that will be necessary from the wider school community together with changes in resources, timetable or accommodation that may be needed. The plan is approved by the senior management team which may require the inclusion of elements that it considers essential. This process is completed by the end of the term.

In the subsequent terms there is regular monitoring of progress in delivering the plan which leads by the end of the second term to a statement of what has been achieved and what remains to be done. This could lead to a revision of the plan or to other action; inevitably changes in personnel require amendments to priorities and targets.

Whole School Development

There is a need to ensure that all departments are involved in a process of review and development even though only one at a time can be the subject of close scrutiny. To this end the senior managers undertake a systematic review of various areas of the school's work each term. For example, a national focus on the need for more careful and systematic lesson planning has led the school to choose that as an area to be addressed. Every department submitted all the lesson plans prepared for its teaching programme in a particular half term. These were evaluated and recommendations made for improvement where appropriate. Other areas of focus include a review of students' work samples, a programme of lesson observations, scrutiny of departmental documentation such as schemes of work and analysis of examination performance.

Difficulties

The need to seek to involve staff in an unthreatening way has been noted above. Many teachers accept the need for change and the assistance that systematic observation, using established criteria and protocols, can bring. There is inevitably a degree of stress in this and it is the business of those involved to find inter-personal strategies for minimising it.

A second serious difficulty is striking a balance between the need to bring about changes and the degree to which they have to be required. It would be easy to introduce a system that entailed the consent and agreement of all parties. There are those who are reluctant to agree to change and this kind of consensual approach would not bring it about. On the other hand change that is entirely imposed is doomed to fail. The effort has therefore to be to seek to demonstrate the efficacy of changes for the teacher as well as for the student. All proposed actions have to have a rationale and to be based on demonstrable good practice. This approach is when necessary: "try this, you might not like the look of it, but I know it works".

A third problem is resource availability. This process absorbs time and requires expertise, particularly in inter-personal skills and professional evaluation. These are scarce resources and this constraint was important in our decision to have a focused approach. A related difficulty is that the process may reveal the need to increase or change resources deployed within a department and this inevitably will impact on others, perhaps negatively. The general approach has to be that change can be effected from within what is already available, it easy to blame under-performance on inadequate resources but occasionally it can be true!

The greatest difficulty is when there is a demonstrable need for change in the practices of an individual who is operating at the margin competence. This is exacerbated when that person has managerial responsibilities and may be the leader of others. Any process of review or evaluation will in truth pose a threat to that individual. The approach has to be to declare from the outset that the procedure is designed to assist and that it should be constructed in that way. As has been noted, however, the individual may not agree that there is a need to improve. Consequently the SEADS approach is that the process is not optional.

Outcomes

This process is relatively new and it is too early to evaluate the long term gains. Our first evaluation is that the planning of lessons and the quality of the assessment of their effectiveness by teachers has improved- this has been across the school as a whole and is not confined to the departments that have been the subject of concentrated attention.

There has been a demonstrable improvement in the quality of classroom practice in the departments that have been under scrutiny but it is too soon to say whether this is a short term effect.

It has been possible through this procedure to identify specific training needs and these are being addressed.

Conclusions

This is a large and time consuming commitment but it is difficult to see how the school could bring about significant change without targeted, followed-through action of this kind. Although it is very much work in progress, it incorporates in a systematic way simple, tried, and tested management principles that have clear objectives. At the very least it enables the identification of good practice that can be shared more generally within the school and raises further the ethos of professionalism that is essential in our quest for excellence. Although it is acknowledged that it puts the more marginally performing teachers and managers under stress a clear gain is the ability to identify and encourage the achievement, expertise and dedication of those who are doing well.

The most important gain is to the culture of the school as a learning institution- learning about itself and improving in consequence. At the lowest, mundane level it yields a capacity accurately to assess the quality of its performance. Self review of this kind is a dynamic activity that replaces the snapshot approach of external inspection and our expectation is that the confidence in our own competence and judgement will be enhanced. The test in a relatively short time will be whether this is borne out in the performance of our students.

References

Mullet, S. (2002) *The OfSTED Handbook for Inspecting Secondary Schools.* London: Stationery Office.

Shân Mullett is Headteacher of The Folkestone School for Girls, UK.

CHAPTER 17

DISO: A DIAGNOSTIC INSTRUMENT FOR SECONDARY SCHOOLS

Luk Van Canneyt, Helmar Vyverman

Situating the instrument

Global context for adequate use of the instrument

The instrument is placed within the process of school-development. This means that:
- the school tries to get an idea of what goes on in the school
- this will be done in view of decisions to be taken in the near future
- the goal is: the process of a school that acts as an autonomous unit in which every-one is involved
- one is prepared to examine, after a certain time, to verify whether the aims are actually achieved.

Therefore, the diagnostic instrument is not limited to the presentation of a list of items nor to merely listing the answers. The diagnosis- as a phase in the development-process – is a complex event of which the questionnaire is but a small part.

This development-process is essentially a school-bound issue that is supported by the self-evaluating ability of the school. 'To make decisions' is the autonomy of the school, and only of the school. This is also the case as far as the way of working with the (or any) self-evaluation instrument is concerned. The

Counselling Service of the catholic schools only wants to help schools to get a thorough view of its own functioning. The involvement of the staff is crucial: all teachers should participate in the process.

Vision

The diagnostic instrument is based upon several concepts that have been verified through research (Mintzberg, Marx, Decaluwé, Petri). This makes the interpretation of the results easier. The frames of reference offer a serious hold.

The second pillar of the instrument consists of the principles of the learning organisation, transferred to the learning school. This means that we want to apply the learning disciplines:

- **Personal Mastery:** Personal mastery' is the practice of articulating a coherent image of your personal vision-the results you most want to create in your life-alongside a realistic assessment of the current reality of your life today. This produces a kind of innate tension that, when cultivated, can expand your capacity to make better choices and to achieve more of the results that you have chosen.
- **Shared Vision:** This collective discipline establishes a focus on mutual purpose. People with a common purpose (e.g., the teachers, administrators, and staff in a school) can learn to nourish a sense of commitment in a group or organisation by developing shared images of the future they seek to create and the principles and guiding practices by which they hope to get there. A school or community that hopes to live by learning needs a common shared vision process.
- **Mental Models:** This discipline of reflection and inquiry' skills is focused around developing awareness of attitudes and perceptions -your own and those of others around you. Working with mental models can also help you more clearly and honestly define current reality. Since most mental models in education are often "undiscussable" and hidden from view, one of the critical acts for a learning school is to develop the capability to talk safely and productively about dangerous and discomfiting subjects.
- **Team Learning**: This is a discipline of group interaction. Through such techniques as dialogue and skilful discussion, small groups of people transform their collective thinking, learning to mobilise their energies and actions to achieve common goals and drawing forth an intelligence and ability greater than the sum of individual members' talents. Team learning can be fostered inside classrooms, between parents and teachers, among members of the community, and in the "pilot groups" that pursue successful school change.
- **Systems Thinking:** In this discipline, people learn to better understand interdependency and change and thereby are able to deal more effectively with the forces that shape the consequences of their actions. Systems thinking is based on a growing body of theory about the behaviour of feedback and complexity-the innate tendencies of a system that lead to growth or stability over time. Tools and techniques such as stock-and-flow diagrams system archetypes and various types of learning labs and

simulations help students gain a broader and deeper understanding of the subjects they study. Systems thinking is a powerful practice for finding the leverage needed to get the most constructive change.

Schools are comparatively complicated structures in which a lot of components are distinguished. These components are both pedagogical and organisational. Both components are interrelated. The vision about teaching and learning is connected to the way student counselling is organised. All these components make a dynamic equilibrium that exactly reflects the uniqueness of each school.

Petri assumes that schools, to a certain extent, can be classified into five models. These models show a whole of coherent features that make improvements (or optimisation) or changes possible. He made a questionnaire of 270 items in which he described all these features.

The General Counselling Service of the Catholic Schools in Flanders, the makers of the DISO-instrument, have reduced the items to a set of 82. We took the 41 most important features and wrote about each of them two statements. Each of the statements represents a different (often opposite but not excluding) opinion about the feature. E.g. about the way of composing the classes (groups), you can choose for the homogeneous or the heterogeneous way. Each of the options reflects a basically different view about dealing with classes: if your starting point is: achievements and results, you will choose a homogeneous class. If you want to start from equal opportunities for all pupils, you may choose the heterogeneous group.

Themes of the questionnaire

The instrument can be used for the analysis of the following components:

Pedagogical components:
– vision about pupils and learning
– aims of education
– choice, coherence and handling of the subjects
– way of composing the classes
– way of assigning classes (why this teacher in this class?)
– didactics
– differentiation of interest
– role of the teacher
– function, integration and co-ordination of student counselling
– testing and reporting
– evaluation

Organisational components:
– function, aims and influence of the departments
– tasks in the counselling of students
– assignment of classes (which teachers are put together in a class?)
– teacher autonomy
– rules and instructions

- growing as a teacher
- rules of the schools
- supervision
- communication
- perception and position of the principal
- staff
- management
- complexity of the organisation

As all these components are connected to each other, the first intention is to get a global view of the school. Later, we will deal with the components themselves.

Minimal conditions for a meaningful use of the instrument

First of all, the management and the staff must be prepared to go through the process and to accept its consequences. That is why we always begin with an intake. All the teachers will be informed and will get a view of the global process: they will know where it begins, where it ends and what they are expected to do. The most important feature of the DISO instrument are the feedback talks. These talks are vital. They are the so-called 'communicative validation' of the instrument.

The reason is that we do not believe in two-way communication. No checklist, no questionnaire, however long and complicated can give a correct and complete idea of what the teachers want to say. We see the use of any instrument as a mere step in the global process of school evaluation. The processes are as important as the naked results: they are part of the results.

Experience

Since 1996, we have worked with about 45 schools. Self-evaluation is a comparatively new phenomenon in Flemish schools. Today it seems that suddenly all schools want to evaluate themselves. i.e. they want to perform a SWOT-analysis in order to do some plastic surgery. They want quick answers to quick questions. That is not what we want. We want schools to be responsible for the quality they pretend to offer. That is why we emphasise so strongly the process. The result is not the same in every school; in spite of the meticulous information process, they underestimated the problems and the co-operation of the teachers.

The instrument itself

Concrete aims

The instrument is a global one. This means that it can only give answers to a global question. In this development process, the school goes from the global analysis to the specific analysis of a determined priority. In some schools, the process can be reversed, which means that they start with a specific problem and end with a global view that rephrases the school priorities.

The global approach means that the teachers are asked to reflect upon the common practice in the school: at the moment, in our school we ask a description of the present situation, not an assessment, not wishful thinking. We do not value the answers: that is up to them in the next phase. What we want to know is: what school are you and are you happy with it. If not, what do you want to change, and in what direction (a reference to the five models by Petri).

Form

A list of 82 items is presented tot the teachers. They can say whether they disagree completely (1), rather disagree (2), rather agree (3) or agree completely (4). There is a possibility to score (0) for items that are not applicable. The 82 items are listed at random, i.e. the pairs are not kept together. A positive answer to the first item of the couple should give a negative to the second. 'Should', because this is not always (or seldom) the case. We only conclude (we do not interpret) that the statements are contradictory. In the feedback talks the teachers can explain their answers. To us these answers show whether the image of the school (for this particular item) is consistent or not. It is up to the school to draw conclusions.

Results

The answers are scored and put in the right order (the couples of items are put together). We, the counselling service, 'translate' these figures into words and send them to the schools. The schools organise the feedback talks per group of about 15 –20 teachers.
After these feedback talks a summary is presented to the school. In this summary smaller components are combined into 12 main components.

Target groups

The target group of the instrument is the secondary school.

Concrete use of the instrument

Preparation

The actual use of the questionnaire is preceded by an intake talk. A mutual agreement is the result of this intake talk: both the counsellor and the school must know what they can expect from each other. Information about the teachers and staff is the most vital issue.

The questionnaire

Filling in the questionnaire takes about 30 minutes. Most of the schools have their teachers fill in the form during an organised meeting.

Handling the results

The school send the scores per section / grade / class to the General Pedagogical Counselling Service who handles the results. This means that they translate the figures into sentences. E.g., "Most of the teachers of the first grade think the board of directors has great impact upon the principal. 30% has no idea about the relation between the management and the board of directors." The translation is only a description and not an interpretation: the counselling service does not make a judgement about the correctness of the answers. It is up to the schools to judge whether they consider the answer a good or a bad one.

Feedback talks

These are organised per section / grade / class to verify whether the teachers have to complete, change or refine their answers. One should not forget that the teachers are confronted with the sum of the answers of their colleagues. These may differ from the 'common opinion'. The first remark in such a group often is: 'did we say that?'. Indeed, they did.

Summary

The General Pedagogical Service draws up a final report. This report consists of two major parts:
- the conclusions from the questionnaire after the refinement and a 'comment'. This comment is not an evaluation, it is rather a framework in which the component can be situated. We show that there is more than one way to get what you want, depending on the criteria you use. We always give this example: when you are used to go from a to b by the same way, we display a map on a larger scale: there you can see that there are different ways to reach your destination, depending on how you want to travel.
- the second part places the school within the Petri models e.g. taking into account the different components, your school has features of model 1 for the component 'leadership', model 2 for 'student guidance', model three for 'communication' etc. The important thing is that schools can see whether they are consistent. If the want to develop, they get an idea of the direction they want to choose.

Implementation

After this 'confrontation with themselves', schools have to make their choices. They cannot change everything at the same time. Therefore, they must make priorities. They can do this with the help of their Local Counselling Service.

Epilogue

Following the presentation of the DISO workshop, delegates were provided with a short extract from the results of one questionnaire and asked to discuss the results presented for one pair of questions. Following this exercise delegates were given the opportunity to ask questions and then provided with the interpretation of two further pairs of questions. The following points are a précis of this question and answer session.

In response to concern from some delegates that the answers given by teachers will merely reflect opinion and not the direct knowledge of the respondent it was explained that the answers reflect what people in the organisation think, not what is really happening. In order to fully understand the process the instrument needs to be set in the specific context of the country where it was developed. General discussion centred upon the difficulty of interpreting the results obtained from the use of the instrument and it was pointed out by the presenter that what is missing in the instrument is the willingness to change.

Some delegates voiced the view that the use of the instrument is related to the fact that it serves to get people thinking and then move on. The presenter emphasised that it is for the school to judge the outcomes and decide what the priorities for development should be.

In response to an enquiry as to why the schools were not allowed to interpret the raw results for themselves it was explained that it is very difficult for them to analyse the results – they are too close to the school.

General discussion then ensued on the mechanistic nature of the instrument and it was agreed that if there was no history of self-evaluation in the school then the school should begin with something else. Schools who undertake the exercise are given one week to discuss the results and often their response was, 'Did we really say this?' Again the point was raised that it is very difficult for individuals to complete the questionnaire because they don't always know what the school is doing. However, this in itself tells you something about the school.

Requests were made for some indication of how it had helped schools to take successful actions to improve and the examples quoted included a) improved collaborative working and b) improved communication.

If you want to contact us about this instrument, you can always send an e-mail to: helmar.vyverman@skynet.be
Or write to
Algemene Pedagogische Begeleidingsdienst
t.a.v. Helmar Vyverman
Guimardstraat 1
1040 BRUSSEL

References

Serge, P. (1990) *The Fifth Discipline*, New York: Doubleday.

Luk Van Canneyt and Helmar Vyverman are advisers for secondary education at VSKO, Belgium.

CHAPTER 18

CRITERIA FOR SCHOOL QUALITY AND ITS INDICATORS

Karl Blüml

To facilitate quality assurance and development work, the Austrian Federal Ministry of Education, Sciences and Culture launched the project "QIS" (quality in schools) in 1999.

They suggested, in order to give a help for structuring the rather complex matter, the following quality areas which they had in turn developed on the basis of international literature and several smaller projects in the country:
– Teaching and learning
– Class and school climate
– Internal and external relations
– School management
– Professionalism and staff development

We, in the Vienna School Board, decided to break down this very complex matter on the basis of the QIS-programme.

The department for higher secondary education decided to offer schools a "real" handbook which they could use as a reference guide when they started on a quality-evaluation job.

On a very broad basis of democratic cooperation (and consulting international literature) we made up a **list of criteria for school quality for each quality area** the ministry had set out in their QIS-programme.

In order to make it real handbook or reference guide we then tried to find **"indicators" for each and every quality criterion**, by which one could to a certain degree tell whether this quality criterion applies for the school or not. Our aim was to supply schools with an instrument, so that they would be in position to be able to start on a project of self-evaluation without the need of having to engage expensive help from external experts.

Schools are strongly invited not to go through the whole handbook, but to take out one or the other aspect and start upon it. Our experience tells us that trying to "do the whole thing" in one great effort will inevitably end in frustration! We, the Vienna School Board, have, however, established one major "rule": Whatever field a school might want to have a closer look at – one aspect of "Teaching and learning" should in any case be included, because we consider this as **the very central aspect of school quality**. However important aspects like "School management" or ""Class and school climate" might be.

We think that the handbook enables schools to assess at least parts of their qualities accordingly. School inspectors are asked to have a look at the results and see whether the methods of assessing were appropriate ("meta-evaluation"). One condition, concerning the methods is that school partners (parents, students and – of course – teachers) should be involved. Statements of head teachers and small groups at the schools are not considered as a basis broad enough.

Criteria for School Quality and its Indicators
a helping hand for schools in facilitating self-evaluation

prepared by the department of Academic High Schools of the Vienna Board of Education

A   TEACHING AND LEARNING

I   Learning goals / teaching methods

I. 1.   Cognitive learning goals

CRITERIA	INDICATORS
There is **agreement** among the subject teachers over which **learning goals** are definitely required to be reached in the year (core subject matter and elective subject matter). This is true both on the subject and working levels	• Teachers, students, and parents are all **aware of and clear about** the **learning goals**, because they have been formulated in writing and have been explained and discussed in the appropriate committees. • It has been ensured through specific measures that a change in teachers does not have any negative effects on students.
The relating of subjects to one anther as well as interdisciplinary instruction are standard. A dovetailing of academic and extracurricular learning is sought and encouraged	• The teachers of a particular graduating class know about the subject matter and about the methodology / didactics of the other subjects and can make reference to them. • Methods such as PING, Team teaching, etc. are used.
Socratic curiosity is a learning goal: wanting to learn – amazement – mentally following the lesson – being creative.	• Students are not afraid to ask questions. These questions are incorporated into the lesson.

CRITERIA	INDICATORS
Self-initiated, individualised learning and the individual responsibility of the students are declared learning goals as much as the ability to work in a team.	• The integration of new learning technology is of particular importance and is actively encouraged in all subjects. • Methods such as project oriented instruction, "open learning", "direct presentation of achievement", portfolio assessment etc. are both known and used.
The teachers intentionally use a wide repertoire of methods	• As wide a variety of methods and media as possible are used according to the size of the class and the goals. • Students can identify various methods of instruction and are able to apply them to their own independent work (oral reports, for example)
Students are appropriately (and according to individual need) **supported and encouraged** as well as **challenged** according to their abilities/situation.	• Teachers are aware of the background and knowledge of their students. They are prepared to adjust themselves accordingly. They have the methods and the tools to analyse them. • There are educational clubs, extra help courses (numeracy), differentiated approaches applied within a class • The instruction is designed to fit the situation of the class and teaching goal. • Learning techniques are taught regularly, both those specific to the subject and those that can be applied generally.

I. 2. Social learning goals

CRITERIA	INDICATORS
The social development of the students is also a learning goal.	• Just like cognitive learning goals social learning goals are decided upon together with the students and are known by the parents. • Methods like 'social learning' and the like take place. • The class teams regularly discuss social development, problems, and conflicts in class. (class conference).

I. 3. Affective learning goals

CRITERIA	INDICATORS
Affective learning goals are taken into account. Teachers respect the feelings of their students and encourage them to deal with emotions in a positive way.	• In the context of cognitive and social learning goals the students also achieve affective learning goals: dealing with success – failure, triumph – defeat, recognition – criticism, feelings and fears. • Students can express their fears and learn how they might overcome them. • The teachers endeavor to create and maintain a positive atmosphere in the class. • The school doctor is the person to contact in the case of health problems and also psychological difficulties. He or she advises the teachers in dealing correctly with students who have health problems.

II Teacher behavior – Student behavior

CRITERIA	INDICATORS
The expectations of teachers with respect to student performance and ability to learn is generally positive and high.	• In a very positive way students "are not to be underestimated" • Praise, encouragement and reward are the main forms of motivation • Students and teachers laugh at least once a lesson. They like to go to school
Instruction is recognizably student oriented Teachers maintain a balance between leading and following in the lesson. The goal is not handling of (getting through) as much subject matter as possible, but rather the assured academic success of as many students as possible. Teachers are generally good at explaining and at asking questions.	• Teachers are for the most part able to make their explanations and demands understood by students. • The students for the most part both follow and understand the explanations and demands of the teachers.

III Homework

CRITERIA	INDICATIONS
The purpose of homework is made clear and is recognized (in general) by the students.	• Homework is generally (punctually) done.
Homework corresponds to the abilities of the students.	• It does not have to be done by parents or extra help teachers.
Homework corresponds to the time that students have available.	• There is a co-ordinating of homework according to number and amount. • Afternoon classes are taken into account.
Homework is applied to further study in a clear way.	• Homework is promptly and regularly checked and corrected by the teacher (for the purpose of serving as an aid to learning or a guide to learning).

CRITERIA	INDICATORS
Tests are there to monitor the achievement of learning goals and learning progress. They have no purpose in and of themselves, they are not a disciplinary measure.	• After tests students are given the feedback they need, specifically which measures (steps to take in their learning) in order to improve their performance (expert advice). • Test results (tests, exams) are used by the teachers as feedback and further instruction is planed on this basis. • Students are trained and disciplined to correctly assess their own performance.
Students are encouraged to participate in regional, national, and international comparative tests.	• Such tests are at the very least made available.
Students are given the chance to show their strengths.	• The amount of stress and test related anxiety tends to be low. • A greater role is to be played by class participation (in the broadest sense). Similar to praise there are other (=LOA, i.e. learning goal oriented performance assessment) ways besides tests to demonstrate acquired knowledge.
There are binding agreements concerning academic standards and core learning goals.	• Standards particular to the school are also known by parents and students. • There are school wide and subject wide agreements concerning principles of correction and evaluation
Expressing a positive conception of achievement.	• School administration and teachers express a positive attitude towards work, creativity and achievement. The thereby give their students a positive example.

The success students have in school is also an important goal of the school.	• School achievement of any kind is appreciated (Yearbook, exhibitions, awards, prizes for excellence and achievement). • The teachers know how many of their students get (need to get) extra help and try to keep this percent of students as low as possible. • If there is an increase in the number of students failing or needing to take extra help classes, counter measures are introduced.

B   THE SCHOOL AS LIVING SPACE

I   The rooms in a school are optimally designed and utilised

CRITERIA	INDICATORS
The school utilizes rooms in a creative way.	• School design is done according to a recognizable total concept (Allocation of rooms for example according to age, or type of school. An appropriate allocation of meeting rooms, special purpose rooms ...) • The entrance area of the school is designed to be inviting. • There are orientation aids for parents, students, and visitors. • There are additional special function rooms (working and lounge rooms). • There are discussion rooms, where conversations between parents, teachers, and students can take place undisturbed. • There is adequate access to library and computer rooms so that there is little inhibition to make use of them. • Hallways and rooms are adequately lit. • There are waiting rooms for free lessons.

	• There is a cafeteria that accommodates the needs and the budgets of the students.
The rooms take into account the needs of the students. The students have the obligation / opportunity to take part in decorating, and designing the living space of the school.	• The students can decorate their classroom and take responsibility thereof. • There is enough freedom of movement. • Attention is paid to neatness and cleanliness (also in the area of sanitation) • There is no vandalism or there are strategies in place for preventing it. • There is the possibility of engaging in free time activities (interest groups, sports clubs, student clubs and others).
The rooms take into account the needs of the faculty.	• Every teacher has an adequate working space. • There are flexible seating arrangements in the classrooms that can be adapted to the form of instruction in use at the moment. • The number and equipment of the special function rooms correspond to the instructional requirements or the requirements of the learning strategy that is being applied.

II   Activities offered outside of the regular school routine

CRITERIA	INDICATORS
In general school assumes the role of a place of encounter and of open dialogue between teachers, students, and parents.	• Administration, teachers, students, as well as parents identify themselves with the school.
There is therefore the appropriate festive atmosphere and tradition.	• There are celebrations which all members of the school community can attend. There are exhibitions and project presentations taking place to which all parents and friends are invited.
The cultural potential of the school is made use of. The school views itself as a regional cultural center.	• There are musical, athletic and literary events taking place. • There are (regular) contacts with outside (cultural and athletic) organizations. • There are student, teacher, and parent initiatives that carried out and documented that address regional problems

III   Handling problems and conflicts

CRITERIA	INDICATORS
Problems are not necessarily to be seen as disturbances, but rather can serve as an impulse for positive change. The solved problem ("now we finally have got our peace and quiet back!") is not the goal, but rather the conscience process of getting there. Conflicts are taken seriously and are handled in time in order to avoid escalations. The school endeavors to improve overall conflict solving ability.	• The administration views the creating of a positive working environment to be one of their duties. • The principal and the teachers have a basic knowledge of group processes as well as methods of setting up groups and teams so that they can have a positive effect on the climate among the faculty and in class. • There are students/teachers who are available as conflict mediators when called for. Conflicts are occasionally tackled with the help

CRITERIA	INDICATORS
	of specialists from outside the school.
The school is interested in developing reasonable strategies for handling problems.	• There are pedagogical conferences, SCHILF-, ARGE and other events to respond appropriately to problem situations.
There is a policy for preventing violence which is also known to the parents.	• In the case of constantly recurring problems within the school the school takes the opportunity of calling in outside opinion and consultation. • There is an arbitrating committee that is effective in the preparation of a disciplinary conference.
The teachers demonstrate exemplary behavior to the students by their handling of conflicts.	• Conflicts between teachers are not to be carried out through students or classes, but are to be addressed and settled between the parties involved. • There is no extreme building of cliques among the faculty, but rather a working environment of mutual respect and co-operation.

IV   Stress management

CRITERIA	INDICATORS
The administration takes measures to alleviate stress among students and faculty.	• Teachers and students know and learn methods of overcoming stress. • Teamwork is encouraged as a forum for the collective handling of open questions and is valued as a factor in psychological hygiene. • Teamwork consultants are available when needed.

CRITERIA	INDICATORS
There are "safety nets" for teachers and students in difficult life situations. The school can respond to personal.	• Use is made of student counselling and other forms of support in the school. • Students take their problems and academic planning questions to the guidance counsellor.
Motivation is achieved by the setting of goals.	• Teachers and students are aware of why the are doing something.

V   Social climate in classes and school

CRITERIA	INDICATORS
Teachers and students feel good in school.	• Cases of illness are not common. • Students only seldom miss class.
School partners treat one anther with respect. Teachers greet their students in a respectful way (and vice versa), students are treated as equals.	• Teachers and students greet one another. • Teachers express themselves in a neutral or respectful way when referring to colleagues or students when speaking to parents or students.
Parents are seen as partners in co-operation. The administration is open to questions and criticism on the part of school partners.	• Teachers maintain an intense contact with parents. • Parents and legal guardians are informed about learning and behavioral difficulties in a timely fashion. • There are frequent SGA (PTA) meetings, • The administration takes part in parents' evenings.
The process of putting together a class is carried out according to clear criteria that are sustainable to the social architecture of the class.	• There are hardly any "problem classes".

VI   Integration

CRITERIA	INDICATORS
Within the pedagogical capabilities of the school's location there is a willingness to integrate minorities. These include the following: gifted students, ethnic minorities, students in special education, physically handicapped students, certain types of behavioral disorders, for example hyperactivity, and others.	• For the integration of certain groups of students certain conditions and resources are made available (such as training, assistant teachers). • The public is aware that there is a particular integration focus at the school.

C   **SCHOOL PARTNERSHIP AND EXTERNAL RELATIONS**

I   Flow of information

CRITERIA	INDICATORS
The school partners are regularly and sufficiently informed about school processes (budget, events, changes in students' schedules, new issues in the program ...).	• Regular class parent evenings take place at which learning and social problems of the class are dealt with. Appropriate space is provided for this. • Information is clear and presented in a slightly way. • Parents evenings are moderated. Class teachers have been trained for this. • Parent days are arranged so as convenient as possible for parents and teachers.
The early warning system is not to be seen as an annoying obligation or alibi, but rather as an opportunity once again to show the parent or guardian ways for his or her student to be successful. Parents are informed promptly of important changes in their child.	• Teachers are easily reached by parents in their office hours. • Cancellations are done in time, • Individual appointments can be made. • The principal, administration, are generally available for teachers, students, parents, and officials, and are legal representatives of the school.

II   Decision making

CRITERIA	INDICATORS
Decision making is done in partnership	• The school partners are involved in school decision making at the very least to the degree which is prescribed by law. • The school partners participate in the creation of school programs and have a say in them. • The school partners participate in the additional course offerings (electives, practice sessions, autonomous class divisions, autonomous class sizes)

III   Partnership and reliability

CRITERIA	INDICATORS
Students and parents are seen as partners in a "educational contract". Teachers, parents, and students feel collectively responsible for achieving the desired education of the students, whereby as the students get older the responsibility of the parents decreases and that of the students increases.	• Representatives of students and parents are respected in their functions (Rolls) and not seen as annoying or disturbing. • The students can depend on the agreements made with teachers. • One knows, one acknowledges what it is that parents are afraid of. • Criticism is dealt with in a respectful way. • The demands made by the teachers of the students are clear and unmistakable.

IV   External relations / PR – measures

CRITERIA	INDICATORS
The school is open and friendly towards the outside world.	• Visitors / guests are welcomed and are shown through the school with pride. • Parents / visitors / guests are greeted by teachers and students in the hallway.

	• Waiting time is kept to a minimum. • Telephone inquiries are answered courteously and accurately or are passed on, messages are passed on, calls are returned promptly.
"We are a friendly school that is respected by all." – that applies to the relationship between non-teaching personnel and the rest of the school partners.	• The non-teaching personnel work constructively together with administration, principal, and faculty and is aware of the general priorities of the school.
The school is incorporated in the cultural concept of the district.	• There is co-operation between the following: School – sports club, school – adult education, school – other schools in the district. • The school presents itself regularly to the public for example with a show of achievements in sports, art, and culture. • Teachers and students are aware of these activities.
For the direct benefit for the students, the school maintains ongoing contact with, businesses, employers, employee associations, employment office, technical colleges and universities.	• Sponsoring and the renting out or school facilities are agreed upon together. The associated financial transactions are made public to the school partners. • Advertising in the school is not disturbing aesthetically or pedagogically. • Are informed regularly and competently (by the appropriate office) about career opportunities and the requirements of various jobs.

D   SCHOOL MANAGEMENT

I   Interaction with teachers – parents – students:

CRITERIA	INDICATORS
Students, parents, teachers are taken seriously as bringers of ideas and are all motivated to perform specialized work or get involved.	• The administration sticks to its agreements. • Commitment is rewarded.
The administration tries to maintain a good working climate with students, teachers and parents. It possesses a high ability to motivate, which it uses.	• The administration is in principle prepared (and in reality most of the time) to participate in parents' association meetings in order to acquire the latest information. • It is there to witness school events. • The school administration is available for students, parents, teachers, and officials, and if necessary, arranges for a representative to do so.
The school administration possesses conflict-solving abilities and uses them on and between all levels (students, teachers, parents, and management personnel).	• The school administration does not behave at all passively when it perceives conflicts / conflicts are brought to its attention. • The school management can gives students, parents, teachers and management personnel con-structive feedback and is able to give praise. • In order to prevent possible conflicts, teachers, students and other people who are new to the school are familiarized with the rules, the school program, etc. There is an institutionalized procedure for this.
In the event of conflict the administration sees itself most of all as conflict moderator.	• The school administration determines the goal to be reached after the working out of the conflict. • It moderates the conflict solving process, does not prescribe or order any arbitrary solutions.

CRITERIA	INDICATORS
School partnership is practised.	• The school administration engages competent decision making help from parents, teachers, and possibly students. • It delegates responsibility and decision making power wherever they belong.

II Questions of substance and quality assurance

CRITERIA	INDICATORS
The school administration is the guarantor of the quality control process. The school administration has visions, ideas, and goals with regard to the school program. All work at the school is understood to be a process subject to permanent change.	• The school administration formulates its ideas clearly, but is also ready to alter or further develop them with students, teachers and parents.
Further education is highly valued.	• The principal is also open to further education; he or she encourages and demands the further education of teachers and administrative personnel. • It supports and encourages SCHILF measures.
The school administration endeavors to establish quality control measures by means of various instruments.	• The administration also requests feedback and processes it openly. • It pushes teachers to seek feedback from colleagues, students and parents. • The administration also assures quality assurance and improvement by means of monitoring.

CRITERIA	INDICATORS
The administration encourages the creative and innovative potential of its students and teachers.	• The administration allows for unusual activities, allows the trying out of new things and even puts up with mistakes without giving up right away. • The school administration provides resources for pedagogically useful initiatives. • In the writing of class subject allocation and schedule of classes pedagogical considerations have top priority.

III   Management and leadership quality

CRITERIA	INDICATORS
The school administration lets students, teachers, and parents know that it is prepared to run the school and to take on the basic responsibility thereof.	• The school administration reaches decisions quickly when this is required. • The administration does not put off various problems, but rather addresses them head on. • In order to realize certain tasks, projects, etc. clear and binding agreements on goals are made with all participants. • In the case of certain leadership tasks the administration also calls in teachers and informs everyone of this. • It does not delegate as a rule but only when necessary. The administration delegates the correct task to the correct person.

CRITERIA	INDICATORS
Conferences and meetings are organized properly, and the agenda is distributed in time.	• Conferences begin and end on time. • The subject (reason for!) a conference is generally known. • It is clear who is holding the meeting. • There is a sharing of responsibilities (moderating, protocol, etc.) moderation material, visuals. • The school administration avoids unnecessary general conferences and tables points on the agenda that can be better dealt with separately in small groups in smaller meetings (time saving!)
The school administration provides sufficient openly available information to students, teachers, parents and to the general public.	• There are letters to parents and an appointment calendar at the beginning of every semester / school year, special parents' information, obligatory class parents' evenings for all classes in autumn and in occasional circumstances bulletin boards for students possibly with class schedule substitute plan, cancelled office hours, etc. • The school administration takes care of creating and distributing current information material for prospective students (PR, school profile, customer information ...). SA also passes on interesting information to the media (The Press, TV, Homepage...) • The school administration is actively involved in the planning and carrying out of the "Open house" day.
The school administration draws a distinction between its essential and non-essential functions in conducting its work.	• The tasks of the administration team (school management, administration, representation, secretarial work, time schedule

CRITERIA	INDICATORS
The staff are also able to see these distinctions.	preparation, custodial work, class (home room) teacher administrational work, janitorial supervision, ...) are delegated in a clear way, so that there is no wasted energy due to an unclear division of responsibilities. • The school administration possesses sufficient knowledge of school regulations, so that the daily operation of the school can be maintained without problems and that decisions enjoy the appropriate level of certainty and don't have to be reversed by the school authorities.

IV   The school administrations supports the infrastructure needed for the work of students and teachers

CRITERIA	INDICATORS
The school administration takes care of the working conditions of teachers and students. That is to say it clearly takes care of the necessary steps in order to – secure space – renovate space – furnish time resources – upgrading of furniture – procurement of equipment – procurement of material	• The school administration provides money for experts, project organization, special acquisitions and the like by means of sponsors. • The school administration uses its contacts, experts in education, companies for career orientation, and rooms in order to organize conferences/pedagogical events. • The school administration has asked the time scheduling personnel to find a set time in the week when there are no classes to create a time for meetings that all can attend (for example Tuesday, 2:00 PM to 4:00 PM).

E PROFESSIONALISM AND HUMAN RESOURCE DEVELOPMENT

I The education and training offered by the school

CRITERIA	INDICATORS
The teachers and administrators address issues concerning their profession, reflect on their own practices, and endeavor to develop them further.	• Teachers and administrators are willing and able to get feedback form outside. • The feedback from outside becomes the basis for further (developmental) measures.
Using the state curriculum as a guide, areas of specialization are agreed upon, to which everyone can contribute and for which everyone feels responsible. (a common understanding about quality standards)	• The "school program" is there in writing and familiar to parents and students. • The compliance and effectiveness of agreements is tested at regular intervals.
The school and the individual teachers keep an eye on the current challenges confronting graduates.	• Contacts with institutions of higher education and with the business community and internships for teachers are used in order to increase the range of experience. • The knowledge acquired thereof is taken into account in the educational and training program of the school.

II   Measures for promoting professionalism

II. 1.   On an individual basis

CRITERIA	INDICATORS
In principle teachers are generally willing to learn and apply new things.	• Every teacher has his or her own personal program of further education. • The professional, methodological, didactic, and personal development is taken into account as is the ability to guide social processes in the classroom. • There is a balance between personal interests and school interests and school program.
The school administration promotes the individual continuing education of teachers and of the rest of the personnel.	• The continuing education in the interest of the school is supported financially.

II. 2. On a team basis

CRITERIA	INDICATORS
A regular, professional, structured exchange takes place with regard to pedagogical questions.	• There are subject as well as subject group meetings and meetings of the teachers of a particular class. • The collective planning and co-ordinating of on basis of subject and class is seen as part of the preparation work. • The co-operation is supported by organizational measures (for example, time slots in the schedule).
Within the teams there is agreements on goals and clear lines of responsibility.	• Meetings are organized are organized and conducted efficiently. • Training courses are used to improve the attitude and habits with regard to meetings.

II. 3. On the organizational and management level

CRITERIA	INDICATORS
There is a general training concept that corresponds to the goals and areas of specialization of the school.	• There are collective measures for continuing education for the entire school. The continuing education activities are related to the school program. • There is someone to co-ordinate the continuing education of teachers.
There is a functional division of tasks. Redundant activities and unclear lines of responsibility are avoided.	• The authority, responsibilities, and functions of the principal, administration, school representatives, student advisors, parents' representatives, secretaries, and custodians, are put down in writing, well known, and are utilized as a resource.
There are opportunities for continuing education in the field of school organization and management.	• The principal regularly participates in training seminars, when possible together with members of the staff. • The administration personnel receive training and continuing education.

III. Utilizing of resources and potential - Internal information management

CRITERIA	INDICATORS
The knowledge and ability of every individual is available to the school. Experience is passed on. For this there is organisational support.	• If is known among the faculty who has taken which course of continuing education. One is able to find out about their course content. • The principal and faculty members know what kind of specialized training and strengths each teacher has. These are valued and utilized. • New teachers are taught specifically about the special features of the school.

CRITERIA	INDICATORS
The school endeavors to learn from positive examples.	• The school maintains exchange with other schools – also on an international level.
The potential of the school at hand is utilized for the further development of instruction and advice from outside is called in occasionally.	• Everyone is aware what projects there are at school (for example, Toward a New Teaching Attitude, Toward Social Learning, LOB). • There is a contact person for each of these projects. • There are opportunities to obtain information about projects that one is not him or herself engaged in. • Projects are also open to "new comers". • There is a pool of materials that all teachers contribute to and make use of.

Karl Blüml is head of the Department for Higher Secondary Academic Schools in the Vienna School Board, Austria.

PART 7

INVOLVEMENT OF PUPILS AND PARENTS

CHAPTER 19

IMPROVING THE QUALITY OF EDUCATION THROUGH STRUCTURED DIALOGUE WITH PARENTS

Jackie Denis

Abstract

Parents are privileged discussion partners for schools as they are our clients. Consequently they are key agents for an ongoing review of our quality aims. We consider that it's only normal to question them about the quality of our services.
We didn't choose questionnaires to be filled in, but the formula of open debate between parents, teachers and school head.

The context: our school being a learning organisation

As in other sectors of society, our school also started reflecting upon the quality of its service a few years ago. We do this in a systematic way. We want to head towards a school where everyone, individually and as a group, wants to learn, towards a school that evolves towards a 'learning organisation'. We want to promote a learning attitude and self-reflection, to increase flexibility and to stimulate creativity on all levels. So we have to work on processes of permanent improvement that are the basis of continuous innovation. Recurring questions have to be: *What are we doing? Why? Can we do those things better? How can we do that?*

We have found inspiration in the EFQM-model (European Foundation for Quality Management), a model that improves quality through self-assessment. This means that we have to work with an analysis of our strong and weak points, specific objectives, feedback …

Our annual hearings

In our core business we present to pupils and parents which services we want to offer, and how we intend to do these. The relationships in which we want to realise our mission are also made explicit in our core business. Our own "Mode of Life" makes this clear to everyone involved in the school. This core business is the first realisation of our educational project and our mission statement.

In the conception of what we consider a learning organisation, it is important to know to what extent we really do what we promise to do. The best way to do this is to ask our 'customers', in this case the parents of our pupils. Therefore, we organise an annual hearing. Until now, we only have these hearings with parents because they made the choice to send their children to our school. We are also considering having hearings with pupils in the future.

An open debate

Because an open dialogue and consultation are key notions in our mission statement, we have opted deliberately for the formula of open debate during these hearings. So no questionnaires or statistics.

The strengths of this formula are evident. We have a round-table debate with different partners (parents, teachers, tutors and school management) who talk about different aspects of school life. Every participant listens to the others, questions can be asked, parents can express their concerns and the school can explain its policy.

It's very important to prevent the debate evolving into a discussion about particular cases or individual complaints. In this way, we get a real dialogue (which we don't get with questionnaires) with 'ordinary customers'. Parents, teachers and management learn to know and understand each other and can work together on the same project.

A dialogue with the 'average' parents

… and not with the members of parents' committee, because we already have regular contact with them and we know their points of view. These parents are involved in a constructive but critical way in our school project.

But it is also essential for us to hear the opinion of the 'ordinary' parents. As we organise 4 hearings a year (in 4 different levels), we can reach about 100 parents a year. 2 parents for each class are contacted at random, with attention to following features: they are not members of parents' committee, there are parents of boys and parents of girls (boys and girls often feel and see the school life in a different way); parents from villages nearby and further away (they have other kinds of problems and mostly other reasons for choosing our school).

A close co-operation with the parents' committee

Although the hearings are the school's initiative to meet the 'average' parents, the co-operation of the parents' committee is essential. Fortunately we have a very motivated and dynamic parents' committee.

In this case, the role of the members consists of contacting other parents by phone to invite them to participate in these hearings. They are the necessary go-betweens and their task is not very easy. Parents mostly don't react with enthusiasm about this kind of invitation. They are not interested when it doesn't concern their own individual situation, or they are afraid that everything they say will be used against their child. It's not easy for many of them to participate in a dialogue with the school about the strong and weak points. For the 'average' parent the barrier is still high, and particularly for those having children in the technical and vocational options. But even when they refuse to participate, they feel involved just because we call them and inform them about the initiative.

So, the members of the parents' committee have a very important role in changing school culture.

The first step: the announcement

On the last day of the first term (December), all the parents get a letter in which the annual hearing is announced and explained. So they are already informed if they are contacted by the parents' committee.

Letter enclosed.

sint-ursula
INSTITUUT

Bosstraat 9 2861 Onze-Lieve-Vrouw-Waver
Tel. (015)76 78 60 Fax (015)76 01 32 E-mail info@st-ursula-instituut.be

Onze-Lieve-Vrouw-Waver, 20 December 2001

Care for quality 2002

Dear parents

It is becoming a tradition in our care for quality. Every year we invite four groups of parents to talk with teachers, co-ordinators, and school board about the functioning of our school. The subjects of the meeting are the learning and well-being of your child at school, the organisation and communication.
This is not a traditional parents' meeting to talk about individual problems of your child.

As a school, we annually ask the opinions and advice of the parents in a systematic way to learn more about the quality of our services.
On such a meeting we learn what we do well, but also what we could do better. So we can correct these points. We also get the opportunity to explain what we are doing. Parents as well as school can express their expectations and worries.
We will make a complete report of each meeting, which will be given to all the participating parents and all the teachers.
In previous years we learned a lot from these meetings and we have adapted a lot of things: school reports, information meetings about educational trips and integrated tests (3rd grade), parents' meetings with class teachers in 2nd and 3rd grade …

To organise these four evenings we can count on the help of the parents' committee. Members of the parents' committee invite other parents for the meetings. They contact at random parents from each class. So each class and study option will be represented on such a meeting.
Parents who agreed to participate will get a letter with more information in January.

The four groups are:
- parents of pupils in the 1st year
- parents of pupils in the 2nd year
- parents of pupils in the 2nd grade
- parents of pupils in the 3rd grade

Each group consists of 25 to 30 parents, 2 to 4 teachers, a staff member of the pupils' secretariat, the co-ordinator and the head of the educational department.

You will notice that we attach great importance to an open dialogue between parents and school. We would like to ask you to consider your co-operation if you are contacted before long.
We thank you for the confidence that you have in our school and we count on your co-operation to help us in deserving that confidence.

Yours truly,

J. Denis
Head educational department

M. Hofkens
Principal

The Treasure Within

Tweede graad

Bosstraat 9 2861 Onze-Lieve-Vrouw-Waver
Tel. (015)76 78 60 Fax (015)76 01 32 E-mail info@st-ursula-instituut.be

Parents' meeting on Tuesday 5 February 2002

Dear parents,

You accepted our invitation for a meeting between parents and our school. The purpose of this meeting is to talk about your experiences about learning and school life in the second grade. Some members of the parents' committee and teachers prepare the agenda of the meeting. We would like to give you some questions in order to prepare the meeting. If you could go through the questions with your son or daughter you could also include his or her opinion.

1. **The second grade**
    - how did you experience the step from the 2nd to the 3rd year?
    - how did you experience the step from the 3rd to the 4th year?
    - what do you think of the support for the choice of study options?

2. **Learning in the second grade**
    - what do you think of the school diary as a means of help for planning, reports, exams, study pressure ...
    - does the meeting with the teachers of you child meet your expectations (time, frequency, organisation)
    - what do you think of the tutoring system?
    - what do you think of the extra-curricular activities (school trips, sports day, theatre, film, projects ...)

3. **School life in the second grade**
    - What do you think of the participation of the pupils in every day school life. Do you think pupils should have more to say? Do you know there is a pupils' council? Do you know there is a sports council?
    - What can the school do for more social and cultural engagement of the pupils? How do you think this can be organised?
    - Does the new cafeteria system work properly? Are there enough activities?

4. **Communication**
    - Is there enough communication towards the parents? (School diary, letters, activities, rules ...)
    - Do you have the impression that you know what is going on at school? Are there enough possibilities to contact the school?
    - How does your son/daughter feel at school? Can he talk to someone in school about problems?
    - Does this meeting meet your expectations? Suggestions?
    - Do you know the enquiry possibilities in our school? Do you know whom to contact?
    - Do you know about the parents' magazine SCH-ouder? What do you think of it?

5. **Miscellany**
    If you want to raise other points please contact 015/76 78 62 or e-mail hvanuytsel@hotmail.com

H. Van Uytsel
Coordinator

J. Denis
head educational department

Chapter 19: Improving the quality of education

Preliminary questionnaire

Parents who have agreed to participate get a preliminary questionnaire in January. This questionnaire is drawn up by teachers, co-ordinators (middle management) and some members of the parents' committee. It concerns 3 or 4 main themes of our core business. The questionnaire enables participants to prepare the debate and makes that some parents discuss school life with their children: this discussion on itself is already very useful.

Above is an example for the middle years of secondary education.

Organisation of the hearing

Short plenary meeting
- Welcome by school management
- Purpose of the evening: starting from the questionnaire we want to draw up a list of the strong and weak points of the school regarding learning and school life, organisation and communication
- Some basic rules are explained: this is not an individual parents' meeting. Personal problems, difficulties with an individual teacher are not a subject to talk about.

Group work
- The parents are divided into 4 groups, each with one teacher or tutor and one member of the parents' committee. They lead the discussion and make a report.
- Each point of the questionnaire is discussed in group: What *is good? What can be improved? What is not clear? Is there a problem of communication?* The teacher gives extra information about school life and answers questions.
- Advantages of the group work: all the parents can say what they think, the commitment is very high, and the barrier is low.
- Each group selects two items for the plenary session.

Plenary session
- The selected items are discussed one by one in a structured debate, led by the headteachers.
- The co-ordinator keeps the records.
- Teachers and school management are a panel that enters into dialogue with the parents.

Follow-up

Report
We draw up a complete report of each hearing. The two parts are reported, so nothing that was said in the small groups is lost, and also the plenary session with more difficult and touchy items is recorded in detail. All the interventions and readings from the school management are reported as well. Every participant and every staff member concerned gets a report.

Discussion of the report
After reading the report, groups of teachers, together with their co-ordinator, can start an internal debate. *Are we doing the right things? Do we do them well? What can be improved?* From the report some items are kept which will have to be improved by the following year. Since there are 4 different hearings for different age groups, there are different groups of teachers working on different items. The report is also discussed in a meeting of the parents' committee. The school management also reports about the items the teachers want to improve. The parents' committee reports in their magazine. In this way everyone in the school knows about the hearings and their results.

Some tangible outcomes

The list is not exhaustive but gives an idea of the most important changes or improvements after 5 years of consultation of the parents about the quality of our services.

In the junior years of secondary school, the pupils work together with the tutor on learning to learn and independent learning. They are supported in their choice of study options. What about the continuity of that process in the second grade? Parents consider planning as being a major problem of students.
The tutoring-hour can't be organised. Nevertheless, from this year (2001-2002) on, the pupils in the third year are working on planning. They also reflect on the choice they made. Two co-ordinators designed workbooks and planned different activities together with the team of tutors. The support for choice has been reconsidered for the pupils of the fourth year. In the future, we want to work on reading strategies with the fourth year and on learning styles with the senior pupils.

Before 2000, the parents were not so happy with the organisation of the parents-meeting in the first term because of a lack of privacy and long waiting times.
On Friday afternoon, just before the Christmas holidays, the parents can meet the tutor individually in a classroom by appointment. In January the parents can

meet subject teachers. All the parents meetings are now organised in the same way for all age levels.

We also became aware of the parents' need to know the tutor and the other parents, the need for extra information about report systems, about specific problems and issues related to the age and to the specific year to come etc.
So we started with class meetings at the beginning of the school year: parents and tutor can talk about relationships within the class group, about organisation and school life, about everything but school results. Now, parents know the tutor, they are informed about the year to come, they feel involved. They can better interpret and understand the information they get from their child and – most of all – they can guide and help her/him in a complementary way.

Parents have to wait until November to see the first school results. Sometimes it is too late.
First, we changed the timing of the report: daily work results are no longer communicated at the same time as exam results, but earlier, before the exams.
Second, we introduced a sheaf of subject charts. All the pupils' work that contributes to the result is noted on a subject chart. These charts are gathered in a booklet. The parents can ask at any moment for the booklet of their child to see how he/she is working.

School trips to foreign countries are expensive.
We inform the pupils and the parents a long time in advance, so that they can begin a saving scheme.

In the senior years pupils have to perform tasks by means of group work. Sometimes pupils who live far away from each other work in the same group. It is difficult to meet out of school time.
From next year on, pupils can work in a "learning centre", that will be open also on Wednesday afternoon and each day until five p.m.

In the technical and vocational education, the pupils have a "GIP" (integrated test). Parents are not well informed about it.
From this year on, we organise a parents' meeting to explain what the "GIP" is about. What do we expect from our pupils? What about the timing, the evaluation, communication of results?

Pupils in technical and vocational education feel discriminated. Their classrooms are in a separate building. Twice a week they have a school day of eight hours of lessons instead of seven. Why can't they have a similar schedule as the pupils in general education?
Concerning the classrooms, the classes have been mixed since two years. We see to it that all the pupils are involved in activities in the same way: from this year on they also participate in a school trip to a foreign country. The schedule cannot be changed.

Examples of recurring requests that cannot be complied with

Can pupils other than those in the Latin-classes be admitted to the Greece trip?
Can schoolbags of the younger students be made less heavy?
Why doesn't the school organise a weekly tutoring-hour in all grades?

Conclusion

We notice that this form of self-assessment on the school level stimulates self-reflection, internal debate and the taking of initiative among teachers.

The hearing formula is a tool to help us get rid of the 'us and them feeling', and to enhance mutual understanding. Teachers feel that parents want to participate in a positive, constructive way, they are not just there to criticise. We noticed that, unlike in the beginning, parents are very understanding and subtle. They are critical and ask questions, but they are not aggressive, on the contrary. This gives the teachers a good feeling. Parents (those participating in the hearings as well as the members of the committee) feel that their remarks are taken seriously and that they can make things change.

In the beginning, parents and teachers confronted each other and experienced the other party as threatening. Today these hearings are considered as a normal course of events and they are not questioned anymore. Most participating teachers see these hearings as a positive experience. Every year we try to find new teachers to participate in these hearings so that more teachers get involved.

We are convinced that this kind of participation leads to more involvement and to a shared responsibility.

What parents say at the end of the evening

'A very open and interesting debate.'
' Other parents have the same questions as me!'
'I learned a lot tonight.'
'A very courageous initiative!'
'Too many questions to discuss.'
'I hope the school will take our input into account.'

Epilogue

During a workshop in which the project on improving the quality of education through structured dialogue with the parents was presented, the following questions and issues were raised:

– Where did the initial stimulus come from? It was explained that it had come from the evident needs and difficulties of the new intake that always experienced problems settling in. This seemed a very good place to start.

– A question was asked about how to make the groups effective. This involved good group management e.g. of not allowing some parents to dominate and ensuring that the discussion was both retroactive (evaluating the impact of previous decisions) as well as forward –looking and planning. The school set the agenda as a starting point.

– As regards parents' complaints, this was a way to mediate complaints but more important was the culture of openness, helped by a very active group of supportive parents.

– A question was asked about the extent to which the parental representation was in fact truly representative of all social strata and e.g. ethnic groups. It was agreed that it is harder for some parents to participate but it was hoped that these parents would feel able to reach out to those parents who did offer themselves. This did need monitoring it was agreed. Every effort had been made to reach out to parents e.g. with posters which said 'Bring a parent to school'!

In conclusion, it was stressed that the underlying purposes were to make partnership a reality and to work in this partnership to improve the quality of schooling. It was considered that this was one of the '1000 ways' (Jones' key note speech) in which a school could improve by stopping to think and discuss improvement together.

Jackie Denis is the head of the educational department of St.-Ursula Instituut, O.L.V.-Waver, Belgium.

The Treasure Within

CHAPTER 20

FEEDBACK FROM PARENTS OF SCHOOL LEAVERS TO THE SCHOOL

HOW DO YOU RATE OUR SCHOOL?

Peter Van de Moortel

Some general ideas

The motivation

'At noon or at the end of the school day as a head teacher you notice that several parents are waiting to take their child back home. Why are they coming so early, why do they talk so vividly or animated and … what are they talking about? Sometimes I want to be a fly to hear what they say about the school. I am interested in their feedback on how the school operates. What image do they have about school life? Are we doing a good job? What is their opinion of our educational organisation? Let's listen to our customers ….'

In the framework of 'self-monitoring' and the 'learning' school, the idea of organising parental feedback about the school has become a target. As I write this article I realise that the process of arriving at the stage where we are now was never structured or even planned. It was imbedded in the 'flow' of the interplay between teachers, parents committee and myself as architect of the pedagogical and didactic framework in school. The match that lit the process was a small event: I was at a conference of 'schools involved in local communities' where a professor said: 'keep it simple and just do it'. This will be more rewarding than waiting for the ideal and perfectly worked out model.' We were mentally ready so we embarked upon a never ending story …

Aims, goals and targets: Why did we organise feedback?

Reflecting on your activities is a learning experience. It makes you think about questions you want to ask, issues you want to have feedback on. So a discussion starts between school management (head teacher) and teachers on the process and content of the feedback. This thinking process can turn your work into a more conscious process. Creating the questionnaire is in some ways as important as obtaining the results.

Achieving participation in the organisation of the school and contribution to the school climate by giving parents a voice is also one of our aims. Parents are the prime educators of their children so they can give valuable feedback on the role of the school in this process.

Improving school quality in general is the final goal. Working on the strengths, weaknesses, opportunities and threats, improving the interplay between what you do in school and what parents think you are doing is part of quality management. Working with feedback is working as a 'learning organisation'. It is learning with the participation of all stakeholders.

Basic conditions: What type of school culture is required?

It is important that the school itself thinks of the school as a changing environment. In the long run, change is the only thing we are sure of. Schools are no longer the only place where knowledge is acquired. The concept of a 'learning organisation' is essential for success in the future.

Open-mindedness and flexibility are essential in a school environment.

Case study: What happened in our school?

Our first feedback module was aimed at parents of pupils leaving the school at the age of 12 years, the end of primary education.

We are now developing several other modules: pupils' feedback to teachers, as self-reflection to teachers, teachers to the organisation, ...

Some general characteristics of our model

Simple:
We think the feedback form should be simple, straightforward and have a limited set of questions. So we avoid academic language and we keep the questionnaire short.

Adaptable:
The content of the questionnaire should be adaptable so questions and statements can be easily changed. Also the timing and the content of different modules should be flexible and adjustable to every local situation.

Computer aided:
Computers are tools which help us simplify the job. When changes are necessary, retyping is minimal. Storing the results and creating reports to the team and participants is easier with the computer. But most of all, the computer can help us to visualise the results so they are easier to comprehend and

discussion afterwards is more focussed. This is why we use a computer generated spreadsheet with easy to comprehend charts.

Thought provoking:
The construction of the questionnaire is designed to be thought- provoking. There are 3 essential parts to the questionnaire: in the first part we provide information about the questionnaire. In this part we explain why we set up this feedback, what we can do with it, how to fill in, why now, etc. The second part contains a series of polarised statements about several school matters on which we are seeking feedback. The polarisation of the statements is very important because it makes people think in two different directions (extreme possibilities). They are asked to mark the statement that matches their personal opinion best. This polarisation opens the mind. The answers to this section are easy to categorise and visualise at a later stage. The third part is a section with open questions. Here people can write freely and express personal opinions and make suggestions. These answers are more difficult to summarise but give more feedback content-wise.

Learning by doing and a bottom up approach.
The content of the questionnaire is changed on a regular basis. The questions are not fixed and can be adapted to current issues. The questions are fieldwork based and derive from our local experiences. They are not based on academic teachings. This makes them strong and recognisable but may lack a scientific basis to a certain degree.

Some implementation ideas

1   Steps in the production of the questionnaire
    1.1 Introduce the idea with the teachers' team. Explain why you are organising the feedback, start a brainstorming session to produce polarised and open questions. Discuss the right words to use.
    1.2 Work the ideas into a proposal and have the teachers provide feedback on this first draft. Adapt and improve the first model.
    1.3 Learn from experience. Do a trial run. Think about appropriate timing. For example in our school we organised the parents feedback at the end of elementary education (after 9 years school education). We do this because by this time parents have an overview of a completed part of the educational process.
    1.4 After the trial run, adjust and improve the questionnaire. Make it into a continuing process.
2   Steps in the use of feedback modules
    2.1 Inform the target group of the aim of the feedback.
    2.2 Set up a schedule for distribution, filling in and bringing back the questionnaire.
    2.3 Enter the results, use the computer software to generate a report.
    2.4 Crystallise the main discussion topics. It is important here not to focus only on the weak or negative points but stress the positive.
    2.5 Report the results back to the people who need the feedback. This can be the whole school team or certain individuals depending on the topic

that needs the focus.

2.6 During the discussion it is important to examine the content of the responses to distil from this a target and an action plan. Also put into words how some of these targets can be achieved and how you plan to follow up.

Modules and target groups

Our first module is aimed at parents of children who are leaving the school.
Below we present the fully worked out version of the questionnaire with some screen shots.

Introduction

Dear parents,
Your son or daughter is leaving our school. Some of you have had your children in our school for the past 9 years. We realise that school has an important influence on both success in school career and continued education at home. That's why we ask you to give us some feedback. We appreciate an open communication and we can learn a lot from your comments about our school. How do you rate the school?
Please fill in the questionnaire. We assure you that your answers will be confidential and treated anonymously.

Questionnaire

Polarised section

Our school is …	2	1	0	1	2	Our school is…
A disciplined school						A school with a lot of freedom
A progressive school						A school behind the times
An active school						A boring school
A religious school						A non-religious school
A school for everyone						An elitist school
An orderly school						A disorderly school
A small school						A large school
A school with a child focus						A school without a child focus
A warm school						A characterless school
An open school						A closed school
A school with team spirit						An school for individuals
A school with a unique character						An ordinary school
A school focused on academic achievement alone						A school that aims at total development
A school with good child guidance						A school with minimal child guidance

An expensive school						A cheap school
A school with a high entrance barrier						A school with a low entrance barrier
A school using good open communication						A school using formal communication
A school for weak pupils						A school for strong pupils
A welcoming school						A less welcoming school
A school with good results						A school with bad results
A school with a good teaching approach						A school with a bad teaching approach
A school with a large package of services such as catering, nursery, reception						A school with a limited package of services
A school with a good infrastructure						A school with a poor infrastructure
A school with a good homework-approach						A school with a bad homework-approach
A school with a good pedagogical approach						A school with a bad pedagogical approach
A school with a modern approach						A traditional school

Questionnaire

Open questions

– What suggestions would you like to offer the school?

– What has been your most positive experience?

– Did you have negative experiences? Please explain.

– Would you recommend our school to other parents? Why?

Screenshots of inventory and charts

#	ONZE SCHOOL IS ...	1+	0-	0+	1+	ONZE SCHOOL IS ...	#
4	een gelovige school	1,39				en ongelovige school	4
5	een school voor allen	1,45				een elitaire school	5
6	een ordelijke school	1,14				een wanordelijke school	6
7	een kleine school		0,35			een grote school	7
8	een kindgerichte school	1,26				een niet kindgerichte school	8
9	een warme school	1,41				een anonieme school	9
10	een open school	1,23				een gesloten school	10
11	een teamgerichte school		0,94			een individugerichte school	11
12	een school met eigen gezicht	1,06				een alledaagse school	12
13	een school enkel voor 'punten' en hoge scores op rapport				1,05	een school die totale ontplooiing nastreeft	13
14	een school met goede kindbegeleiding	1,23				een school met weinig kindbegeleiding	14
15	een dure school		0,29			een goedkope school	15
16	een school met hoge drempel			0,20		een school met lage drempel	16
17	een school met vlotte communicatie		0,96			een school met stroeve communicatie	17
18	een school voor zwakke leerlingen			0,33		een school voor sterke leerlingen	18
19	een school met goed onthaal		0,96			een school met zwak onthaal	19
20	een school met goede resultaten	1,08				een school met zwakke resultaten	20
21	een school met goede onderwijsaanpak	1,10				een school met zwakke onderwijsaanpak	21
22	een school met voldoende diensten als opvang, maaltijden, aanbod, ...	1,43				een school met zwak dienstenpakket	22
23	een school met goede infrastructuur (gebouwen)		0,94			een school met slechte infrastructuur	23
24	een school met goed huiswerkbeleid		0,98			een school met slecht huiswerkbeleid	24
25	een school met goed opvoedingsklimaat	1,33				een school met slecht opvoedingsklimaat	25
26	een vernieuwingsgerichte school	1,12				een traditionele school	26
27							27
28							28
29							29
30							30

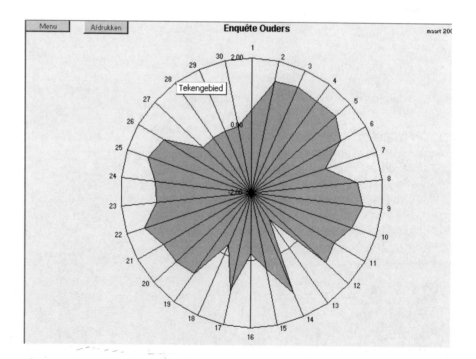

The Treasure Within

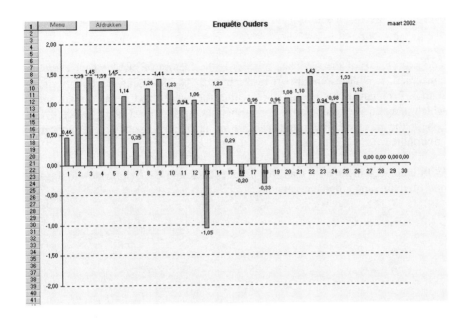

Note:
While using the first module (feedback from parents with children leaving the school) we realised the possibility of producing modules for other target groups or relating to hot topics.

The following modules are under construction:
1   Feedback from pupils to teachers: after each school year we could organise feedback on pupils topics such as teacher-pupil relations, class climate, pupil and class results, school aspects, etc.
2   Feedback from teachers to teachers based on teacher function profiles. As a mirror for teachers.
3   Feedback from teachers to school organisation on topics such as working conditions, school culture, teambuilding, leadership, teaching style, school effectiveness linking aims to results, etc.
4   Feedback concerning stress management.
5   Feedback concerning change management.

Conclusions

What we have learned is that designing the questionnaire and generating the report are rather easy. However, coming up with the appropriate questions is a very useful exercise and in a way acts as a personal survey of what you think is important for your school. That's the reason why we see the questionnaire as an open adaptable system. It makes one think and reflect.

The difficult part is to focus on what to do with the results. The challenge here is to find the right balance during the design of the action plan. In my opinion not every point needs an action plan. Awareness alone is often enough of a spark to instigate a change (if needed!).

The main result of the feedback process is the feeling of involvement everyone concerned. It is an essential part in the process of improving the quality of the school. It enhances both team spirit within the school and parents involvement which is again very stimulating for further action. Finally it is the children who benefit the most by living and learning in an open, respectful and supporting environment.

With thanks to my school team for the feedback and the help in developing the questionnaire and computer version.

Peter Van de Moortel is Head Teacher of Zedelgem De Leeuw Primary School, Belgium.

CHAPTER 21

STUDENT
DEMOCRACY

OR ARE STUDENTS AGENTS OF CHANGE?

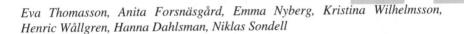

Eva Thomasson, Anita Forsnäsgård, Emma Nyberg, Kristina Wilhelmsson,
Henric Wållgren, Hanna Dahlsman, Niklas Sondell

Background

Schools in Sweden are based on democratic values, as is our society. I quote
from the curriculum for the non-compulsory school system LPF94:

"Democracy forms the basis of the national school system. The education act
(1985:1100) stipulates that all school activity shall be carried out in accordance
with fundamental democratic values and that each and everyone working in
school shall encourage respect for the intrinsic value of each person as well as
for the environment we all share (Chapter 1 §2 and 9). The school has the
important task of imparting, instilling and forming in pupils those values on
which our society is based. The inviolability of human life individual freedom
and integrity, the equal value of all people, equality between women and men
and solidarity with the weak and vulnerable are all values that the school shall
represent and impart. In accordance with the Christian tradition and Western
humans, this is achieved by fostering in the individual a sense of justice,
generosity of spirit, tolerance and responsibility. Education in schools shall be
non-denominational. The task of the school is to encourage all pupils to discover
their own uniqueness as individuals and thereby actively participant in social life
by giving of their best in responsible freedom."

At Sundsta-Älvkullegymnasiet in Karlstad, Sweden, we want to ensure that our students get an education based on democratic values. Our way of trying to improve this development is to have the students of the school formally organised in a students' council. The students' council is elected once a year at an annual meeting where every student at the school is represented by a class elector. The students' council participates in the school's development on different levels together with the staff and the head masters. Sundsta-Älvkullegymnasiet is an upper secondary school located in the mid-west of Sweden. The 2500 students are attending a variety of national programmes such as for example the social science programme, the natural science programme, the media programme, the health programme.

Why student democracy?

We all live in a democratic society. Therefore this should also be obvious in schools where students spend most of their days and are getting their education. With student democracy the students gets a basic democratic education that will be very important and useful in their forthcoming lives. We are convinced that if students get the knowledge of how to improve their education and are trusted to participate in the development of the school, they grow with the responsibility.

When they get to know their democratic rights they begin to reflect upon their environment. One aspect of student democracy is that the students learn to be critical while searching for new and different ways of shaping their education.

This way of working demands a lot of respect, with the respect for other people's opinions we learn to co-operate. The most important conclusion of this is that student democracy prepares students in a realistic way for adult life.

The school plan for upper secondary schools of Karlstad

Vision
School in Karlstad is a meeting-place, where people will grow and develop to build tomorrow's society. The school experience will lead to an increase in the students' confidence in their own learning, and their desire to continue to learn.

Operational goals
General
The guiding principle for all school-related operations is to create as favourable conditions as possible for students' learning and development. The students' best will always come first.

School will provide students with the best conditions for developing into democratic citizens with good knowledge and the ability to put it into practice. All students will be supported in their personal development regardless of sex, age and cultural or social background.

In order for students to incorporate the values on which the democratic society is built, they must be *treated* as colleagues in a school where they are actively trained in influencing and taking responsibility for their job situation.

School will be a social and cultural meeting-place, in which the working methods and the social interaction between people are crucial to the knowledge, values and qualities the students develop. The school actively repudiates all forms of violence, racism and abusive treatment. The school promotes health and the environment, and therefore opposes all types of drug use.

In a changing world, the working methods used at school must be continuously reviewed. All colleagues will develop in their roles in order to meet the demands and challenges of the future.

What is student democracy?

This is how it is defined by the education board in Karlstad.

Pupil Democracy Plan for Upper Secondary Schools in Karlstad
Goals
Pupils will be involved and feel a sense of responsibility at school.
Pupils will be able to actively control their study situation.
Pupils will be educated in the fundamental principles of democracy.

Pupil influence - general
All schools will have functioning forums such as Pupil Councils/boards and class/mentor committees.
Pupils will be involved in developing the school's local work plan.
The school's local work plan will show how pupil influence, involvement and responsibility are increased through various forums.
Pupil Councils raise issues for discussion on the class/mentor committees.
The class/mentor committee should meet weekly. An agenda should be kept and submitted to the school management and Pupil Council for follow-up/measures.

Head teacher – Pupil Council
The board of the Pupil Council will participate in budget work and be updated about changes on a continuous basis.
The head teacher and Pupil Council will meet at least once a fortnight, and inform each other about past and planned events.

Pupils – personnel
Pupils and personnel will be considered colleagues and should therefore treat each other with respect.
The school management will investigate and follow up pupils' views on personnel and the working environment.

Pupil representatives
Pupil Council representatives will be educated in school issues for their assignments. Pupil Council representatives will be involved when new posts are

filled at the school. Pupil representatives are entitled to teacher-led lessons to compensate for those they miss due to assignments. Pupil representatives will receive certificates from the head teacher for their assignments.

In lessons

The mentors/form teachers will present the Pupil Democracy Plan to the class and discuss the contents. The teacher is obliged to present programme goals, course goals and grading criteria. The teacher and pupils will jointly discuss the structure of the course, content and work methods. The teacher will take into account the pupils' requests for varied tuition and alternative teaching aids. Pupil-led work methods will be stimulated, and pupils encouraged to increasingly seek and evaluate information themselves. The teacher will, in dialogue with the individual pupil, evaluate study results ahead of awarding grades.

Teaching will be adapted to the individual: as far as possible, pupils who are willing and able will have the chance to pursue studies beyond the standard curriculum, and pupils with studying difficulties will receive help and support.

Knowledge can take the form of facts, proficiency, understanding or in-depth familiarity – not exclusively one or the other form.

Evaluation

The school's work will be evaluated on a continuous basis, and the pupils' views are important in all aspects of evaluation. At the end of the course, the teacher and pupils will evaluate the tuition and discuss the results. Pupils will be encouraged to express views on the tuition they receive. Criticism and suggestions for change will not be allowed to have negative repercussions of any kind. The school management will continuously inform the Pupil Council's board of the various evaluations carried out at the school, and discuss the evaluation results.

The Upper Secondary Education Board

The Upper Secondary Education Board's working committee will convene to hold discussions with each Pupil Council at least twice a term. The Board's Sponsors will meet the Pupil Council board and representatives continuously for information and discussion. The Pupil Councils are the official referral body to the Upper Secondary Education Board. The Pupil Councils' chairpersons and deputy chairpersons will meet the Secondary Education Director at least four times a term, to be informed about decisions and their follow-up. Pupil representatives will be involved in recruitment for management positions. Pupils will receive free school dinners and access to free teaching aids. Pupil representatives will be involved whenever the municipality's school plan is revised. Observance of the Pupil Democracy Plan will be monitored annually.

The Pupil Democracy Plan will be reviewed at least every three years.

How establish student democracy?

The establishment of student democracy requires time, commitment and patience.

It is also a necessity to have an ongoing discussion concerning democracy and democratic values.

How does a democratic society work? What privileges and obligations does democracy bring? What do students need to learn in order to become active citizens, finding it important to maintain a democratic dynamic society?

How does student democracy improve quality in school?

We think that when you are being involved and have the possibility to affect the school environment, as a student, you feel secure.

Several surveys show that security improves the quality in school.

How is student democracy established?

The establishment of student democracy requires time, commitment and patience.

It is also a necessity to have an ongoing discussion concerning democracy and democratic values.

How does a democratic society work? What privileges and obligations does democracy bring? What do students need to learn in order to become active citizens, finding it important to maintain a democratic dynamic society?

So, start by convincing the school board and the teachers that student democracy is a matter of course. Without their support it will be impossible. Student democracy is about mutual respect and it is based upon the fact that everyone at school has a positive attitude towards it.

Once the school board and the teachers are convinced it is time to involve the students. Start by discussing what democracy is. How does a democratic society work? What does it take from a person to live in a democratic society? What privileges and obligations does democracy bring? What do you need to learn to become an active citizen in a democratic society?

Then transfer these conditions to the school. What does democracy mean in the teaching and in the classroom? What does democracy mean for the encouragement of students' initiative? What does democracy mean for the possibility of discussion and argumentation?

A great deal of questions will probably be raised and with the encouragement from the teachers the students will understand the advantages of student democracy. But it is going to take time. You will have to take one step at a time. The introduction of a students' council and a student board will come eventually – when you are ready for it.

And remember, even if you feel like you are not making any progress, do not give up. Change takes time, so be patient.

From the curriculum for the non-compulsory school system LPF94:

"It is not itself sufficient that education imparts knowledge of fundamental democratic values. It must also be carried out using democratic working methods and develop the pupils ability and willingness to take personal responsibility and participate actively in civic life. Opportunities for pupils to exercise influence over their learning and take responsibility for their studies assumes that the school clarifies the goals for education, its contents and working forms, as well as the rights and obligations that pupils have."

Our organisation

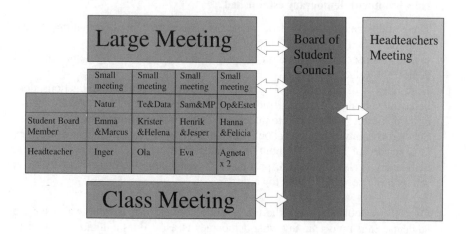

Eva Thomasson is Principal, Anita Forsnåsgård is a teacher, Emma Nyberg, Kristina Wilhelmsson, Henric Wållgren, Hanna Dahlsman and Niklas Sondell are pupils at Sundsta Älvkullegymnasiet Upper secondary school, Karlstad, Sweden.

PART 8

THE PROCESS OF LEARNING AND TEACHING

CHAPTER 22

HOW TO MAP UNDERSTANDING

Anna-Lena N Groth

The purpose

The purpose of the developmental work aims to visualize and to create increased understanding of how teachers and head teachers lead pupils and teachers respectively in learning about teaching and learning. Data collecting, within this project, will be used as a starting point for a dialogue about the task of leading learning and to create a deepened understanding of the mission.

Background

Karlstad – a municipality with the ambition to create a learning organization

The municipality of Karlstad has an ambition to develop pre-school and school into a learning organization. The ambition and the definition of a learning organization is expressed like this in the management philosophy of the organization:

"A school is a learning organization when it is capable of creating, obtaining and spreading knowledge and moreover has the ability to change its behaviour as a consequence of new knowledge and new insights. But a learning organization is not an abstract phenomenon – it consists of and is developed by its participants."

The foundation of a learning organization, for personal learning as well as for the learning of the organization, is the everyday experience of the practitioners. From the staff's experience knowledge is developed which later forms the basis for a different way of acting to get a better result. Therefore, every pre-school and all other schools in Karlstad are supposed to, on an annual basis, report to the board of the directorate not only what results they have achieved and how they have done this, but also what general conclusions and learning have been reached and how this could be used in a developmental way.

Understanding – a central concept

Understanding is a central concept in the learning organization. Understanding can mean various things depending on how you use or interpret the word. Understanding can mean that you acknowledge the existence of something, often followed by sympathy. An example of this is that you sympathize with teachers' complex mission of today. Understanding can also mean that you can assimilate a deeper meaning of different ideas and theories. Here is an illustrating example from the report Lärande ledare (2001):

"Does the head teacher read the curriculum like you read an information sheet at the opera – to understand the story – or does the head teacher read the curriculum to be able to participate on stage, which calls for a deeper understanding of the context of the words and also an understanding for what you can read between the lines? To read the curriculum 'to be able to be on stage' implies understanding the essence of the fundamental expressions."

In a learning organization *understanding the mission* forms the basis for the continuous learning. A distinction is made here between understanding the work and understanding the mission. Understanding the work has to do with how I understand the relationships between cause and effect and this is affected by the way I understand the mission. How I understand what essence I put into the formulation of the curriculum affects my understanding and action at work.

Teachers' and head teachers' learning

In a learning organization, learning from experience is the most important starting-point for learning and developing. But to become experienced and to learn from experience is not the same thing. To learn I need to become aware of and challenge my existing ideas. My new ideas lead to a different way of acting which leads to new experience. To have a reflecting attitude is decisive when it comes to deal with experiences you get.

Practitioners in an organization responsible for children's learning need continuous learning and development themselves. The head teacher's most important assignment is to lead the learning through dialogue with practitioners. The most important assignment for the head of the administration of education will then be to lead head teachers' learning.

The purpose of the development work

The school inspectors' assignment aims to visualize and to create increased understanding of how teachers and head teachers lead pupils and teachers respectively in learning about teaching and learning. Data collecting, within this project, will be used as a starting point for a dialogue about the assignment of leading learning and to create a deepened understanding of the mission.

Method/Accomplishment

As to the method for the assignment, qualitative interviews was chosen. This was done because both this technique and the mapping technique are designed to elicit teachers' and head teachers' own ideas and thoughts. The intention is that all head teachers and approximately 5-7 teachers within each pre-school and school area will be interviewed. This makes a total of 51 head teachers and 105 teachers.

The interviews are run individually at each school with a starting-point in certain questions. One of the questions is shown in the form of a graphic mind-map. The mind-map has its theoretical background in constructivism and figure theory about teaching and development and can be seen as a graphic representation of an individual's idea of a certain phenomenon. Letting the interviewee create a graphic mind-map helps deepening the interview as well as making the interviewed person's conceptional world clearer and more complete. The conception given by the individual is however connected to the actual time and the actual situation. The construction of the mind-map is followed by questions aiming to illustrate, explain and strengthen the map. The questions aim to identify underlying causes for comprehension. One of the questions is meant to shed light upon the point at which understanding is turned into action by teachers and head teachers.

The interview starts with a couple of question areas designed to highlight certain background factors. The answers to these open questions are written down in a traditional way. The first questions aim to make contact between the interviewer and the interviewee but also to collect information about contextual factors. The interview continues with the question: "What does it mean to you to lead learning?" answered with the interviewee and the interviewer together constructing the mind-map. First, the interviewee writes a couple of key words on small notes and attaches them to a bigger piece of paper. After that he/she is asked to prioritize, link together and/or group the words in a meaningful way. The purpose of this is to make the interviewee create a whole out of the small parts. Next step in the interview is a conversation where the interviewer is supposed to try to understand the meaning of the map. The interviewee explains how he/she thinks with the help from the key words and the interviewer writes word by word on the map what he/she thinks is the essence of what is said. The interviewee can see his/her words "grow" and realizes that certain connections and prioritizing may not always be obvious for the interviewer. Every mind-map is unique and different from the others. At last, the interviewee is allowed to make necessary corrections and confirm the result.

Every interview is summed up in a text to be read and confirmed by the interviewee. Collected material is supposed to be studied to see if there are any connections, patterns or differences in the teachers' and head teachers' understanding and factors that are important for this understanding. Feedback on results in different schools is given continuously to each leader team and partial reports of the project are shown in the annual quality report of the municipality. The whole project will be presented in a final report.

Result

So far, 22 interviews have been carried out during 2001-2002. Due to the project having been started so recently and that the material consists of only two of the 21 school areas in the administration. There are no possibilities to draw any conclusions from the project. Of the existing material, interviews with 6 head teachers and 16 teachers, the following components can be distinguished.

The most common component in the understanding of leading learning is:
- teaching must derive from each and every individual
- sensitivity for the pupil's/teacher's needs is important
- to start from the pupil's level and way of learning is important
- learning should be fun
- to challenge and question existing notions is essential.

When it comes to how the interviewee behaves when leading other people's learning the following strategies are most frequent.
- individualizing learning
- careful planning on how to do it
- to be exemplary towards pupils and teachers
- forming platforms for dialogue between teachers, practitioners and school management

Some examples of what has turned out to be important for the interviewed person's understanding of the mission are:
- everyday experience from their work
- discussing with colleagues
- further education
- undergraduate studies for teacher's certificate
- their own education

Discussion

The above mentioned developmental work, aiming to map teachers' and head teachers' understanding of how to lead learning, has just started. The mapping is expected to be carried out during a three-year-period with a final report in 2004. The aim of the mapping is to shed light on the staff's understanding of their mission and to add knowledge concerning leadership of other people's learning and contribute to an increased concordance in the interpretation of the assignment and that way reach an increased fulfilment of the goals and hereby an increased quality in pre-school and school.

Despite the developmental work having just started and that no results can be drawn, the mapping is already today contributing to the development of the mission and its understanding. In the areas where interviews have been done they have been the natural staring-point for an on-going discussion about the mission. The ambition is that the mapping should formulate unspoken knowledge so that it can be used in the organization and be a part of its collective memory.

The advantage of using this kind of interviewing method is that the interviewee sees his/her "answer image" grow and can, during the interview, check with himself/herself and the interviewer that everything was correctly apprehended. By using open questions and by illustrating what is said, there is space for direct development of thoughts. The purpose of the mind-map is to make the interviewed person's pattern of thoughts clear and that it is produced in co-operation between the interviewed and the interviewee. The method puts considerable demands on the interviewer in the way that he/she must be able to see the interviewed person's perspective and not transfer his/her own personal opinion. The method in itself implies that the interviewer interprets the interviewee's answers during the interview. The starting-point for the interviewer at every occasion is that he/she doesn't understand what he/she wants to understand. To make sure that the interviewer has understood the content of the question there can be need for several attendant questions. Here you can see that the interviewer's ability is decisive for good reliability.

In the education department of Karlstad there is a striving for pre-school and school to go from a "doing-culture" to a "learning-culture". The developmental project mentioned above can be seen as a part of the administration's leader strategy to affect practitioners understanding of the mission to hereby create increased concordance of how the practitioners take care of their mission with the starting-point in the means of control. The developmental work will hopefully lead to the management of the administration acquiring more knowledge about the practitioners' understanding of the mission and what means of influence have been more fruitful than others.

References

Karlstad kommuns, barn- och ungdomsförvaltning (1999). Översyn av barn- och ungdomsförvaltningens fältorganisation.
Utbildningsdepartementets rapport (2001). Lärande ledare – ledarskap för dagens och framtidens skola.
Scherp, Hans-Åke (2001). Problembaserad skolutveckling och den lärandeorienterade organisationen.

Addendum

Interview questions for teachers
Background
Tell me a little about yourself – teaching background
What does your work situation look like?
– class, subject
– the number of pupils
– team work
– co-operation climate
– preparedness for alteration
– general atmosphere

1 What is leading pupils' learning to you?
2 How have you reached this understanding?
3 What has been of importance for your understanding of leading learning?
4 What do you do to lead your pupils' learning?

Interview questions for head teachers
Background
Tell me a little about yourself – professional background
What does your school look like?
– the number of pupils
– staff
– organization/management
– view of learning/teaching/knowledge
– co-operation climate
– preparedness for alteration
– general atmosphere

1 What is, as you see it, as a head teacher to lead teachers' learning?
2 How have you reached this understanding?
3 What has been of importance for your understanding of leading learning?
4 What do you do to lead your teachers' learning?

Anna-Lena N Groth is a school inspector in Sweden.

CHAPTER 23

THE WRITER
WITHIN

Phil Whitehead

I write so I can write story and poems

I write because I like it.

(Year 4 pupil, Binfield)

Abstract

The paper is a review of one strand of a current, longitudinal study into the effects on pupils' writing of professional writers working in schools. The 'Writer Within' is at one level about the physical presence of a writer working within a primary school. At another level it is premised on the belief that all members of the school community - pupils, staff, parents/carers and governors, can be motivated to discover the writers within themselves and write with a sense of purpose, audience and **success.**
The full study will report on the impact on the quality and standards of writing and on the effect on attitudes to writing within school communities in three English primary schools following a series of writer residencies over a one-year period. The study will also review the wider literature on writers and artists in schools and consider the rationale, organisation and effectiveness of writers and artists in schools projects.
Despite the concerted efforts of government agencies, schools and local education authorities since the introduction of the National Literacy Strategy in 1998 (NLS, 1998), standards of writing in English primary schools remain too low and lag far behind attainment in reading (Ofsted, 2001). The recent data on pupil progress and performance also indicates a sharp difference in attainment in

writing between boys and girls. By the end of the primary school phase, for pupils aged 11, the attainment of girls has remained significantly ahead of boys, with a persistent 15% gap since 1999 (DfES, 2001).

For the purposes of this paper, the Writer Within strand reports on the impact of a writer in residence in one primary school after two full school terms, September to March, 2001-2002. It is an interim review using a case study approach. The overall findings will not be available until September 2002.

Initial findings indicate a positive shift in pupils' attitudes to writing, particularly in younger pupils and lower ability sets, increased confidence amongst staff in the target class groups, and an improvement in the quality of writing based on an analysis of pupils' scripts. The profile of writing has also been raised within the school community and key principles in writing have been highlighted.

Context

The study is part of a collaboration between Oxford Brookes University and three partner primary schools. One of the teachers/schools involved is supported by a Teacher Training Agency (TTA) Best Practice Grant (see website for TTA). One of the researchers and the author of this paper, is also the writer in residence. An important element in validating the research findings is the use of a triangulation process whereby the data will be analysed and verified by the writer, a University supervisor and the teacher/literacy co-ordinators in the three primary schools. The study will be completed in September 2002.

This paper is an interim report based on the work of the writer in residence and the teacher/literacy co-ordinator in one of the primary schools.

The key questions raised are:
- Can an extended writer in residence project make a significant and sustained impact on standards of attainment across the school?
- Can the project improve attitudes towards writing within the school and improve staff confidence in teaching writing?

The main hypotheses are:
- one-off or short term writer residencies in schools can have many benefits but they rarely change classroom practice, indeed they are not designed to;
- pupils in English primary schools generally have negative attitudes towards writing and this is because they do not experience writing with a clear sense of purpose, with a sense of audience beyond for the most part their classteacher or any sense of success as writers;
- longer term writer in school residencies can change pupil attitudes and teacher practices, raising the confidence of writers and encouraging the writing process, including the important element of drafting to improve quality.

Binfield School is accredited with beacon status for writing (see DfES website for beacon school status descriptions) but is concerned with maintaining standards of writing, particularly in the face of staff changes. The school is also concerned that the original status was conferred on the school on the basis of an able cohort of pupils who produced a very high writing score in their national tests and skewed the overall attainment profile. (National test information for schools in England and Wales is available on the Qualifications and Curriculum Authority website: www.qca.org.uk - Key Stages 1 and 2). The school contacted the writer following the attendance by the literacy co-ordinator, Jill Hanson, at the Bristol 'Writing Together' conference early in 2001 (Booktrust website). Although the school had, for many years, been involved in writer visits they had not worked with a writer over a longer period of time. Jill, in a recent article for Booktrust, commented on the reassurance she felt from speakers at the conference who were promoting the benefits of having writers in schools. In a keynote address Andrew Motion, the poet laureate, stressed the importance of writers working with pupils, (Writers are)... 'People who can change the landscape.' (Motion, 2001). Jill was looking for ways to change the landscape in her school and the idea of a longitudinal residency took shape.

'One new idea that I took away from the conference is that of having a writer in residence throughout the year – this is having an immediate positive impact on our school.' (Hanson, 2002)

There is, however, a wider context to this one school's concerns over their pupils' standards in writing.
The National Literacy Strategy (NLS) was launched in England in the summer of 1998. It followed on from the new government's White Paper in 1997, 'Excellence in Schools' (DfEE, 1997). Excellence in Schools highlighted the need to drive up standards of literacy in English schools. The issue was not that standards in literacy were falling but that they were not high enough. In 1996 official figures for pupils at the end of their primary education, aged 10 and 11 in year 6, indicated that 57% were achieving the expected national standard in English overall of a Level 4 or above. Worryingly this meant that almost half the pupils in the country were leaving primary education with insufficient literacy skills to cope with the demands of secondary education. (The National Curriculum website gives details of level descriptions in English and the Department for Education and Skills; DfES, website offers a breakdown of standards year on year.)

Alongside the introduction of the NLS, the government set a challenging target for the year 2002. Standards in literacy were to rise across England to 80% attaining Level 4 or above. Since 1996 attainment in English has progressively and impressively improved year on year to the 2001 figure of 75%. The overall figure, however masks poor standards and progress in writing.

Table 1 shows the percentage of pupils achieving Level 4 and above in 1999-2001, indicating overall progress in English, but also highlighting significant differences between achievement in reading and writing and between boys and girls.

Table 1. Percentage of pupils achieving Level 4 and above in 1999-2001 Key Stage 2 tests.

Subject	Boys			Girls			All			Change	Difference
	1999	2000	2001	1999	2000	2001	1999	2000	2001	2000-2001	Girls - Boys
English	65	70	70	76	79	80	71	75	75	-	+10
Reading	75	80	78	82	86	85	78	83	82	-1	+7
Writing	47	48	50	62	63	65	64	55	58	+3	+15
Mathematics	69	72	71	69	71	70	69	72	71	-1	-1
Science	79	84	87	78	85	88	78	85	87	+2	+1

(Source: DfES website – National Statistics, released September 2001)

Whilst 82% of all pupils achieved or exceeded the national standard in reading in 2001, including 78% of boys, only 58% of all pupils achieved this in writing. 50% of boys achieved the standard and 65% of girls.

Half the boys in the country are leaving primary education with underdeveloped skills in writing and have remained 15% points behind girls for the last three years.

Achievement in writing and specifically the achievement of boys is a cause for national concern. It appears that the NLS has been remarkably successful in raising standards of reading but has signally failed to address poor standards in writing (see Ofsted, 2001 and Fullan et al, 2000, 2001).

Moreover teachers in primary schools are now expressing concerns that the tight structure of the curriculum framework and the daily literacy hour promoted by the NLS (NLS, 1998a) and the emphasis on skills, is inhibiting both their own creativity as teachers and the opportunities for pupils to be creative in their work. A review of the literacy hour as a key element of the NLS, reported the following observations by teachers, literacy consultants and student teachers:

'It didn't always allow for expressive/creative writing to develop due to the need to keep up pace and vigour.'

'There was insufficient time for extended writing'

'Children don't get any time to think... I know myself that if I'm composing something, I like thinking time.' (Fisher & Williams, 2000, p. ix)

This perception is supported by data collected for the current Writers in Schools study.

Concerns over standards in writing and teacher perceptions that there is too little opportunity to develop creativity and the use of the imagination led to a study by the Qualifications and Curriculum Authority (QCA) into creativity in schools. Data and case studies on school projects involving creativity are currently being compiled in order to report on the essential elements of creativity. (The QCA website, reference Alistair West, for further details.) The NLS has also sought to address both the issues of low standards in writing and the perceived threat to creativity (Creativity in Writing Conference, autumn 2001; Writing Fliers, see DfES website – standards.dfes.gov.uk/literacy). The Director of training for the NLS, Laura Huxford, opened the conference by stating, 'Creativity is on the lips of everyone' (Huxford, 2001). The keynote speaker at the Creativity Conference, Roger Beard, presented a research survey from over 300 international sources on writing. Troubled by current concerns, he asked 'what is going wrong?' when all the research data is available on successful approaches to teaching writing (Beard, 2001, unpublished conference notes; see also Beard, 1999 & 2000).

Perhaps the most significant recent development, in the sense that it is groundbreaking in national government terms, was the organisation of the 'Writing Together' conferences in the spring, 2001 (see Booktrust website for the conference report). Six regional conferences were sponsored by the Department for Education and Employment (DfEE) and supported by a wide range of national organisations promoting literacy such as the NLS, BookTrust, The Poetry Society, National Association of Writers in Education (NAWE), the Arts Council of England and QCA. The aim of the conferences was to encourage schools to set-up writers in schools projects as a means of enriching the curriculum and to help children to become successful, creative readers and writers.

'...We believe that the opportunity to work with a professional writer in school can be a real inspiration for many children... We want as many schools as possible to give children this experience...' (Anwyll, 2001, Director, NLS, Writing Together conference report, p. 1)

In part this demonstrates the commitment to drive up standards, it also demonstrates the urgency and almost sense of desperation to meet the 2002 target. At the end of each conference the teacher delegates were presented with a cheque for £130 to 'half fund' a writer in school for a day. The conferences certainly provided the main catalyst for this study and were a breath of fresh air to many of the delegates, including this writer/researcher.

The tradition of the professional writer visiting schools in the United Kingdom can be tracked back thirty years or so when the Arts Council of Great Britain began to develop a scheme to promote author visits. (See Jones & Lockwood, 1998; Dooley, 1996; Harries, 1983.) The provision of writer visits has, however remained patchy and uneven across schools and local education authorities. Schemes and projects to promote writers in schools have come and gone without any clear national picture or lead, although the regional arts boards in England have provided advice and part funding to schools over the years. There is a general feeling that they are of tremendous benefit but little quantifiable evidence of this is available. The Writing Together conference report, 'Writers in the Classroom, Why a writer?' offered fourteen reasons for having a writer in the classroom. The first reason was:

'Having a writer in schools... is inspiring and exciting for pupils and teachers.' (Booktrust, conference report, 2001, p. 4)

Conference speakers from the Arts Council of England and from the QCA admitted that the actual research evidence on the effects of writer visits was rather 'thin on the ground'.

The Case Study - Writer in Residence project, Binfield School, September 2001-July 2002

The school is in a residential area of a rapidly expanding 'new' town development in south-east England. Around 400 pupils attend the school aged from 4-11 years. Pupils in primary schools in England are organised in age-banded classes from reception (R aged 4-5) up to year 6 (Y6 aged 10-11 years). Although pupils are classroom based with one main designated teacher for most of the day, the practice of ability grouping pupils in different sets has become widespread since the introduction of the NLS. This means that pupils may move to another teacher in another class mainly for daily lessons in English and mathematics. This is mostly the case from Key Stage 2 (ages 7-11) although increasingly the practice seems to be extending into Key Stage 1 (5-7 years). Binfield has a two-form entry from the reception class upwards. Ability setting is practised throughout Key Stage 2 as described. Class sizes range from the mid 20s in Key Stage 1 and reception to around 30 pupils in some Key Stage 2 classes. This is fairly typical of many English schools. (See the DfES website for the 'Autumn Package' - a wide range of statistical information on schools in England and Wales.)

The school is designated a beacon school and as such is allocated additional funds by central government to develop and share good practice. The funds have allowed the school to buy in a writer to work within the school throughout the year. Eighteen sessions will be spread over the three school terms during the academic year September 2001 to July 2002. This is an unusual approach, as most writers in schools projects in England have traditionally been one-off, one-day visits (Jones & Lockwood, 1998 and Dooley, 1996). Funding organisations, such as the regional arts boards, have preferred more extended visits or mini-residencies but schools and writers do not always wish for this (Jones & Lockwood, 1998). The first term was thoroughly reviewed by the writer and the literacy co-ordinator from the school and on the basis of its success was extended.

It was decided to focus on poetry writing as the genre throughout the first term for a number of reasons. It was the writer's published and preferred area; it was also felt to be a more manageable genre for the situation where the writer would not be returning for two to three weeks. The writer had also developed a number of writing workshops that worked well as models for writing for both pupils and teachers, especially the 'Keepers' workshop (see below). Jones and Lockwood (1998) record some interesting comparisons between author visits and poet visits to schools. Their findings certainly support the experiences at Binfield and justify the choice of poetry.

The rationale for the Binfield project has recently been published in an article for Booktrust by the school literacy co-ordinator, Jill Hanson (Booktrust website

2002). The Booktrust website also contains detailed advice on how to plan, run and follow up a writer visit to a school (Booktrust, Writing Together conference report, 2001).

The visits occurred around every two to three weeks and followed a pattern agreed between the writer and the literacy co-ordinator:
Session 1 Week 1 – Whole School Performance followed by writing workshops of around one hour in duration in Y2, Y4 and Y6 classes with a shorter reading session in R. Staff training session led by the writer, 3.30-4.30 pm.
Week 2 onwards – writing sessions in the same classes as week 1 for one hour throughout the day.
Week 6, final week – preparation for a performance of works to the whole school followed by a performance of writing by the pupils and the launch of the 'Binfield Poets' anthology. This was planned to coincide with the school's biannual Bookweek, when other writers, publishers and illustrators visited the school.

Working with the same classes each session meant that a relationship could be built up with the pupils and teachers and ideas could be followed up.
Term 2 has just been completed and followed a similar pattern, this time with the parallel R, Y2, Y4 and Y6 classes. Performances again took place at the end of the final session to the whole school and the new anthology is being prepared for publication. The Y6 focus was more on narrative writing, as the teacher was concerned about the national tests in May. Poetry has not featured as a writing form in the tests since they were introduced in the mid-1990s, the emphasis has been on narrative and non-fiction writing.

Outcomes and Evaluation

This is an interim evaluation of the project so far. Two terms of data are available in the form of pupils' scripts, teacher and pupil comments, two internal reports and video material from pupils' performances and a staff training session. Further evidence informing the evaluation includes a literature review, collated as part of the wider study, unpublished data collected from post graduate teacher-trainee students in 1999 and information accumulated over the past 14 years from the writer's visits to schools.

Has the project made an impact on pupil and teacher attitudes to writing and has confidence been enhanced?

'...individuals who hold positive writer self-perceptions will probably pursue opportunities to write, expend more effort during writing engagements, and demonstrate greater persistence in seeking writing competence.' (Bottomley, Henk & Melnick, 1998)

'I read to get information. I write for my teacher.' (Y5 pupil, Buckinghamshire school, 1999)

Initial findings and comments collected from pupils, teachers and parents, indicate that attitudes generally are more positive towards writing. Pupils who performed or featured in the anthology certainly see themselves as 'writers'. However, this question can only be partly addressed at this stage. More in-depth writer self-perception instruments have been used in one of the other study schools and this will be reported in at the end of the full study (Bottomley et al, 1998).

A simple research instrument was devised to elicit pupils' views on writing at various points in this project. Their views were an indictor of the sense of purpose they felt when writing. Both Graves (1983) and Browne (1996) comment on the importance of this sense of purpose and meaning. For many pupils at the end of their primary years writing is seen as a 'pointless' exercise (Graves). Roger Beard in 'Clarion call for another century' (Times Educational Supplement, 2000) offers a very pertinent comment from the opening of the twentieth century by Sir Philip Hartog. Writing in 1908 Hartog suggested that 'much writing in school does not go beyond writing something, about anything, for no one in particular'.

Boys in particular, in my experience, need a real sense of purpose, working on finite tasks with clear and achievable outcomes. The lack of this kind of experience in their writing and the resulting disaffection may explain to some extent the low attainment of boys and the disparity in national test results at the end of KS2 between boys and girls.

Two basic questions were asked of Y2 and Y4 pupils:
- Why do we read?
- Why do we write?

There was no lead in to the question other than to say that the writer was interested in their opinions. The Y4 group was the lower ability set. Around 60 responses were collected and analysed in the first term, repeated at the start of the second term with the new cohort.

The majority of comments by pupils in Y2 and Y4 at the start of the project focused on the ideas that we write to 'get better at handwriting', 'to learn to spell' or 'so we don't rub out' (Y2 pupils). 'I write so I can write quickly'. 'I write so I can improve my handwriting.' (Alina, Y4)

'I think we write to learn to write', a comment by Eleanor inY2, summed up much of the thinking. Pupils saw writing as a means of addressing the secretarial aspects. Children were writing to get it right – 'it' being spellings, handwriting and neatness.

The Y6 group was a higher ability set and had engaged in discussion from the outset about the sense of purpose and audience and for the most part they were confident writers in terms of mastering the secretarial aspects. This group was more sophisticated in their thinking and produced a wider range of answers –

'We write because sometimes writing a poem can help us say what we feel about something.'

'We write so we can get all those ideas from reading into our writing.' (Emily)

The second cohort of pupils had the benefit of the performances by their peers and the anthology of poetry, which had a positive impact on the school community. This was reflected in their comments which focused much more on 'I write so I can write stories and poems' type comments.

The main difference between the first cohort and the second was in the Y6 group. This group was the lower-ability group and their confidence and approach to writing was markedly different to the higher ability group of the previous term. They were much more reluctant to write and to talk about their writing.

The same instrument was used with a group of 70 post-graduate students on a one-year teacher training course in 1999. As part of an assignment on children's writing the students were encouraged to ask pupils in their school experience classrooms the same two questions as above and to elicit their pupils' opinions and attitudes towards writing. Fifty percent of the student collected data and reported on their pupils' views. The overwhelming majority of pupils were not positive about being asked to write. Boys in KS2 were clearly the least positive group.

The very act of asking pupils to focus on why they are writing was a useful starting point for the writer. With the first group of Y6 pupils it led into a discussion about who we write for. The pupils were able to identify around twenty different audiences for their writing but admitted for the most part they wrote for their teacher.

The key principles of writing with a sense of purpose and audience, principles that underpin successful writing seem to be persistently omitted in too many English lessons. At least that has been the experience of this writer in the many classrooms worked in and observed over the last fourteen years. Even in a beacon school for writing these elements are often missing. Each session in the Binfield project focused on whom the writing was for and why we were writing in this particular way.

An unexpected outcome from the work has been to reveal elements of the impact of ability grouping on attitudes. The ability grouping within the school in KS2 did not have a positive impact on the perceptions of the lower ability pupils in Y4 and Y6. For the most part these pupils did not have positive views on writing or see themselves at the outset of the project. The Y4 group had clearly changed their views by the end of the sessions and had become enthusiastic and successful writers. It would be difficult to claim this for the second Y6 group.

'Has the project improved the quality of pupils' writing and raised attainment?'

Again a longer-term perspective needs to prevail before a definitive answer can be provided. In the short term however the overwhelming evidence from pupils' scripts, their revisions, published pieces and performances indicates a clear improvement in the quality of writing for those pupils engaged in the project. Many pupils have surprised their teachers and parents in this respect.

Towards the end of the second term I asked Mitchell in Y6 if he was still writing. Mitchell was in the first Y6 cohort and had produced several very well written pieces (see Poem War). 'Of course I am!' he replied, implying that it went without saying. Mitchell's mother had approached me at the end of the first term, after the performance, to express her amazement at the quality of his work and his engagement in writing.

A key feature of the success was the approach through poetry. The 'Keepers' workshop best exemplifies this approach and produced excellent results with the Y2 and Y4 pupils.

'Keepers' was one of a suite of poems commissioned for a poetry poster pack for schools based on the world of work (SEEN, 2001). The following is an explanation of how a typical Keepers session of around one hour would go.

'I initially talk to the children about the commission and how I was struggling for ideas with a deadline to meet. I explain how I went for a walk along the Thames at Oxford to see if any inspiration was forthcoming. When I reached the locks at Godstow a canal boat was going through with the assistance of the lock keeper. The idea of different jobs around the idea of a keeper – lockkeeper, goalkeeper, shopkeeper, suddenly struck me and I began to record the ideas in my idea/notebook. I show the pupils my notebook and explain how important it is for a writer to keep a note of ideas and thoughts that later may become the basis for poems or stories. (Pupils in Y2, Y4 and Y6 have been encouraged to keep notebooks from the outset of the project. This has worked best where the teacher has been active in promoting the idea.)

Next I show the children the poetry poster and they listen to the poem.

Keepers

I keep the goal.
I keep the ball out.
Often it goes whizzing in!

I keep the shop.
I keep the groceries in.
Hopefully they get wheeled out!

I keep the bees.
I keep the buzz in.
Frequently I scoop the honey out!

I keep the lock.
I keep the water in.
Usually it gushes back out!

I keep the change.
I keep the money in.
Rarely does it roll out!

I keep the books.
I keep the figures in.
Occasionally they wriggle out!

I keep a diary.
I keep my words in.
Never should they slip out!

I keep secrets.
I keep hopes and wishes and fears in.
One day, be sure, they'll
BLURT RIGHT OUT!

I keep the time.
I keep the hours and minutes and seconds in.
Unfortunately, they just trickle out
And before you know it,
TIME'S UP!

(Phil Whitehead 2001)

Listening first is my way of modelling reading behaviour. It is the starting point for shared reading (NLS, 1998). I also try to provide opportunities for children to discuss ideas with a partner and share them with the whole group. This is important, not only in developing their speaking and listening skills within a tightly structured model, but it also reinforces the idea that they are working along the 'right' lines, enhancing motivation.

I explain that I had so many keepers ideas in my notebook that they could not all fit into the poem. The illustrator added some of them to the poster. We then search for more keepers from the poster. The children are asked to come up with more keepers ideas. I challenge them to find 10 new keepers. Boys in particular respond to a quantified target and enjoy the challenge. I encourage them to talk to a partner and to write their ideas down on a white board. The use of white boards is widespread now in primary schools. A year ago if I requested white boards there may have been one or two sets in a school; often I took my own set. In just the last year most schools seem to now have a set in each classroom. The use of white boards is a major motivator for many children who feel freer to write without the constraints and worries of accuracy whilst working on initial ideas. This relates very closely to the pupils' views on writing – the secretarial idea that writing is about getting it right. This is a powerful idea that fixes itself from an early point in a child's schooling.

In a matter of a few minutes the children usually collect enough keepers to fill their boards. As soon as I spot an unusual one I praise it highly and request more unusual ones. I ensure all children have a least one keeper on their whiteboards and request that every child shares their favourite with the class. From the outset this is valuing their ideas and giving them a sense of success. Amongst the keepers suggested, typically are: rainbow, stars, rain, smiles, chocolate, zoo, peace, lighthouse, school, park, house, cemetery, dream, sea, words, books, cars… a whole range of unusual and imaginative ideas come out from this simple request.

I ask a teacher to write the ideas down on a large piece of paper for future use. This further values their work, instantly displaying their ideas (and providing spellings for those who become desperate for accuracy). Twenty or more new ideas are thus generated and easily available for reference.

Now I explain to the children that I want them to help me to write a new verse for the poem to put in a small, pocketbook of Keepers. I show them the simple pocketbook made from A4 paper folded to A5 size and stapled together. I explain that each of them will have their own book in which to write new Keepers verses. The classroom assistant makes them up in a matter of minutes from a template provided, although it is good practice for the children to begin making their own books.

Before I begin writing I ask the children if they can tell me anything special about the way the poem was written. I ask if they can see any patterns, any structure to the poem. This tells me immediately how familiar they are with poems and the language of poetry. Usually, from Y2 upwards they spot the 'I keep the ___' pattern for the first two lines of each verse. They notice the 'in/out' pattern at the end of the lines, the mostly three-line pattern of the verses and by Y5 they are able to talk about the connectives that open line three of each verse.

I model the opening to lines two and three on the class whiteboard and add in the in/out pattern:
  'I keep the____
  I keep the _____in

  _ _ _ _ _ _ _ _ _out'

I then look at the new list of keepers collected and explain to the children that I am now going to do some thinking out aloud. I am letting children into my thinking processes as a writer, the metacognitive elements and demonstrating shared writing – modelling writer behaviour. (Beard, 1999 references the important work of Bereiter and Scardamalia on the importance of shared writing and the thinking process.) I have already pre-selected a keeper and prepared my new version for the whiteboard as part of my planning for the session. I explain this to teachers during training sessions. If teachers are to demonstrate shared writing most effectively and model the writing process they need to plan through the elements. They are being teachers as well as writers at this point. Writing is hard work, nobody denies that and one of the greatest challenges to improving writing in my experience is the reluctance of teachers to engage in the process and model writing behaviour (Frater, TES, 2001).

Hopefully somewhere on the collected and displayed list is a zookeeper – it hasn't failed yet. I explain that I am thinking about a zookeeper and ask the child who supplied it if they mind if I borrowed their idea? Only once has a child said 'No – it's my idea!' I also talk about the notion that writers borrow ideas from everywhere, as Pie Corbett puts it, 'Writers are thieves!' (DfES 2001). So my verse becomes:

> 'I keep the zoo
> I keep the ___in'

What am I going to keep 'in'? Children quickly suggest 'animals', occasionally but not often they suggest a specific animal. I write in the suggestion:

> 'I keep the zoo
> I keep the animals in'

Now a final line. There are variations but something like this emerges:

> 'I keep the zoo
> I keep the animals in
> Sometimes they get out.'

I read the verse through and ask the children if it fits the pattern – 'Yes'.
I ask them if I am satisfied and ready to put the new verse in the pocketbook – 'Yes'
'No!' is my response and at this point I explain to the children that they are working as writers during this session and must behave like one. Writers are never satisfied with their words and continually seek new, better, more interesting, more exciting choices. Indeed if children are to attain Level 4 their vocabulary choice must be adventurous and interesting.

I return to the verse. I am happy with line one but not with line 2.

> 'I keep the animals in'

I go back into metacognitive mode – When I say this line in my head I have a picture of a zoo and lots of animals but it is a blurred picture, nothing clear comes into my mind. I need something specific. Soon the children come up with specific animals – lions, tigers, elephants and I continue until eventually I get 'snakes', because this fits in with my plan.

> 'I keep the zoo
> I keep the animals in
>   lions
>   tigers
>   elephants
>   snakes ⎤
> Sometimes they get out.'

Now to concentrate on the final line. I am not happy with snakes getting out. Tell me some more ways that snakes could escape from the zoo. Soon I have a selection:

'Sometimes they get out
　　　　sneak
　　　　squeeze
　　　　squirm⎤
　　　　wriggle
　　　　slip
　　　　slide

I choose a favourite from the suggestions that starts with the letter 's'. I re-read the whole verse and say that I am now satisfied. I ask if they notice anything else about the verse now? It does not take long usually for someone to comment on the alliteration of snake, sometimes and squirm and a further teaching point can be made.

The final step is for the children to now complete their own versions in the same way. The key elements I want the children and their teachers to focus on in their own writing now are:
–　to concentrate on specific nouns in line 2, ones that put a clear picture in your head;
–　to work on choices for powerful verbs in line 3;
–　and with KS2 pupils attention to their choice of connective at the start of line 3.

In variably the children rush off a new verse and have to be encouraged to work on choices. This is often the element that teachers say children are most reluctant to work on – the redrafting of writing. Once the children see a point to this and the task is not one of redrafting whole chunks of text as in elements of narrative writing, they will readily and effectively revisit their work. I say to them – ' Show me choices on your white board, behave like a writer' and they do! Only when they have demonstrated hard thinking are they allowed a pocketbook to write in. For some children the sheer effort of getting something down on the whiteboard that resembles the structure is a massive achievement and is highly praised. For others nothing but five or more alternatives for verbs and connectives will suffice. The challenge can be set for individuals depending upon their ability.

Children then work through the next few literacy sessions to complete the new book of Keepers. I encouraged Y2 and Y4 at Binfield to take the idea home and ask their parents to write a Keepers poem in the book. This was particularly successful with the Y2 children in the first term with around 80% of parents responding.

This activity is transferable to any text where pupils can begin to improve their work by focusing on verbs, nouns and connectives, looking for patterns, such as alliteration and not being afraid to risk-take with their choices. If left without consolidation and follow-up work the children will go back to using weak verbs and simple connectives such as – and, so, but, and then. They do this because they can spell these words not because of a lack of ideas or a wide enough vocabulary. The emphasis again for them, first and foremost is on accuracy.

The improved quality of pupils' work could be seen within sessions let alone over time.

Keepers is so simple a workshop yet effective at many levels. It starts with meaning, has a sense of purpose, has an audience when the finished pocketbooks are shared or displayed or performed, and as I haven't had a failure yet in a very wide range of schools, abilities, challenging behaviours… This includes a boy in Y5 in a school in Streatham, London who was refusing to do any work for anybody. I had been advised by the teacher to leave him alone because he was at the point of 'exploding' and running off. He spent the whole lesson with his head down on the whiteboard but I caught him at one point trying to write his version from under his arm. As soon as he saw me he wiped the board clean. I still count his as a success! It provides a good model for redrafting and has direct links to teaching pupils knowledge about language, the grammar or sentence elements of literacy (NLS 2001). Neither is it threatening to teachers or pupils. Often the teacher has written her version as I am explaining the idea to the children. Although often she has to be prompted and prised open to share the work!

On the evidence of the Binfield project there can be no doubt that writers in schools can have a very positive impact on attitudes to writing and on attainment. The key element of the Binfield project is the longitudinal aspect. This is also a pitfall as it can be expensive. (See Writing Together conference report, p. 6 'Five ways to help raise £250 in a writerish way'.) The writer could go back into the classroom every few weeks and revisit ideas. This was a motivating influence for the teachers too who knew that follow up work was important. The pupils realised that they were working towards a goal – writing for an anthology and writing to perform their work to a whole school audience. In every session all children wrote something from R. to Y6 and felt the sense of success.

The project became one where all pupils had the opportunity to write exceptionally rather than a focus on exceptional pupils writing. The reality however, remains that in too many English primary schools too many pupils are unsuccessful in their writing, do not meet national expectations or standards and do not enjoy writing. The Writer Within seeks to emphasise and address three basic conditions or 'senses' that need to be met in order for primary aged pupils, 4-11, to meet national expectations:

Writers need to have a sense of purpose, a sense of audience and a sense of success. Writers have a right to know from the outset – why are we writing (rather than talking, drawing, miming…)? Who is it for? And how are we to go about it in order to be successful?

These 'senses' are not new ideas. They are within the statutory English orders as part of the National Curriculum and are regularly and explicitly stressed within the guidance issued by the National Literacy Strategy. Schools clearly find it difficult to include these essential ingredients. Writers in schools project are one way of helping to release the writer within the teacher and the child.

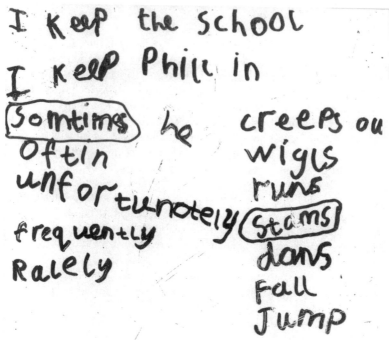

I keep the school
I keep Phill in
Somtims he creeps ou
Oftin wigls
unfortunately runs
frequently Stams
Ralely dans
Fall
Jump

(Year 2 pupil Binfield School)

I keep the clouds
I keep the rain drops in
Normly thay rush out
Relly Slid
usly Creep
patter
Normly Sawes
talk
run

(Y2 Binfield)

The Treasure Within

POEM WAR

I WANT TO GO BOLDLY
WHERE NO POET HAS GONE BEFORE
TO FIGHT IN HUGE GREAT BATTLES
AND WIN HUMONGOUS WARS
I'LL FIGHT WITH MY ALLITERATION SWORD
AND USE MY SIMILE SHIELD
I'LL DESTROY YOUR ARMED FORCES
AND USE WORDS OF PURE STEEL
I SHALL BEAT YOU
I WON'T LOOSE HEART
DO THE SAME
AND BE SMART.

BY BEN CHRISTMAS AND MITCHELL CARPENTER (YEAR 6)

Poetry is like a music tragedy,
Building the passion,
Disaster strikes,
Suddenly the sound falls in your mind,
Ideas spilling out of the violin box.

by Victoria Tay   Year 6

References

Beard, R. (1999). *The National Literacy Strategy: Review of research and other related evidence*. London: DfEE.

Beard, R. (2000). *Developing Writing 3-13*. London: Hodder & Stoughton.

Beard, R. (2000). *'Clarion call for another century'*, Times Educational Supplement, Curriculum Special, October 6, 7.

Bottomley, D., Henk, W. & Melnick, S. (1998). Assessing children's views about themselves as writers using the Writer Self-Perception Scale, *The Reading Teacher*, 51, 286-293.

Browne, A. (1996). *Developing language and Literacy 3-8*. London: Paul Chapman Publishing.

DfEE (1997). *Excellence in Schools*. London, DfEE Publications.

DfEE (1998). *The National Literacy Strategy: Framework for Teaching*. London: DfEE.

DfES (2000). *National Literacy Strategy: Grammar for Writing*. London: DfEE.

Dooley, M. (1996). *A Beginning, Middle and End?: A study of the work of Writers in Education*. London: Arts Board.

Fisher & Williams (2000). *Unlocking Literacy*. London: David Fulton Publishers.

Fullan, M. (2000 & 2001). *Evaluation of the Implementation of the National Literacy and Numeracy Strategies*. University of Ontario, OISEUT/DfEE Publications

Graves, D. (1983). *Writing: teachers and Children at Work*. London: Heinemann.

Harries, S. (1984). *Writers in School: A report on the scheme in England and Wales up to 1983*. London: Arts Council of Great Britain.

Jones, D. & Lockwood, M. (1998). *The Writer in Education*, Children's Literature in Education, 29, 199-210.

Whitehead, P. (2000). *World of Work Poems for Key Stages 1 and 2*, Buckinghamshire: SEEN.

Websites

Many of the references are contained within the websites for ease of international access.

http://www.booktrust.org.uk (for Writing Together conference report, 2001; Anwyll, S. 2001, Welcome; Hanson, J., 2002 Writer in Residence; & Motion A. 2001 Foreword, & Literacy Entitlement)

http://www.canteach.gov.uk (for Teacher Training Agency and Best Practice Grants)

http://www.dfes.gov.uk (add- /statistics for attainment of pupils 1999-2001; also for information reference beacon school status)

http://www.nawe.co.uk (for database on writers in schools)

http://www.nc.gov.uk (for the National Curriculum and information on Level 4 attainment)

http://www.ofsted.gov.uk (for National Literacy Strategy: The third year, 2001)

http://www.poetrysoc.com

http://www.poetryclass.net

http://www.qca.org.uk (for links directly into literacy add-/ca/subjects /English/literacy)

http://www.standards.dfes.gov.uk/literacy (for National Literacy Strategy information including fliers on writing, including Corbett, P.)

Phil Whitehead is principal lecturer in education at Oxford Brookes University, UK.

CHAPTER 24

TEAM BUILDING IN INTERNATIONAL PROJECTS

FROM IDEA TO PRODUCT

Jezerka Beškovnik

Introduction

Since 1995 our school has been involved in various international projects. When talking about international projects I mean co-operation with schools around the world, intercultural and multicultural exchanges using e-mail as a tool and having in mind a final product.

To make such a project successful takes more than just effort of an individual teacher or student. It needs a team, it needs teamwork. In schools, teams are used to accomplish many tasks. On this occasion I am talking about building teams that will join international projects and carry out all the activities in such a way that their final goals or objectives will be reached.

To be successful, the team members must have clear goals in mind and the goals must also be shared by all the team members. However, this is still not enough. Each of the team members is supposed to show a sense of commitment to the group and to the final objective. Each of them has to be willing to work with the other members of the team, share ideas, resources, skills. To make it simple, all the work has to be interlaced, directed towards meeting the needs of every individual in the team and the team as a whole. But most of all, it has to be directed towards the final objective. In this case this is the successful completion of an international project.

How are the teams built and how are the international projects carried out?
What steps do we take?

The idea

I remember our students' first attempts at writing letters to friends in different foreign countries. They had to be taught how letters are written, how the letter is organised, how to start and finish it. They also had to practise writing quite a lot in order not to make so many spelling and grammatical mistakes. But they were motivated and did not mind the efforts.

The next thing to do was to find schools and classes which would be interested in writing to us. It was quite difficult to find such classes that were willing to co-operate with students from non-English speaking countries. Everybody was looking for penpals from such countries so that they could practise their English with native speakers.

I had to do quite a lot of research to find out students who would be willing to correspond with us. But I did it and the exchange of letters began. At first, they were thrilled about the idea of having friends all around the world but the motivation soon 'vanished'. Why?

It lasted for a while, the students were happy to have penpals, they wrote letters regularly and waited impatiently for the answers. But after a few months the replies didn't come so regularly any more, the motivation fell to minimum and the interest to write was getting weaker and weaker. Finally, we decided to stop writing. The disappointment was such that I didn't have the courage to ask them to try again with another group of students.

Everything changed with the introduction of IT in our schools and the possibility of using e-mail.

Now letter writing has suddenly become more interesting, challenging, enjoyable and motivating. Communication is faster now, the exchange of e-mail messages does not take so long any more and the students are much more motivated to write them.

So, why not start an international project?

There are lots of ideas of what could be done in the future project e.g. exchange of cultural issues, legends, poems, weather reports, issues dealing with pollution of the environment, climate changes, democracy, tolerance, xenophobia and many many more.

Let's say that the idea is to design an international electronic students' magazine. The idea is here. What comes next? It has to be explained to the teaching staff and the head teacher and approved. After that it has to be advertised among the students.

Advertising the idea

The students are informed about the idea of creating an electronic magazine and asked whether they are willing to contribute. Normally, there are quite a few interested in joining the project, but they lose interest very soon if it is not them who suggest ideas, articles, topics, the layout of the magazine and so on. That's why a meeting has to be organised during which ideas are expressed, explained and shared. The best ideas are chosen democratically - by voting. The basic team is now formed, but there are still things to do.

Looking for partners

If we want the project to be an international one, we have to find partners in other countries. There are a lot of sites on the internet where schools and classes are looking for possible partners. Some of them have already decided on what to do in the future projects and are looking for partners to join them. Some schools suggest ideas for future projects and invite other schools to join them. And there are also such schools that would like to join a project but have no ideas of their own. They just register on the internet sites and wait to be invited. That's how it is possible to find our future partners.

Finding partners

Once the project is advertised on the internet, you have two possibilities. Either you contact schools that might be willing to co-operate or wait to be contacted. In both cases the result is usually positive. Once the possible project partners are found and the contact has been established, the idea has to be evaluated, developed, upgraded, and improved by all the interested parties. In order to do that, teams of teachers and students are formed to discuss the issues and share new ideas and new solutions with all of us.

Correspondence

To be sure, that the possible partner is really interested in the future co-operation a certain time has to be dedicated to correspondence during which other important issues that have come out are discussed, possible problems dealt with, and important matters decided. During this time the idea for the future project is not an idea any more, it has become a joint objective. It is only now that the real co-operation starts, that the real teams are formed and the tangible results can be expected.

Deciding on the joint project

We can say that now all the most important issues have been discussed and all important decisions have been taken. As everything has been decided by the teachers and students together, by all partners together, it should not be difficult to proceed. We have all decided on what our joint project should be. What still has to be done is to form international teams of students who would work together on the topic they choose and to decide what roles would the teams of teachers have. Again, the future topics are advertised by e-mail, and the students decide what they are going to write about and which team they are going to join.

The teachers, as a team, have to decide what they will do to help the students, how they will monitor the work, how they will act as facilitators and how will they motivate the students so the outcomes will be reached and the work successfully completed.

Setting objectives and deadlines

Each team has to decide on the amount of work to be done, the responsibilities of individual members and the way to solve possible problems. Each team has to set their own objectives and decide on the deadline. The time limit is very important as, we all know that, by postponing the work, the motivation fades and the results are harder to achieve.

Team work

Building the Magazine Web Team
Once they have learnt the first steps the students find creating web pages a very exciting experience. The excitement does not last long when they discover the first steps are not enough and that there is much more to know if you want to build a really good web page with an attractive layout and all the links functioning.

When creating an electronic magazine, the web pages have to be made by a team and not by individual students or teachers. That way the work is done much more easily. In order to facilitate the work the team members must share responsibilities. Clear goals and expectations have to be stated for each member of the team and the progress has to be constantly monitored.

What roles will the members of the web team have?

Organisation Team
The members of this team gather ideas from students and teachers, do research and suggest the content to be included in the magazine. This can be: presentation of the school, school calendar, school activities, projects, extra-curricular activities, etc. The representatives of this team should be students, teachers, school management and also those parents who are willing to co-operate with school. If the school has an IT teacher, he or she has to be available as well in order to help create and design the web pages.

Material Writing Team
We all know that some students enjoy writing materials while others can be creative in many different ways. When the school magazine is started, a team of writers is the first thing to be found. Their role will be to create materials suggested by the organisation team. This team should include all, teachers, students and parents.

Web Master Team

The students and teachers in this team are responsible for creating web pages and uploading the material to the web server. They are monitored by the IT teacher and / or by the project co-ordinator.

All the members of the teams must have an active role, they all have to share responsibilities and pay attention to the deadlines. The members of the three teams also need to collaborate with each other, otherwise the work cannot be completed properly.

The teams have been formed, they are working together and creating material to be published on the internet. Each team has an equally important role in the creation of the final product, each of the teams has to perform a specific task.

It can be to write articles about the country, city, school life, youth problems, culture, free time activities, etc. to do research and suggest new topics or design and create the web pages.

Each team has to start and complete the task they have been assigned or they have chosen during the time limit that has been previously set.

We must not forget that we are working with students who constantly need to be supervised, monitored, helped, encouraged and motivated. Only with the help of the teachers can the objectives be obtained and the work successfully accomplished.

The final product

The final product has been created. In order to show how committed the students and the teachers have been in the course of the project, the work has to be published on the internet or in the traditional way. Video films and CD-roms can be created. The work has to be presented to the teaching staff, students who have not been involved in the project and, last but not least, to the parents and the local community. Again, teams of students can do the presentations and explain how they have reached the objectives. The results of the project have to be disseminated, otherwise all the work has been done in vain.

To conclude

The final product should not be the only objective that the teachers and students have to bear in mind. By joining an international project, new friendships and new relationships are formed, new cultures are discovered, new perspectives are seen, new horizons are opened up. New teams can be built to start new and even better projects.

We have planted a single tree which will once grow into a forest if we only give it the chance to grow.

Example: European Youth Electronic Magazine created as an international project

Jezerka Beškovnik is a language teacher at Lucija Primary School in Portoroz, Slovenia.

CONCLUSION

THE USES OF VARIETY:
REFLECTIONS ON THE TREASURE WITHIN

Pieter Leenheer

In the plenary closing session of the Prague conference Pieter Leenheer made some personal reflections concerning the developments in *The Treasure Within*. Below you find a slightly revised version of his speech.

I can imagine after attending several workshops some of the conference participants might wonder what The Treasure is about. Even apart from the fact that this conference was a mix of several conferences, I cannot deny that the workshops actually belonging to The Treasure as such, perhaps showed more differences than similarities as for themes, outcomes and what not. Actually, however, for me that variety is exactly what makes The Treasure worthwhile.

That such a variety is absolutely indispensable is, as far as I am concerned, one of the lessons of the last fifty years. For shortness sake, the overview of the developments in that period I give below, is, to say the least, rather crude. I trust, however, that it is sufficiently clear for the point I want to make.

After World War II two developments that have been of the utmost importance for the developments in education have become exponentially intensified. First: in quite a few countries there has been a massive influx of pupils and students in education, due to the democratisation process in society as a whole. As a consequence especially secondary education had to learn how to cope with pupils for whom learning doesn't come easy. Second: the modernisation process in the sociological sense of the word speeded up and as we all know things like industrialisation, urbanisation, secularisation, individualisation and what not drastically changed society's landscape in a few decades time. And it goes without saying that all that had far-reaching consequences for the curriculum.

During the sixties, seventies and part of the eighties most governments and politicians tried to cope with these developments in what we now see as a traditional way. That is: top-down, by imposing changes on people, on schools. Helped, as a matter of fact, by researchers, teacher trainers, In-service trainers etc., who at that time were fond of research and development strategies and took quite some pleasure in designing programs, in telling people how to teach and so on.

Turning over

But gradually governments, researchers and even politicians began to realise: this top down strategy doesn't work. So, in the eighties and nineties in more than one country we have seen a movement towards decentralisation due to the fact that governments realised that central steering didn't work. In that context we now see all over Europe that schools are getting greater autonomy or at least that people are thinking about that.

By the way, I am well aware that the motives of governments and politicians for decentralising and giving schools greater autonomy sometimes might be somewhat improper. But to me that is irrelevant. In itself this development is very fruitful and I hope the relatively autonomous schools (I speak of 'relatively autonomous schools' in view of the fact that of course complete autonomy is impossible on earth) - I hope, the relatively autonomous schools of the (near) future will be so strong as to prevent politicians from retracing their steps.

As for the researchers: even as early as the seventies of the last century, but certainly in the eighties they began to publish articles in which they admitted their ideas didn't work as well as they had hoped for, and meanwhile we have at our disposal a massive amount of literature proving that. As a matter of fact, in the last decades we have seen an important switch towards constructivist learning psychology. That is, a psychology that envisages learning not so much as passive reception of the wise words of experts but as a matter of creating possibilities for active construction of knowledge.

To summarise, all this means we have finally realised what Shân Mullet, one of the Treasure partners, nicely stated in her article for the first Treasure publication: real improvement comes from within and is not externally imposed or mandated. Or to quote Spanbauer, the man Rudi Schollaert referred to in his keynote speech during the opening session, we have learned that 'change happens by degree, not by decree'. And in addition to that, I would like to quote Jane Jones' quotation in her keynote, a word of Block's: schools improve and get changed in a thousand little ways.

Agency

The development in which schools get greater autonomy can also be described in the terms Rudi Schollaert introduced in his keynote during the opening session: by giving them greater autonomy you promote the agency of schools. However, that, in its turn, presupposes schools to be or to become learning organisations. And that is what The Treasure is about: helping schools to become learning organisations.

Actually, I am fully aware that learning organisation is a fuzzy concept. But as for me, the fuzziest concepts often are the most inspiring and intriguing. Anyway, I do not intend to give you a complete lecture on the topic; just for the sake of clarity I will just say a few words about what I understand by the term. In his opening speech Rudi Schollaert quoted David Hopkins' definition in which the learning of students was the focus. In her keynote on practitioner research

Jane Jones offered a sketch of the Research Engaged School – definitely a learning organisation! – in which the reflective practitioner is the key focus. In my turn I mention some characteristics from a slightly different perspective, in a somewhat impressionist order:

– In a learning organisation, or preferably in a learning school, there is a shared vision about what the school is or should be.
– The management is not of the planning and control type but displays real educational leadership and shows genuine interest in the learning of teachers.
– Agency doesn't get stuck in the upper regions of the organisation: self-managing teams are seen as important.
– The organisation fosters its external orientation: it is constantly in search for inspiration, for possibilities for benchmarking, for feedback from all sorts of stakeholders.
– Self-evaluation is seen as something of great importance.
– And finally, a learning organisation gives plenty of room for reflective practitioners, and creates, as Jane Jones perfectly described in her keynote, a rich variety of possibilities for practitioner research. In other words, a learning organisation realises that learning processes are like a pinball machine: you may know where the pins are, but you can never predict the route the ball will take. So the best thing you can do is to offer a rich variety of learning opportunities, not just the odd in-service course but also - or rather: preferably – quite a lot of quite different strategies.

I leave it at that. The point is how do we get there.

Voyage of Discovery

Many politicians and managers would prefer - for actually that is how they are built - to know beforehand exactly what a learning organisation looks like. Moreover, they would prefer to know exactly what steps to take so as to be able to exactly plan the way (or ask people to do so) and keep things under control. But that is - to say the least - a problem in many respects. There certainly is no blueprint, no standardised European model that could be imposed on each and every school. As a matter of fact, in my opinion that is an advantage. Schools differ from each other, as national conditions do; so what fits in one case, does not necessarily fit in another.

All in all, it is more or less as Rudi Schollaert phrased it in his opening speech: people looking for the learning organisation resemble pilgrims in quest for the grail or something equally important and elusive. The development of a learning organisation doesn't resemble your odd trip to the Balearics or Tunisia: planned from the first to the last minute, even where free time is concerned, while the goal is exactly known beforehand. The search for a learning organisation is a journey of discovery, more or less like the ones Columbus organised, including sometimes arriving at quite another place than the one you had in mind.

In this respect, participation in a project like *The Treasure Within* can be of great help. As a matter of fact, not only by offering opportunities for exchanging solutions or inspiring and comforting each other. But also where the more dark sides of the journey towards a learning organisation are concerned. That journey will not always proceed smoothly. On the contrary, to all probability some chaos and some mistakes are unavoidable. So, a certain degree of chaos tolerance plus a willingness to learn from mistakes are a prerequisite. But let's face it, managers and teachers don't like chaos, and professionals in general tend to avoid making mistakes or to conceal them. In your own school or even in exchanges with schools next door the climate often is unfavourable to talk freely about problems. *The Treasure Within* might offer a safer environment. I realise, however, for most partners and members the possibilities for exchanging ideas and co-operating in the development of strategies are far more appealing. In that respect *The Treasure Within* has undeniably much to offer.

Variety and connections

Some of the conference participants might have found some difficulty in coming to grips with what *The Treasure Within* is about. They attended some workshops, they talked to several colleagues, and I can imagine, they didn't detect the connecting principle, the thread that holds all activities together. But as I said at the start, for me, it is exactly this variety, this mosaic character - or to use the funny term Jane Jones introduced: this Pick and Mix Character - that constitutes the real value of *The Treasure Within*. There are no blueprints or standardised instruments; the development of learning organisations is a journey of discovery, not a trip that is planned and controlled from begin to end; there is no unique most fruitful way of learning, neither for pupils nor for teachers and managers. So, any project that helps schools to become learning organisations has to reflect that variety. That is the variety of life.

Apart from that, there is another (but in fact closely related) reason why I like the mosaic character of *The Treasure Within*. It is in the nature of strategies, approaches, methods and models to wear out. Unavoidably, after some time things like that begin to loose their freshness that once was so attractive, their stimulating and inspiring character. As it seems, variety is an absolute, almost physical prerequisite for learning. And again, that is exactly the variety The Treasure intends to offer.

But however useful all this variety might be, that doesn't alter the fact that at the same time some mutual connections are needed in order to prevent that the project becomes a scattering galaxy in which the stars and planets and meteorites continuously move further and further away from each other. In the Treasure we try to establish the connection by using some focus points like the following:

–   In the end, starting with a certain approach, how difficult it may be, is not the problem. The problem is how do you sustain developments, what factors promote success or cause failure? In *The Treasure Within* we can try to share experiences in different contexts to find common denominators.

- A central Treasure Within question is: what works and why does it work? That makes it possible to look for what is unique and what is more general. To get a picture of what fosters a collaborative culture, to find ways to bridge the gap between collegiality and the role of power in the organisation, or ways to promote shared leadership by creating self-managing teams.

There are, of course, more focus points, but these two might suffice to make clear what we intend to do.

External obligation

Many teachers and school leaders I know, nowadays often assert that peer learning, peer consultation, is their preferred way of learning. Of course they consult experts, they buy and/or attend courses, they read (or at least plan to do so) books and articles. But the real thing – so they say – happens in exchanges with colleagues. However, important as peer learning might be in their eyes, in practice (and I don't blame them for that) the daily pressures all too often prevent them from finding time for it. And that is where a project like *The Treasure Within* comes in for a last time in my story. Participation in such a network boils down to a self imposed obligation to 'stop & think' as Jane Jones phrased it earlier. Educators that know themselves will realise the importance of such an obligation. It is just a matter of sense and sensibility.

Pieter Leenheer is national network co-ordinator in The Netherlands